GETTING STARTED
on Social Analysis in Canada

"Social analysis means raising questions about society and seeking answers. Its purpose is not only to develop a critical awareness of the world but also to lead towards social justice."

To
our elders

Doris Marshall
advocate for the aged

Margot Power, rscj
counsellor to the poor

John Robson
inner-city pastor

Tony Walsh
promoter of community

witnesses to justice
practitioners of social analysis
prophets of hope

Getting Started on Social Analysis in Canada
is dedicated with
admiration and gratitude

Table of Contents

Preface

Who We Are

The Jesuit Centre for Social Faith and Justice occupies the second storey of a white stucco community hall in Toronto's inner city. The building is attached to a hundred-year-old red-brick gothic Presbyterian Church on Queen Street East. Factories define the main streets of the neighbourhood, which is criss-crossed by decaying avenues of row-housing, while small shops stretch east and west along the tramline.

A full array of urban problems abounds in this part of the city. In response, co-ops, community projects and local organizations have mushroomed. Since 1973 a few Jesuits have been living in South Riverdale, sharing in the neighbourhood's destiny.

The Jesuit Centre, founded in 1979, inherited this geography and history as part of its identity. The Centre's goals are severalfold:
- to engage in issues of justice as they emerge in the city;
- to be involved with the Christian churches in Canada, especially in the major ecumenical coalitions;
- to participate with other groups, centres and projects;
- to accompany organizations in their struggles for justice;
- to co-operate with persons and especially groups of similar concern.

The Jesuit Centre staff is a team of seven members, with several part-time associates. We have often travelled in the Third World, where our commitment to social justice has deepened. Trips throughout Canada have nourished our special hope for this country.

At the Jesuit Centre we do research into contemporary social issues. Our main work is to analyze problems as they emerge on the local and regional, national and international levels, and to reflect critically on the grave social obstacles to full human development. The Centre originally focused on health but is now involved in many projects, some of them reflected in chapters of this book: environmental hazards; health care for native peoples; Canadian energy policy; the social impact of microtechnology; and human rights in Central America.

Why This Book?

The Jesuit Centre was born, and this book written, within the intellectual currents of the Christian churches. These currents explain the "social faith and justice" in the Centre's name, as well as the particular slant of *Getting Started*.

Every religion has a social dimension, and Christianity is no exception. The teachings of Jesus Christ led to his own crucifixion and to the persecution of his early followers. The subsequent two millennia have seen the Christian churches playing the widest variety of roles in their social milieux.

Some Christians feel that religion has no social role to play and should not mix in politics and public life. This view maintains, at least implicitly, that economic, social and political life is not only very difficult to deal with, but also quite separate from individual faith — and not worth connecting to that faith. Others feel that religion inhibits social change and necessarily supports the status quo. In fact, Christian doctrine and especially Christian practice have always played a social role, ranging from the profoundly conservative to the utterly radical, and have promoted both social atrophy and social change.

Getting Started does not deal with organized religion's crucial role as a social force and defender of the status quo, or with the effects of social changes on the churches. But we maintain that the authentic Judaeo-Christian tradition — with its roots in the Exodus experience — clearly calls for justice and renewal. That call needs to be applied to the circumstances of today's society. This means that it is first necessary to analyze the concrete situations and difficulties of daily life in society. Only with the help of social analysis, then, can people fulfill their human, religious vocation.

We take our inspiration from the contemporary Christian tradition, the social teaching of the Canadian churches, and the commitment of the Jesuit Order (Society of Jesus) to the service of faith and the promotion of justice:

> As an international body, the Society of Jesus commits itself to that work which is the promotion of a more just world order, greater solidarity of rich countries with poor, and a lasting peace based on human rights and freedom.

We are convinced that all people enjoy inalienable rights, have an inherent dignity and should exercise a say about their lives and society. We believe that human beings can develop more fully as society becomes more just. Without claiming that perfect happiness and perfect justice are possible in this world, the Centre affirms the crucial link between struggling for social justice and promoting full human development.

The Canadian churches have been giving ever clearer expression to the social dimension of Christian faith, life and practice, especially since

World War II. Examples of such analysis, taken from the teachings of the Christian churches in Canada, serve to illustrate the chapters of this book.

Who are You?

Since beginning our work in retreats and workshops with community and church groups, religious orders and teachers across Canada, we have been asked over and over again about ways to analyze — or "read" — Canadian society and the problems that confront Canadians. Accordingly, in early 1982 the Centre undertook to write this introductory book on social analysis in Canada. *Getting Started* is written for:

- members of parishes or congregations;
- teachers in high schools and community colleges;
- university classes and discussion groups;
- trade unionists and associations of the unemployed;
- community and neighbourhood groups;
- adult educators and teachers of English as a second language,
- members of church projects, solidarity groups and social organizations oriented toward justice, such as Amnesty International, the Student Christian Movement (SCM) and Newman Clubs, Ten Days, Share Lent, Development and Peace.

The people we have talked to say they need a social analysis that is clear, Canadian and practical.

- *Clear* — They want to understand how our society functions, with its various forces, groups and institutions. Why is it not working as well as it should?
- *Canadian* — There are helpful educational materials from the United States, and many Canadian activists have been influenced by work from Latin America and the Third World. Still, people want a truly Canadian analysis.
- *Practical* — After starting to both think about Canadian society and learn how to do analysis, people want to consider what they can do. *Getting Started* deals with questions most people have to face regularly and, without specifying actions and responses, the analysis opens up the next steps to be taken.

We hope that *Getting Started* will do these things well enough to be useful to people who are trying to confront social injustice and build a more just society in Canada. The Jesuit Centre is eager to receive feedback on the analysis presented in *Getting Started*.

Thank You

We wish first of all to thank Virginia R. Smith. Throughout 1982 she co-ordinated the initial work on the project, helped to design and plan this book, drafted several of the chapters, and did a great deal of rewriting and editing. Her dedication and enthusiasm have left their mark on *Getting Started*.

Phil Ryan laid the foundations for the economics section with his research and writing. Joe Cassidy, S.J., Pat Doyle, S.J., Tim Draimin, John Foster, Virginia Field Smith and Michael Stogre, S.J., all did early drafts of chapters. Andrew Murray and Martin Royackers, S.J., contributed research, editing and writing. Gordon George, S.J., was tireless in suggesting improvements for every chapter. Bonnie Greene of the United Church, John Duncan of the Presbyterian Church and Béla Somfai, S.J., of Regis College in Toronto provided much appreciated documents and advice. Don Cockburn, Hania Fedorowicz, Judy Giroux and Fran McKenna in Ottawa looked up helpful data.

At the Jesuit Centre, Norine Pigeau managed the office throughout the long haul, Kathy Brouwer helped type and read chapters, and Vicki Butterfield paid the bills. In addition to staff members Tim Draimin and Michael Stogre, Carlos Sebastian prepared some illustrations, Jim Webb, S.J., was a constructive critic and Lois Anne Bordowitz, F.C.J., collated all the critical comments. Ted Hyland, S.J., also contributed to several chapters, prepared the index and developed ways of promoting and teaching *Getting Started*.

Constructive criticism came from Janice Acton, Frances Arbour, Pat Bird, Donald Cole, Lee Cormie, Ferne Cristall, John Dillon, Joey Edwardh, Sean Goetz-Gadon, Beth Haddon, Susan Hower, Michael Kaufman, Doris Marshall, Dan McCarthy, Laura McLauchlan, Mary Beth Montcalm, C.S.J., David Nazar, S.J., Jennifer Penney, Susan Purcell McKenna, Ray Rogers, Abe Rotstein, Janet Somerville, Lorne Waldman and Bill Zimmerman. They improved the book greatly but deserve no blame for any errors that remain.

The Sisters of St. Joseph of Toronto, the Ursuline Sisters of Chatham, the Sisters of Charity of Halifax and the Loyola Jesuit Community of Montreal encouraged the project with their financial assistance. Reverend William F. Ryan, S.J., major superior (1978-1984) of the English-speaking Jesuits in Canada, energetically supported both the founding of the Jesuit Centre and the writing of this book.

Robert Clarke, editor at Between The Lines, helped *Getting Started* find its true expression. Carlos Freire's illustrations serve to communicate what many words fail to say. Finally, may Michael Czerny, S.J., and Jamie Swift, co-authors and co-editors, be as gratified by the book and its reception as the Jesuit Centre is grateful for the creative energies they invested in it.

The Jesuit Centre for Social Faith and Justice,
June, 1984

Chapter One

Welcome to Social Analysis

"Would you like a coffee?"

A friendly way to start a conversation . . . and a good way to begin social analysis. Most of us probably don't think twice about having a cup of coffee (unless it's to heed the warnings about too much caffeine). But if you stop to think about it, a coffee can quickly get some questions going:

- "Yes, I'd like a cup." The coffee may come from one of those small Central American countries always in the news. What does that have to do with Canada?
- "A coffee to go." The drink will come in a cheap, disposable styrofoam cup fashioned from petroleum (there may be a shortage, or a glut). You'll probably also get a plastic stir-stick. When you throw these things away, where do they go?
- "A spoonful of instant." The makings of that instant coffee may have come from Honduras or Nicaragua. But what's the name of the company that is selling it now? Where was it processed?
- "Do you care for sugar?" Another Third World product and, apparently, something that may not be good for you. Recently the government lost an anti-combines suit against the large sugar companies — does that mean *we* lost?
- "Would you like cream?" Dairy farmers work a seven-day week but many have gone bankrupt in the eighties. How do the priorities of business and government affect small farmers?
- "We're out of milk — here's the whitener." Have you read the list of ingredients? Is the whitener an "edible oil product"? Can you guess what the ingredients do to your health?
- "Please pass me a teaspoon." If there is iron in

Schefferville, Que. (mine closed in 1982), and nickel stockpiles in Sudbury, Ont. (over ten thousand jobs lost between 1973 and 1983), why was the teaspoon made in Korea, Japan or Taiwan?

"Good to the last drop." A cup of coffee does not just happen. Many people are involved in getting it ready, from planting the seedling through all the stages of processing to serving the coffee and washing the cup: owner, planter, picker, shipper, buyer, insurer, processor, packer, advertiser, seller, shopper, consumer, dishwasher. How are all these people — and jobs — related to each other?

A Questioning Awareness

Social analysis begins with *questions* like these. As they surface they start us thinking about a particular issue, like Third World exports, or a whole cluster of issues like the "coffee cycle". Similar questions can prompt us to think about Canadian society. Doing social analysis, as we shall see, is acquiring the habit of questioning the world around us.

There are many different approaches to social analysis and many theories. One book is too short to discuss them all. But here is a preliminary definition that will serve people using this book.

Social analysis, as we are using the term, means *raising questions about society and seeking answers*. Its purpose is not only *to develop a critical awareness of the world* but also *to lead towards social justice*.

The process of social analysis also gives rise to further questions about what is going on and who is getting hurt. It thus leads to further research. It discerns the links or connections between different social issues. It encourages group discussion.

Many readers will find this process of social analysis to be familiar. Others just need encouragement to see that it lies within their normal abilities. Many people feel stuck on the surface of society, without finding out what is really going on beneath the appearances and behind the slogans. Social analysis helps people become *critical*. "Critical" does not mean negative, condemnatory or ungrateful. Critical means conscious, aware, questioning. It means developing a discerning attitude, a habit of trying to get to the bottom of things.

All the questions that arise from this process cannot be answered right away. Some open up topics that require *research*. This means taking time to pursue the questions further. For example, after a discussion of the coffee cycle, you might want to look for additional information about: the health hazards of caffeine, sugar or whitener; mining and refining in Canada; the workings of the international coffee and sugar markets; or the situation of coffee-producing people and their needs. It is important at the same time to question the information you gather — to make sure it is accurate and thorough.

Critical questions lead to an awareness of previously unsuspected *connections* between issues. For example, thinking about where a cup of coffee comes from can quickly lead to questions about the Canadian balance of trade, the structure of the food industry, the relationship between mining and manufacturing, and the effects of caffeine and sugar on health. Or another example: a comparative analysis of a particular industry in Canada and a Third World country would soon uncover a common tendency to export relatively unprocessed raw materials. Social analysis tries to trace the links connecting issues, in order to understand how society works and fails to work.

Why raise questions, become critical, do research and trace connections? Social analysis is not motivated by merely intellectual or scientific curiosity. The purpose is to seek the truth of a situation — be it the coffee cycle or unemployment in Canada — in order to lay bare the injustice that characterizes the situation. Social analysis is oriented towards *social justice* — towards taking some action, or promoting change where this is judged necessary. It is meant to contribute effectively to the quest for social justice.

Social analysis is preferably done *in a group*, where one comment can spark new thoughts, and opinions get refined by coming up against other points of view. As a group gains a picture of an issue, it moves easily from analysis to a discussion of possible action, to making decisions, distributing tasks, contacting other groups and acting to do something about a problem that has been identified.

Some people say, "I have other things to do." The alternative to social analysis is to accept the surface-meanings; to think what we are told to think; to consume, not only goods and services,

but also the slogans, meanings and values of society that go along with them. It is to leave the interpretation and direction of society in the hands of others, perhaps others whose values we don't share. One day, seeing that things have gone too far, we might object, "I wasn't consulted!" By then it may be too late.

Towards Social Justice

Social analysis leads to action on behalf of justice. Such action may entail looking up more information, organizing a local interest group, making a small gesture of protest or contributing to a national campaign that is tackling an important issue. Whatever the action, it will in turn raise new questions and involve people more deeply again in the process of social analysis.

It does not take long for social analysis to begin uncovering the deep inequities and structural problems that characterize Canadian society. These matters can be stated very starkly, even simply. Practical solutions, on the other hand, are rarely black or white and usually quite messy. They need to be hammered out in an often difficult process of compromise. In most cases, *Getting Started* poses the problems rather than proposes solutions.

Social analysis opens up the need for political analysis, which is in turn basic to the task of developing political organizations and finding workable solutions. But political analysis is outside the range of this book, which limits itself to raising social questions without proffering political answers; it is an introduction to social analysis. (There is more, however, on the political consequences of social analysis in the conclusion.)

Without making specific proposals, *Getting Started* nevertheless does take a stand. It analyzes issues from the perspective of the many Canadians who feel relatively helpless in the face of social issues. It deliberately opts for their interests. It favours those whose viewpoint is usually not heard and whose dignity is most often neglected and violated.

Some of *Getting Started*'s suggestions may in effect challenge the status quo, for social analysis as defined here is not detached from the social reality under study, but unabashedly involved and committed to greater justice in Canada.

Everyone is welcome

Analyzing the social situations in Canada is a task belonging to everybody, no matter what group, church, school, union or party they belong to. Among all these, the Canadian churches have been especially insistent in calling for social analysis.

The Catholic bishops in Canada explain the task in this way:

> It is up to Christian communities, Pope Paul VI has emphasized, "to analyze with objectivity the situation which is proper to their own country, to shed on it the light of the Gospel's unalterable

words and to draw principles of reflection, norms of judgment, and directives of action from the social teaching of the Church". Applying the Gospel in this way to our own times, we are better able to identify and evaluate what is going on around us and make a positive contribution to human development.

In a more recent document the Bishops describe the steps leading to and flowing from social analysis:

a) being present with and listening to the experiences of the poor, the marginalized, the oppressed in our society (e.g., the unemployed, the working poor, the welfare poor, exploited workers, native peoples, the elderly, the handicapped, small producers, racial and cultural minorities, etc.);

b) developing a critical analysis of the economic, political, and social structures that cause human suffering;

c) making judgments in the light of Gospel principles and the social teachings of the Church concerning social values and priorities;

d) stimulating creative thought and action regarding alternative visions and models for social and economic development; and

e) acting in solidarity with popular groups in their struggles to transform economic, political and social structures that cause social and economic injustices.

Accordingly, everyone is responsible for analyzing the situation in Canada. The words of the Gospel appeal to all Christians, whatever their denomination. Social teaching, likewise, makes a special claim on all people of good will who want to contribute in a positive way to the development of their brothers and sisters.

In encouraging social analysis to go on, the Canadian churches have spoken out on very concrete issues, including

- health,
- housing,
- unemployment,
- native rights,
- environment,
- nuclear disarmament,
- foreign policy,
- human rights.

Getting Started does not attempt, however, to present a Christian analysis, but instead a social analysis that everyone — Christians included — will find effective and valid. Moreover, the social analysis is not limited to church-goers, members of particular organizations or experts in any particular field. *Getting Started* is written for all people who:

- feel paralyzed and baffled by the workings of Canadian society;
- are concerned about a particular social issue and want to begin thinking about it;

- are already working on one issue and want to see how it relates to other issues;
- have done some social analysis and want to develop their critical thinking, questioning and reflecting;
- want to teach social analysis to others, lead group discussion or encourage a community response;
- share the desire to make Canada a better, more just country to live in.

How to Use This Book

Getting Started is divided into three main parts, with each part containing three or four chapters of analysis. A chapter of reflection brings each part to a close and prepares the way for the next set of chapters. The parts of the book are arranged in the following way:

Part One — People often run up against immediate and personal problems that seem overwhelming. The analysis in Part One discusses how to connect that basic (and seemingly individual) problem to a larger social issue that helps to explain its root causes.

Reflection — Social analysis is like learning how to understand a language and its grammar.

Part Two — An issue-by-issue approach (Part One) is not enough because interconnected economic patterns keep cropping up. Part Two introduces (in chapter six) some essential ideas about the economy. The three subsequent chapters serve as case studies to illustrate more specifically how economics work in Canada.

Reflection — After analyzing basic issues and economic structures, it becomes apparent that the media are entangled in all those phenomena. The reflection introduces that set of assumptions — or dominant ideology — which is geared to justify what is happening.

Part Three — So far the analysis has dealt with the issues and structures of Canadian society in general. But there are many particular groups of people that suffer injustices of a different and distinct kind. Part Three explores the experience, troubles and contribution of old people, native people and women, and in addition analyzes Canada's role in dealing with people of the Third World.

Reflection — The conclusion reflects further on what social analysis can mean in concrete action. It reveals also that analysis can include victories, not just set-backs. It looks at impediments to analysis, at the issue of priorities and political power, and at steps beyond social analysis.

Many readers will want to work their way through the chapters in the order presented. Others may prefer to go directly to a chapter treating an issue of greatest concern or interest to them. In any case, at least one or two of the appropriate issue chapters should be read before delving into the reflection chapters (five, ten and fifteen).

Each *Chapter* divides easily into three or four sections; each section could serve as one session in presentation to a group or class. Alternatively, all the members of a group could read a chapter and discuss it, one section per meeting.

The *Illustrations* are part of the analysis, too, questioning typical images, cultural expressions, attitudes and stereotypes.

The *Boxed Quotations*, taken from documents of the Canadian churches, are examples of social analysis which highlight or re-state the points being made.

Most chapters end with *Questions* to help begin discussion, as well as to orient further reading or research.

In each chapter, *Resources* are also suggested to follow up the analysis: recommended books, audio-visuals and groups to contact for further information and orientation.

At the back of the book, the *Notes* identify sources of quotations within the text and give details on other sources used in writing this book.

The *Index*, in addition to its normal use, can also suggest themes to develop or new connections to trace between issues.

Because *Getting Started* treats a representative sample of Canadian issues, the treatment of each one is necessarily very introductory. Furthermore, there are many topics which are not treated, for instance: racism and the problems of visible minorities; the handicapped; agriculture, fisheries, forestry and manufacturing; regional disparities and the many issues in Quebec's "quiet revolution"; the role of schools, colleges and universities; militarism and national security; and the list could go on.

In planning the chapters on old people, native people and women, the authors of *Getting Started* faced a particular difficulty that needs to be pointed out, namely, the fact that we do not belong to any one of these three groups. This is a handicap, but one that's widely shared. We believe it is both possible and necessary for social analysts to enter, at least partially, into the experience of other groups and make their concerns our own.

We also debated whether old people's, native people's and women's issues should be treated in separate chapters or integrated into the other chapters. In fact we do both. The advantages of a chapter dedicated, in a frankly introductory way, to some of each group's issues seem to outweigh the risk of tokenism (that is, giving the impression that a separate chapter "took care of" all their issues).

One further note on content: When it comes to the very important issue of abortion, Canadians disagree strongly. Even among the Christian churches of Canada, there is profound disagreement. Similarly, the authors of *Getting Started* could not agree on a common approach to this issue. It has therefore been deliberately omitted.

Resources

- Beginning to do social analysis in a workshop, classroom or group discussion is really no harder than arranging a coffee-mug, styrofoam cup, teaspoon, plastic stir-stick, creamer or whitener, bowl of sugar and jar of instant coffee on a low table. Everyone can be invited to mention the ideas or questions these items suggest — similar to the comments that opened this chapter — and a record of points can be kept on paper or a blackboard. In no time there will be plenty of suggestions for discussion, further research, liaison with other groups, and proposals for action.

- After seeing how quickly questions for social analysis can be generated, another session might consider why anyone would deliberately remain unaware. What is it in people that blocks their analysis of social reality? Why are people reluctant to take part in social analysis?

- The following "Social Paralysis Quiz" has been used successfully in classes and workshops. Each member of the group should get a copy of the quiz and be asked to rate the statements as they apply personally.

Social Paralysis Quiz

[5]	[4]	[3]	[2]	[1]
strongly agree	agree	don't know	disagree	strongly disagree

[ ] Canadian society is too complicated for me to understand.

[ ] In Canada there's a premium on authority and obedience: The prudent thing, whenever there's social tension, is to stay out of it.

[ ] Things are always getting worse and I feel the news is too awful to take in.

[ ] If the experts cannot agree between themselves on any social problem, much less the solution, I haven't a chance.

[ ] Faced with issues too big and complicated for me, I feel overwhelmed — it's better not to start.

[ ] Since decisions about social issues are very personal, I feel alone and isolated in facing the social world.

[ ] There are too many facts to absorb and it's like I'm drowning in a deluge of information.

[ ] I have no control over the important decisions that shape life in Canada.

[ ] Economics is a science so mysterious that even economists cannot understand how the Canadian economy works.

[ ] We will never reach a perfectly just society, since human greed and the lust for power will always reassert themselves, so why bother?

[ ] I want to live a well-ordered life — I keep my world quite small.

[ ] Social analysis might work in a Third World country, where the inequities are obvious, but it's nearly impossible to analyze a free society like Canada with its complex issues.

[ ] People used to understand the world from the viewpoint of a community in which they lived all their lives, but now things are moving too fast for us to understand.

[ ] There are tendencies towards evil built into human nature and, until individual hearts are changed, there's no point in tampering with social structures.

[ ] Political decisions are too weighty for the majority of citizens to grasp.

[   ] Total Score

This is a test of people's disposition towards social analysis. The higher the score, the more one has to struggle against social complacency or paralysis, the tendency to leave social concern to experts, professionals or activists. A lower score suggests that people believe they can understand their society and hope to have some impact on it. In a group, scores could be averaged to see if they weigh towards social faith and hope, or paralysis and disbelief. There could be a discussion of those items that people tended to score on the pessimistic side.

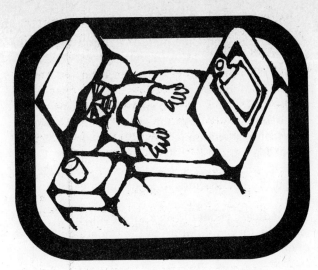

Chapter Two

In Sickness and in Health

"I feel sick!" someone complains.

"Where does it hurt?"

"I have an awful sore throat," comes the reply. "My head aches, I can't sleep."

Now what?

The immediate reaction to a sick feeling is to get rid of it as quickly as possible. We suppress the cough, kill the pain, take a pill. That is how aches and pains are usually handled.

When that doesn't work, we begin to see the cough or fever in a different light. Instead of nagging irritants, they become *symptoms*. Symptoms indicate that something is wrong inside. They are the starting point for a more thorough investigation, which traces its way back to the probable causes, figures out which cause is the most likely and then suggests an appropriate cure. This activity of identifying what's wrong is called *diagnosis*.

The advantage of diagnosis — compared with the immediate elimination of any sick feeling — is that it seeks out the causes and offers a cure. It does not merely treat the effects or symptoms. Diagnosis analyzes symptoms in the context of the whole body, and many factors come into play. Diagnosis is a combination of science and art, experience and intuition, dialogue and consultation.

Social analysis has a lot in common with the diagnosis of illness. In looking at society we run into problems that are urgent and painful, most often to find that they do not yield to immediate solutions. The task of social analysis is then to work back from symptomatic problems to the real causes. This means that a more effective, longer-lasting solution can be proposed and planned, though it is more demanding and harder to achieve than a quick cure.

Everyone has some experience of what symptoms are and how diagnosis works. These experiences help to get social analysis started. According to the old proverb, "An ounce of prevention is worth a pound of cure." Since both prevention and cure are needed, this chapter looks at both. The first part, "A pound of cure", gives healthcare delivery in Canada a preliminary check-up. The second, "An ounce of prevention", considers some improvements in Canadian health care.

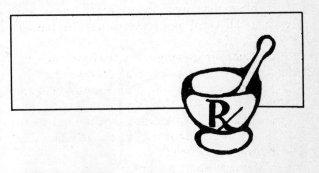

"A Pound of Cure"

In the days before medicare — which really weren't so long ago — the prevailing arrangement in Canada was "pay-as-you-go". Here are some typical experiences under that system:

- Children of poorer families rarely saw a doctor or nurse.
- Severe illness often forced elderly people to sell off their homes or other assets in order to raise cash to pay medical bills.
- Those who could not afford to pay avoided the doctor altogether, humbly asked for free care or credit, or went to the emergency department and the public ward. Patients felt like beggars, and doctors decided who deserved "charity medicine".
- The inability to predict medical expenses and the pressure to budget for expensive health insurance were sources of anxiety for many people.
- Those most in need of medical attention — the poor, especially the borderline poor who did not qualify for welfare — were least likely to get it.

It's worth remembering what the "facts of life" used to be under an arrangement that still characterizes health care in the United States, where twenty-five million citizens lack any health insurance.

Today, under Canada's medicare programme, the situation is markedly different. Medicare is Canada's publicly-funded health insurance system, designed to give all members of society reasonable access to medical attention. Compared with the hardships and inequities of the out-of-pocket arrangement, in which each patient paid for medical services either personally or through an insurance policy sold by a private firm, medicare seems very fair and effective to most Canadians.

Justice Emmett Hall is one of the founding fathers of medicare in Canada. After conducting a

comprehensive review of the system in 1980, Justice Hall assured Canadians, "I found no one — not any Government or individual, not the Medical Profession nor any organization — not in favour of *Medicare*."

But this view is not shared by everyone. In 1982 Dr. Marc Baltzan, president of the Canadian Medical Association (CMA), stated baldly, "There are at least three distinct disadvantages to Canadian medicare: it is a threat to civil liberty, it is a threat to health and it is economically inefficient."

Medicare is obviously controversial. Let's look at the history and nature of the Canadian "pound of cure".

A Health Charter for Canadians

Medicare was first proposed by the Liberal Party as long ago as 1919. The Co-operative Commonwealth Federation (CCF) and all the major labour unions pushed for it during the thirties and forties. But in 1962, when the CCF government in Saskatchewan moved towards a system of publicly-funded health insurance, doctors warned of chaos in medicine and launched a strike to protest the government's action. After a bitter struggle, Saskatchewan residents became the first in the country to be covered by medicare.

Prepaid insurance for medical care, as a right for all Canadians, was established by the federal Medical Care Act of 1966 and reaffirmed in the Canada Health Act of 1984. Although this field comes under provincial jurisdiction, the federal government exercises influence by paying a large share of the costs of medicare in any province whose programme meets five criteria. Of these criteria, the three most important describe qualities of health care that Canadians now appreciate and even take for granted:

- *Universality* — everyone must be covered. Insured health services must be available to all residents, without discrimination.
- *Accessibility* — people must have reasonable access to services, without prohibitive extra charges.
- *Comprehensiveness* — a full range of health services must be available and covered by the programme.

Medicare is sometimes loosely referred to as "free", though it is neither free nor a government hand-out. The public pays for it through taxes; in Alberta, British Columbia, Ontario and the Yukon, individual citizens also pay premiums, like those of a conventional insurance plan, in order to be covered.

Medicare poses no challenge to private practice or fee-for-service medicine. Doctors still operate their offices in the same way as before. They are independent professionals, not civil servants. Ideally, they follow an agreed-upon schedule of fees, although some doctors extra-bill. They simply receive payments for their services from a government health insurance agency rather than directly from individual patients or private insurance plans. The fee schedule is set by each province after negotiation with the provincial medical association.

Why does medicare come under fire? The most frequent criticisms have to do with the public purse.

Have We Run Out of Health Dollars?

Medicare has gone a long way toward "curing" the major financial difficulties that used to prevent the sick from getting medical attention.

In the first year after the introduction of Quebec's medicare plan, poor families in Montreal increased their visits to the doctor by 18.2 per cent. Among low-income, pregnant women, the rate of prenatal consultations more than doubled with the advent of medicare. But once these previously under-served groups were being attended to, the statistics levelled off, indicating that medicare did not lead to over-use on the part of the poor. Research in Alberta, Saskatchewan, Ontario and in Canada as a whole suggests that, while health insurance has improved access to medical care by the poor, average medical services per family still tend to increase with family income.

Accessible, comprehensive and universal coverage solves some of the problems caused by the former out-of-pocket arrangement. Despite the obvious advantages, the programme has been under attack since the late seventies, as governments began to face shrinking tax revenues and swelling deficits. Stories in the media often give the impression that medical costs are out of control, consuming a large and ever-growing chunk of our tax dollars. There are calls for restraint. If social services such as medicare can be made to look "free" or like a kind of "welfare" that the government cannot afford, cuts do not seem hard to justify.

Healthcare expenditures did grow rapidly in the fifties and sixties, helped by government subsidies for hospitals and hospital insurance. But since the introduction of medicare, the total cost of health care (public and private) has been constant, hovering between 7.5 and 8 per cent of Gross National Product. In the United States, where there is no universal health insurance, costs have risen to at least 10.5 per cent of GNP. According to a task force commissioned by the Ontario ministry of health to review primary health care, Canadians "receive a larger package of public health services than before the introduction of government funding, but in 'constant dollar' terms, the amount spent on health care has decreased."

Medicare is too popular a programme to be dismantled, because according to a recent poll 85 per cent of Canadians rate it as one of the most important services provided by government. But there is erosion, as governments introduce or tolerate measures which in fact reduce the accessibility, comprehensiveness or universality of ensured services. These measures are regressive because the burden falls most heavily on those least able to bear it. The major regressive measures are:
- premiums (Alberta, British Columbia, Ontario and the Yukon);
- hospital user-fees (Alberta, British Columbia, New Brunswick and Newfoundland);
- extra-billing (permitted in all provinces except Quebec).

These costs deter the poor, the elderly and those with large families from seeking necessary medical attention. They unfairly discriminate against lower-income people, and probably violate the Canada Health Act.

Health dollars are far from having run out. The controversy seems to centre rather on how the funds are distributed among the doctors, other health workers and the medical industry. Let's look at these.

Healthcare Workers Turn Militant

Doctors have long belonged to the most highly-revered profession in society and most Canadians still see them as deserving of prestige. The image lives on of the selfless country "Doc", working long hours and making house calls during the night. Yet there is a growing feeling among many that the medical associations may be abusing the public trust and greedily demanding too much.

To such suggestions the Canadian Medical Association cries "Foul!" and "Doctor-bashing!" The CMA alleges that public insurance makes poorer medical service inevitable. It cites delays in payment for services as an example of the inefficient public administration of medicare. It argues that its members are falling behind economically.

At the turn of the century a doctor took home four times as much pay as an industrial worker. This ratio has remained quite constant over the years. In the eighties physicians continue to enjoy the highest average income of any group in society. "Don't look now, doctor," joked a headline in the *Medical Post*, "Profession highest paid in Canada." According to 1980 tax returns, self-employed medical doctors held the highest income-generating occupations. They made on average $62,273 that year, up 8.2 per cent from the year before. In 1981 doctors in British Columbia earned an average of $70,000 per annum. Average net professional income in Ontario ranged from $61,000 for general practitioners to $121,000 for cardiovascular and thoracic surgeons.

Some doctors claim that, by controlling their fee schedule, medicare forces them into "factory" or "revolving-door" medicine: To maintain their incomes they must either see an unconscionable number of patients, or provide quality care to fewer patients and extra-bill them. "Extra-billing" means charging patients over and above the amount provincial insurance plans will pay. In some communities so many specialists extra-bill that there is no anaesthetist or obstetrician-gynecologist whose fee is fully covered by medicare. In Nova Scotia more than half of all doctors extra-bill patients. While only Quebec prohibited extra-billing, the 1984 Canada Health Act imposes penalties on provinces that permit it.

Other doctors, who resent what they call government interference in their bookkeeping, prefer to "opt out" and bill their patients directly; their fees are nearly always higher than those of opted-in doctors.

Extra-billing and the adoption of premiums and user-fees are regressive measures that in practice deny Canadians access to the full range of medical services. They violate the spirit of the Canadian health charter and gradually reintroduce a two-tier system of health care — private medicine for those who can afford it, public medicine for those who cannot.

In the eighties the medical associations have been trying to reassert doctors' rights as they see them. Advertisements, educational campaigns and unabashed political lobbying are used to attack medicare as unrealistic, expensive and unfair. Moreover, as one physician put it, " 'Job action' is no longer a no-no with us." In 1982 such job action in both Ontario and Quebec took the form of short-term strikes.

At the same time, other healthcare workers have been demanding that their wages keep pace with inflation. Alberta nurses struck three times between 1977 and 1982. In Quebec, hospital

workers actually faced salary reductions when the provincial government claimed there was no money left in the healthcare pot. In Ontario, striking hospital workers were legislated back to work. Some were jailed along with their leaders.

But it is noteworthy that when doctors stopped working, or when interns and residents withdrew services, they did not suffer similar treatment. Oddly enough, a strike by a union representing orderlies and kitchen staff seems to pose a greater threat to public health than "job action" by professionals, if we can judge by the action government has taken or failed to take. To point this up, hospital staff raise the slogan, "What's good for the doctor is good for the worker!"

The conflict is obviously over money. The government tries to exercise "restraint" at the expense of public service unions representing hospital workers. Doctors try to maintain their income; other health workers struggle to improve theirs. But the conflict also has to do with the distribution of prestige, responsibility, and decision-making in the healthcare field.

Growing Pains or Terminal Illness?

Over 85 per cent of Canadians rate medicare among the best and most important services that government provides. The medical associations, speaking for doctors most critical of medicare, urge a return to the unregulated situation (still operating in the United States) in which the profession alone determines its fees and doctors charge whatever the market will bear. Under this arrangement, the government funds medical schools, hospitals and other essential facilities which are not attractive to the private sector, while the rest of the medical enterprise is conducted like any other business.

But it is worth noting that the vast majority — nearly 90 per cent — of Canada's more than forty thousand doctors participate voluntarily in medicare and accept provincial plan compensation as payment in full. They do not want to go back to "cash register medicine", as the former system has been unkindly tagged.

Obviously, governments win support from the population by providing a system like medicare which most Canadians need and want. At the same time, government policy protects its own long-range political interests by favouring the powerful medical-industrial complex, whose generous earnings and profits tend to undermine the cost-effectiveness of publicly-funded health care. Besides the national and provincial medical associations, the medical establishment includes: the medical schools; private insurance companies, which naturally oppose public insurance; the powerful hospital associations; the medical suppliers and the pharmaceutical industry. Each of these deserves analysis, too.

The present state of medicare may be assessed as follows. Internal to medicare, there are some bureaucratic delays and red tape. The public appreciates the system, practically taking it for granted. Among doctors, some very vocal frustration overshadows widespread but quiet support for the system. Other health workers experience tension with the medical profession and conflict with their employers. The medical-industrial complex is oriented toward profits.

The various pressures result in politicians speaking publicly in favour of medicare while their actual government policy is tolerant of its erosion.

According to this preliminary diagnosis, medicare does have some problems of its own — but its most serious problem is the fact that it is being attacked and undermined. That's why a whole host of people and their organizations — having analyzed Canadian health care in terms similar to the ones used here — have been working to prevent the gradual dismantling of medicare.

Christian health care must include a critical analysis of our attitudes, lifestyle and of the structures of society that inflict suffering on powerless people. For instance, are vast expenditures of money on remedial medicine justified, when basic housing, nutrition, education and sanitation policies multiply unnecessary illness, especially in Third World countries?

Christians need to explore and change the roots of ill health found in the way we organize our society. For example, inadequate and expensive housing endangers the health of the poor. In the field of education we find exaggerated competition among students and staff that places needless strains on people. Unfair and unsafe labour practices threaten the health of workers and their families. Economic policies that increase automation at the cost of rising unemployment neglect people's basic need to find recognition and dignity in work.

The healing of these social ills and the equal provision of health services to all people in our country and elsewhere may be beyond the reach of individual persons, but they are not beyond the reach of people working together.

Canadian Conference of Catholic Bishops,
Pastoral Message on Sickness and Healing, *1983*

"An Ounce of Prevention"

Medicare, the Canadian "pound of cure", is a big improvement over the previous out-of-pocket arrangement. It needs protection and strengthening. It also needs to be questioned and improved, and that is the purpose of the analysis in this second section, "An ounce of prevention".

In addition to medical coverage that is accessible, comprehensive and universal, health care itself should have other qualities:

- *Holistic* — dealing with the whole person, not just with the mechanics of the body looked at in isolation. This includes mental and spiritual ills that can have serious effects on bodily health.
- *Communal* — engaging the person within a broader human and social environment, not just as an isolated individual. This includes occupational and environmental health.
- *Preventive* — avoiding accidents and disease as much as possible, not just repairing sickness once it has occurred.
- *Positive* — promoting health (itself a holistic idea) and including nutrition and exercise, rather than focusing only on illness.
- *Participative* and *Empowering* — increasing people's knowledge of how their bodies work while at the same time enabling them to assume more control over their social and physical environments.

Why do these ideals seem remote from our daily experience? Medicare did not fundamentally change the heavy emphasis on individual and curative medicine, surgery and drugs, high technology and big institutions. For example, hospitals — absorbing over 50 per cent of the total healthcare budget — often prove to be an inefficient and overly-expensive form of healthcare delivery.

Take prevention as another example. The opening reflection on sickness and diagnosis illustrated the importance of tracking down the causes of disease. But the causes are not merely biological, they're also social. In the Third World, for example, poverty means inadequate nutrition, poor housing and a lack of clean water. These factors in turn give rise to widespread malnutrition, rampant infectious disease, high rates of infant

mortality, and so forth. In short, poverty breeds disease — as surely as germs do.

This is true not only in developing countries, but also in wealthy ones such as Canada, the United States and Britain. As income rises, parents are able to furnish better diet, shelter and hygiene for their offspring, and fewer children die in the early years of life. But among Canada's native people, with incomes far below those of most Canadians, infant mortality continues to be a scandalous problem (see chapter twelve). The solution, whether in Canada or in the Third World, seems similar. Alleviate the cause of the problem — poverty — and the infant mortality rate will come down accordingly.

In Canada, many diseases like typhoid and cholera — often spread by contaminated water and food — have been dramatically reduced or even eliminated thanks to the generally higher level of prosperity. Clean water, more hygienic food-handling, improved disposal of garbage and sewage are monitored by public health organizations. Statistics prove that public health measures are the most effective way of preventing disease. Yet paradoxically the public health sector receives only 2 to 5 per cent of all public healthcare expenditures.

Typhoid and cholera used to threaten our grandparents' lives. Now people are afraid of a different killer. Cancer is the most dreaded disease in our society. Will a cure ever be found? Can the disease be prevented?

The Terry Fox Phenomenon

Fear of cancer is one reason why Terry Fox's courageous marathon struck a generous chord in the hearts of so many Canadians. People who had previously felt powerless to do anything against the cancer plague threatening them and their families were moved by Terry's brave gesture. They gave financial support to help find a cure for cancer.

Health and Welfare Canada collects reports of cases of cancer from across the country. The 1970-72 average was 39,741 cases per year and in 1980 this had risen to 52,739 — an increase of over 30 per cent. Deaths from cancer have increased from 126.2 per 100,000 in 1950 to 165.3 in 1980, again by over 30 per cent.

What has caused this dramatic rise? An answer involves diagnosing or analyzing cancer through its root causes.

Modern industrial, technological society exposes citizens to hundreds of potential carcinogens or cancer-causing agents that influence cancer rates:

- diet, cigarette smoking and alcohol consumption;
- pollutants in air, water, food and soil — for example, food additives that give colour, flavour and longer "shelf life" to processed foods (see chapter six);
- toxic chemicals used in the workplace or in manufactured products — for example, pesticides and herbicides, which affect not only agricultural workers but also the public exposed to these poisons once they enter the air, water and food chain (see chapter four);
- exposure to sunlight and to ionizing radiation — for example, the fall-out from nuclear-weapons testing and the waste from nuclear-power plants (see chapter nine).

No wonder that many a cigarette smoker — upon being reminded of the risks posed by smoking — shrugs resignedly and replies, "Everything causes cancer."

While the exact cause of each cancer is still unknown, substantial evidence links 70 to 90 per cent of all human cancer to industrial pollutants in the environment and to habits that are part of our lifestyle. Public authorities have responded in a limited way.

Cigarette packages bear warnings and concerted public campaigns aim at getting people to quit smoking. We are urged to drink alcohol only in moderation, and in Quebec, liquor bottles are put into bags with printed reminders to this effect.

How sincere are these campaigns? Governments themselves are "addicted" to the hundreds of millions of dollars in annual tax revenues from the sale of tobacco and alcohol. A more effective strategy would not only discourage smoking but also encourage the reallocation of tobacco lands to the cultivation of crops such as protein-rich peanuts.

Healthy diet helps to prevent — and might even cure — cancer. By contrast, heavily-processed, additive-laden foods are clearly unhealthy and contribute to the cancer plague. Yet the food industry continues to develop and promote them. More affluent consumers who are conscious of various nutritional Do's and Don'ts can afford to shop carefully for more wholesome and expensive "health" foods; the poor cannot.

Fitness campaigns such as "Participaction" portray an active lifestyle as key to individual health. Of course everyone should try to get exercise, eat properly and avoid harmful substances. But individual action falls short of addressing cancer as the "social disease" that it is. Freedom of choice also falters before the massive avalanche of advertising and marketing techniques let loose on Canadian society by the multi-billion-dollar food, alcohol, and tobacco industries.

In the Third World improving poor health is a matter of "curing" poverty by providing rural families with access to clean water, decent housing and a basic minimum of food — not just teaching them to wash their hands. Similarly, Canadians need to take collective action against the carcinogens from which as individual citizens they cannot escape (see chapter four).

Lead, asbestos, radiation and dioxins are environmental hazards that can cause cancer today and genetic damage in future generations. Taking a preventive public health approach, working to eliminate some of these causes, will prove more effective than only searching for a cure. This is the real hope that Terry Fox ran for.

Organization for Health

Good resolutions on an individual scale — to avoid harmful substances and to take care of oneself — do not add up to a sufficient strategy for promoting health. Are there ways of organizing health care to bring the curative and preventive dimensions together — to cure sickness *and* to promote health?

Let's consider one example of a communal and structural approach that makes the promotion of health more possible than it is in private practice or hospital medicine. The example is the Community Health Centre (CHC) or in Quebec the CLSC (*Centre local de services communautaires*).

The CHC or CLSC (we use them interchangeably here) is an organization or social structure designed to implement or follow the criteria of the Canadian health charter — that is, to offer health care that is accessible, comprehensive and universal — and to address "social diseases" like cancer.

CHCs, though definitely part of the medicare system, differ from both private practice and larger hospitals. A CHC, often located in a refurbished storefront or public building, seems more open and welcoming than a typical doctor's office, far less impersonal and intimidating than a big hospital. The friendly atmosphere, informal dress, and simplified procedures can help to reduce some of the anxiety usually connected with seeking medical aid.

CLSCs offer a wide range of curative, preventive and social services, including pre-and post-natal care, nutrition, mutual help groups, and testing for environmental hazards. Instead of responding only to patients who are sick, the CLSCs try to address the social causes of sicknesses and educate people to take care of their health. Primary prevention and health promotion can be important emphases.

The staff of a CHC is a multi-disciplinary team of physicians, healthcare and social-service workers. This takes an almost exclusive focus off the doctor and makes room for other contributors to the health of individuals and the community. Usually the staff is paid salaries, thus removing financial transactions from the doctor-patient relationship and freeing the staff to provide a more comprehensive range of services.

A community board of directors is selected from among the people who use the centre and so are directly affected by the quality of health care offered. The board is responsible for planning, setting priorities and preparing budgets. In effect, the whole health team is accountable to its patients.

Over a hundred such health centres operate across Canada. Because of their philosophy, staffing, funding arrangements and community control:

- CHCs are more accessible to the poor, elderly and disadvantaged, who are frequently underserved by normal medical practice. This also applies to anyone who cannot afford the premiums in Alberta, British Columbia and Ontario.
- CLSCs can deal with illnesses, not only in medical terms, but also as linked with the patient's family, housing (see chapter three), environment (see chapter four) and economic and social problems. This is more comprehensive care than hospitals or private practice can offer.
- Besides helping patients treat their sickness,

CHCs can actively promote health, develop ways of preventing disease and tackle environmental or social problems in the neighbourhood.

The Community Health Centre is a new kind of structure in Canada. It can deliver "the pound of cure" within medicare. At the same time, the CHC or CLSC goes beyond the merely curative to make holistic, communal, preventive and positive, participative and empowering health care possible. It is a structure within which people — professionals, volunteers, the ill, the poor — can work together on these important ideals.

"I feel better!"

Social analysis, like diagnosis, begins with symptoms or problems on the surface and then works its way back to whatever is causing them. Like diagnosis, social analysis is a combination of science and art, experience and intuition, dialogue and consultation.

In "A pound of cure", the symptomatic problems are financial and full of conflict. Medicare seems to be ailing, but in fact it is being attacked and undermined. Medicare needs the public to maintain and protect it.

In "An ounce of prevention", health care proves to be much broader than medicare. The analysis focused on cancer, diagnosing it as a "social" and not just an individual disease. A public health approach is needed. Canadians have already invented CHCs/CLSCs as better structures for dealing with diseases and promoting health.

Once a disease is discovered, few people say, "It's too difficult to get rid of, I'll live with it."

Social analysis has brought us up against what is causing problems with medicare and what is a grave contributing cause of the dread illness, cancer. Doing something about these causes is obviously essential to the effort of preventing disease and promoting health — even if doing so may challenge things as they are.

Health care at first seems as simple as an individual patient's relationship with an individual doctor. But health care soon proves to be a broader system that affects everyone. And people working in groups can have some effect on that system.

From the beginning of time, communities have recognized certain men and women as possessing the skill and power to heal. These healers might be herbalists, midwives, shamans, priests or physicians. The stereotype is a wild-eyed "witch doctor" mumbling bizarre incantations. Yet healers — from herbalists to neurosurgeons — have this in common: They are commissioned by the community to tend to the sick.

Modern medicine, shying away from the traditional approach, has made medical practice a private affair. It has centralized healthcare services and promoted increased specialization and the use of complex, expensive technology. The medical establishment frowns on the activities of those it sees as "less professional" but competing health practitioners, such as chiropractors and midwives.

A complex society obviously requires a complex medical system with high technology, well-established institutions, efficient business practices. But Canadian communities also need centres of healing in the more traditional sense. The knowledge and resources exist: to learn how to avoid getting sick in the first place, to attack disease in a more systematic way, to develop more effective structures like the CHCs, and to promote health positively by encouraging preventive medicine and public health.

Canadian medicare is a very good beginning: It provides accessible, comprehensive and universal healthcare delivery. When we do get sick, we are glad of the "pound of cure" that pays the bills. But prepaid public insurance is not enough. Must it always be inevitable to get sick in the first place? While we're healthy, let's work to develop many an "ounce of prevention".

Questions

- What do people remember about being sick before the days of medicare? Are similar experiences occurring nowadays?

- Do a survey of your community's health needs and resources. Does everyone in your community have equal access to health care? Do some physicians extra-bill? Does the government allow extra-billing? Your provincial Health Coa-

Resources

- Ed Finn, *Medicare: On the critical list*, Ottawa, 1984. A pamphlet produced by the Canadian Centre for Policy Alternatives, P.O. Box 4466, Station "E", Ottawa, Ontario K1S 5B6.

- David Coburn et al., eds., *Health and Canadian Society: Sociological Perspectives*, Toronto: Fitzhenry and Whiteside, 1981. Nearly thirty studies of the Canadian health industry, devel-

Questions (cont'd)

lition is part of a national movement to preserve the original principles of medicare; for further information, contact the Canadian Health Coalition, 2841 Riverside Drive, Ottawa, Ont. K1V 8X7, ph. 613-521-3400.

- What are the differences between being a unionized health worker (such as an orderly) and a self-employed professional (such as a family doctor)?

- What constitutes a healthy lifestyle? Is yours healthy? What helps people develop such a lifestyle? What are the economic and political barriers? Is there a CHC or CLSC in the neighbourhood? If so, is it community-controlled? If not, to explore setting up such a centre, contact your provincial association of CHCs/CLSCs (address available from Canadian Health Coalition, above).

- Is environmental pollution in your community causing cancer? What measures have been taken to clean up the pollution and prevent the illness? Are there problems with occupational health and safety? For further information, contact the Canadian Centre for Occupational Safety and Health, 250 Main Street East, Hamilton, Ont. L8N 1H6, ph. 416-523-2981.

Resources (cont'd)

oping virtually all the topics introduced in this analysis.

- Erik P. Eckholm, *The Picture of Health: Environmental Sources of Disease*, New York: W.W. Norton, 1977. A very clear essay on the environmental origins of world health trends, with especially good presentation of the social sources of cancer and occupationally-induced diseases. Eckholm argues for changes in social structures, government policies and personal behaviour.

- Martin Shapiro, *Getting Doctored: Critical Reflections on Becoming a Physician*, Toronto: Between The Lines, 1978. A popular account of how medical education transforms the ideals of young medical students into very different views on health care. Problems in the field of medicine reflect broader social issues.

- National Council of Welfare, *Medicare: The Public Good and the Private Practice*, Ottawa, 1982. A concise overview of the state of medicare in Canada in the 1980s, criticizing the trend towards extra-billing and user fees as making health care less accessible.

- "Rich Man's Medicine, Poor Man's Medicine", DEC Films, 16 mm, 43 minutes, colour, 1976. Traditional and modern medicine in two West African countries are complementary. But expensive western ways tend to displace time-tested treatments based on local products and beliefs.

- "Citizen's Medicine," Bonnie Klein, NFB, 16 mm, 30 minutes, 1970. The problems and advantages of a CLSC in Montreal as seen by both patients and doctors.

Chapter Three

The Housing Drama

What does the word *"home"* convey?

"Home" gives most people a feeling of belonging and security. Home is where we grew up, and where we live our personal and family lives. Home is a unique place to arrange and furnish as an expression of one's character, to adorn by decorating a room or planting tulips. Home is a retreat from the frenzy of daily life, it is the place we identify with.

The Universal Declaration of Human Rights states simply that everyone has the right to an adequate standard of living, including *housing*, a minimum of decent, affordable shelter. Housing is a material right and necessity; a home is a spiritual and cultural need. Both are basic to human well-being. People take whatever housing they are able to get, be it modest or extravagant, and use it to create their home.

"Real Estate" is a weekend feature of most Canadian papers. If you look in that section for news about housing in Canada, you find a few stories overshadowed by a tremendous volume of advertising. "Luxurious enclaves of prestigious townhomes" vie with "elegant" or "graceful" houses in new suburbs.

In one ad, a typical couple, in formal attire and sipping champagne, pose in their well-appointed living room. "I guess you could say we move in the fast track," confides the suave husband. "Our full social calendar would certainly suggest it. And we most certainly enjoy it." He goes on to assure the reader: "But make no mistake. It has been earned. When one has paid one's dues, the attendant rewards are richly appreciated. Such as

the sumptuousness of a Rosedale Glen home."

The many ads make it clear that housing is not just a basic right and necessity. Housing is also the product of an industry, a commodity to be marketed for profit. How is accommodation planned, financed, constructed and sold in Canada?

For approximately 20 per cent of Canadian families, finding affordable, appropriate housing is a serious problem. The members of one household in every five cannot find housing they can afford. Do the laws of the market tend to protect or violate people's fundamental right to shelter?

This chapter looks at those involved in "The Housing Drama". After identifying the main actors, we go "Behind the Scenes" to analyze some of the major decisions being made in the development industry and see how these decisions affect consumers. "Consumers Write a New Script" explores various responses to the problems of housing.

> Canada, despite its abundant wealth, has not yet managed to provide all of its population with a decent shelter. . . . Particularly in large cities, behind a screen of skyscrapers, wide avenues sometimes conceal blighted areas teeming with newcomers, unemployed workers, low wage-earners or members of ethnic minorities. The development of suburbia has given rise to similar results.
>
> *Canadian Conference of Catholic Bishops,*
> **Decent Housing For All,** *1976*

Actors on the Stage

Housing is a drama involving many players. Among them are: the dwellers, or those in search of dwellings, who are called "consumers"; the producers of housing, formerly known as "builders"; the financiers; and the government.

Consumers

Budget and financial advisers say that, in order to meet all their other needs, Canadians should spend no more than 25 to 30 per cent of their incomes on housing. But rent or mortgage, utilities and maintenance can easily gobble up much more of the paycheque than that.

Over half a million families who rent — or 18 per cent of all tenants — pay more than 30 per cent of their income on rent, according to the government's Canada Mortgage and Housing Corporation. In 1978, 30 per cent of all women renters were paying more than 30 per cent of their income on rent. By 1980, 38 per cent of women who paid rent spent over the 30 per cent figure. Two out of every three women renters had incomes under $12,000 per year, compared to one out of every four men.

The dream of owning a house seems harder and harder to realize. A magazine article on the housing crisis told readers bluntly, "If you don't own the roof over your head today, you probably never will." The reasons were attributed to an intimidating mix of "population pressures, social phenomena, monetarism and the topography of cities". But the "best reason" for the problems with real estate was that "God isn't making any more of it".

The two Canadians out of five who live in rented accommodation have little control over what they pay for their shelter, because apartments are hard to find and rents are often set by anonymous corporate landlords. For example, a group of tenants in Montreal faced rent increases of up to 44 per cent. At a Quebec Rental Board hearing, they asked their superintendent who owned the building: a firm by the name of Trading Fund Establishment. Who was that? The superintendent admitted that he didn't know. The company turned out to be registered in the tiny European principality of Liechtenstein, which was also the home base of over thirty other Montreal apartment buildings along with a number of commercial properties and other real estate.

One woman described her difficulty in finding decent shelter for her daughter and herself:

> Being a single parent, I was living at the boarding house with my daughter Julia, and that was really hard. I was lucky I could work there and save some money to get out. If I worked, it was deducted off my rent. That was the only way for me. You can't save money on welfare. It's just like a never ending circle. I had lice. Julia had lice. We finally got out and now we're ok.

Finding a dream house in a choice location is not the issue here. "People are phoning to say they can't find a place to live," reported a Toronto alderman, who added that the increase from earlier years was not simply in the volume of calls, "but in the intensity. People come near the breaking point because there is no solution". Vancouver community workers frequently fail to find accommodation for desperate people even for one night and end up giving needy people enough cash so they can spend the night drinking coffee in an all-night restaurant.

A former psychiatric patient describes her housing:

> Right now I get $318 a month for my disability, but my rent is $260 and I have to share my room. The landlord isn't a bad guy, but he charges way too much. That leaves me $58 a month and I give about $20 of that to my friend Fred because they won't give him anything. The rest I spend mostly on cigarettes or coffee. I'm always hungry.

Some people simply lack permanent shelter, spending the night outdoors or in hostels, while whole families are crowded into shabby, often dangerous lodgings rented by the week. What concern are the homeless to the majority of well-housed Canadians, the developers, financiers and government housing departments?

Under the pressure of urbanization, the structure of city centres is once more being completely changed to make it more functional for further-ance of commercial ends. Thus, whole streets are being torn up and low-wage earners displaced. Then on those sites tall impressive buildings are going up, often symbolic of power and wealth, and broad air-polluting speedways are being provided. As a result, mainly for economic rea-sons, dwellings by the thousands have been expropriated and even more citizens uprooted and left to fend for themselves. Even though pub-lic opinion has reproved this destructiveness, the "law of progress" keeps on adding new victims. All of this seems to us inconceivable, especially when the elderly or the helpless are involved.

Canadian Conference of Catholic Bishops,
Decent Housing For All, *1976*

Producers

Things have changed since the days when tenants rented accommodation from landlords who owned a few properties. Until World War II, small businessmen generally dominated the field. Then the post-war population boom of the 1950s lured real estate investors hoping to make money by building much-needed housing. Super profits could be made by *developers* of housing — busi-nesses that organized building projects in such a way that other firms supplied the financing and did the actual construction.

Many small builders and landholders were soon pushed aside or eliminated. By the end of the sixties the housing resources that had for-merly been spread around were consolidated into a modern, big-business industry. This is what economists call "rationalization". The huge Cana-dian development corporations were fully in con-trol.

Today the largest firms in the development industry are:
- Olympia and York of Toronto, privately owned, reputedly the world's largest development firm with assets of over $13 billion;
- Cadillac-Fairview of Toronto, with assets of $3.4 billion;
- Trizec of Calgary, $2.8 billion;
- Daon of Vancouver, $2.2 billion;
- Nu West of Calgary, $1.9 billion;
- Campeau of Ottawa, $1.7 billion.

These corporations spawned the apartments and offices, the malls and condominiums that fed the explosive growth of Canadian cities.

A task force on housing organized by Paul Hel-lyer, the federal minister responsible for housing at the end of the sixties, encouraged the growth of big development corporations. Hellyer's report concluded that "The house-building industry needs more *larger companies*. Not only to ensure sufficient capital . . . but to be able to plan on a rational basis." Some now question whether the process of consolidation and rationalization has resulted in the best plans for our urban environ-ment.

Financiers

Developers who construct mammoth highrise apartments and sprawling suburban communities require even larger amounts of capital than they themselves can supply, so another player appears in the housing drama.

The country's financial institutions are crucial to both the first-time homeowner and the multi-million dollar development firm. The chartered banks, trust companies and insurance companies all lend substantial sums to support construction

of commercial and residential buildings. This lending permits developers to do what they otherwise could not afford.

For financial institutions, real estate and its exploitation form a fundamental part of business. As ManuLife asserts in an advertisement showing sketches of highrises across the continent: "A leader in Life Insurance . . . Now an innovator in Real Estate."

Despite advertisements depicting houses and apartments, financial institutions are not primarily concerned with exploiting housing as a commodity. Their major interest is in the land, which is bought, developed and sold for profit, for the sake of a healthy balance sheet. The financial institutions like to be assured that the funds borrowed by developers, plus interest, will be fully recoverable.

Those who invest in land are speculating on a unique resource, because "God isn't making any more of it". The steady demand, or ever greater need for space to live, tends to make the price rise. The value of the land appreciates. But does the treatment of land and buildings as commodities respond sufficiently to people's basic need for decent, affordable shelter and security?

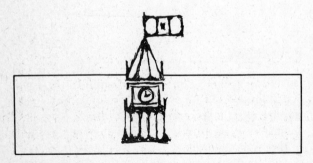

Government

A fourth actor comes on stage. Unwilling to let the majority of the population go without shelter, all levels of government have stepped into the housing field.

The most active intervention has been by the federal government, whose role began in 1935 with the National Housing Act. Since then and until the early seventies, the federal government tried to stimulate construction by providing incentives which favoured large developers. This promoted corporate concentration in the housing industry.

The provincial governments have intervened less dramatically. Their principal contribution was the slum clearance and urban renewal projects initiated in the fifties and sixties. These programmes — oriented towards the poor — resulted in what's known as public housing.

During the seventies more and more consumers became unable to afford the price of housing. The federal and provincial response was to offer an array of programmes aimed at both consumers and developers. Such programmes include:
• AHOP (Assisted Home Ownership Program);
• RHOSP (Registered Home Ownership Savings Plan);
• RRAP (Residential Rehabilitation Assistance Program);
• ARP (Assisted Rental Plan); and
• CRSP (Canada Rental Supply Plan).

The titles sound resolute; but the policies have often been short-term, inconsistent or even conflicting. This confusing wealth of direct incentives and indirect subsidies to entice builders into constructing houses and apartments is now seen as a fairly vain attempt to solve the real housing problem.

For example, under the CRSP the government supplied interest-free loans to induce reluctant private developers to build apartments. This resulted in the construction of twenty-one thousand new apartments. Although a third of all such apartments were earmarked for low-income people, very few were actually ever occupied by those in need because provincial governments were reluctant to play their designated role by providing on-going subsidies. So less than six hundred of the twenty-one thousand publicly-supported units wound up as low-cost housing. Developers were very enthusiastic about CRSP, especially since they were free to convert the buildings into condominiums once they repaid the loans.

In 1979 the Ministry of Housing and Urban Affairs was abolished and its functions integrated with those of the Ministry of Public Works. From 1976 to 1981 the budget of the Crown-owned Canada Mortgage and Housing Corporation was cut from $1.6 billion to $326 million. By 1983 the money available for housing had again risen to over a billion dollars, only to be cut down to half that amount in 1984.

Rather than direct loans for housing, the government is encouraging loans from the private financial sector. But when Ottawa proposed elimination of the Multiple Unit Residential Building (MURB) programme, which provides tax breaks for investors in large residential projects regardless of availability of apartments for the poor, it met with strong opposition from developers and financiers. The government permitted the MURB programme to continue, although MURB mainly subsidizes condominiums that are well out of the price range of those most in need of housing.

Federal law allows big developers a tax deduction for depreciation in the value of their rental properties. But the properties may actually increase in value, thanks to a rise in the market and the ever higher cost of construction. One study estimated the effective rate of taxation in the development industry at much less than 10 per cent, well below the average rate for large corporations in other sectors.

The industry has periodically failed to produce sufficient basic accommodation for purchase or rent. At such moments the government tends to intervene, but with the understanding, as one Ottawa housing minister put it, that: "The private market is the best tool for providing housing for most Canadians. . . . The federal government is determined to let market forces operate for the broad majority of households who can afford to choose what the market offers."

The results are haphazard — of the now-you-see-us/now-you-don't variety — and rather inconsistent. In practice Canada's housing policy does not primarily serve the interests of consumers.

Behind the Scenes

Canada, one would think, has the *means* to provide everyone with decent shelter, yet the housing squeeze seems dramatic. Why does the potential for decent, affordable housing for all remain unrealized? Identifying the actors is one step of analysis towards understanding the whole drama. Another is to focus on the changing interests and roles of the development industry, to see their effect on housing.

Developers Leave the Stage

Until the 1920s, half of all Canadians lived in rural areas. In town, small entrepreneurs built stores and offices along neighbourhood commercial strips. Rapid growth in the urban population — now well over 80 per cent of Canadians — has meant changes in the character of Canadian cities and their builders.

After a boom during the postwar period, the development industry began to shift its money out of housing in search of higher profits. By 1976 every major Canadian developer who had started business in the residential field was trying to corner a portion of the commercial market: office buildings, sports complexes, shopping malls. Moreover, even in the housing field, developers' dollars were apt to be invested in the construction of expensive condominiums rather than single family dwellings or even highrise apartments.

This major shift in strategy involved wholesale sheddings of residential properties and land holdings. The capital was diverted into the

> **Right now our country must tackle the major problem of housing. To avoid swelling the ranks of the needy it will not be enough to build thousands and thousands of houses. We will first need to know where to build them, where to find the required capital, and what types of dwellings are necessary for human community. That is why Canada must urgently adopt policies calculated to protect its citizens, especially its low-wage earners, against galloping inflation of house building costs: rising mortgage rates, real estate speculation, increased costs of building materials, higher rents, etc.**
>
> *Canadian Conference of Catholic Bishops,*
> **Decent Housing For All,** *1976*

commercial sector where it could be used for the financial schemes and leasing arrangements that generate the highest profits. A tenants' rights advocate put the matter succinctly.

It all boils down to a business decision. Why should a major developer bother with tenants and all the problems of dealing with residential properties — all for a lower return — when he can move into shopping centres and other commercial properties with almost no equity and no big problems?

In 1982 the Nu-West group of Calgary announced plans to cut its housing inventory down to zero and move its money to land devel-

opment and commercial building in the United States. Later that year Cadillac-Fairview sold off over ten thousand apartment units in its strategy to concentrate on mixed properties, shopping centres, major office buildings and business parks. This caused a major furor. Tenants would have to support the new owners' borrowing through higher rents. Subsequently, the three trust companies involved in the deal were placed under the control of the Ontario government and investigated for violations of Ontario laws. In the midst of the controversy, few questioned whether by shifting its investments Cadillac-Fairview had betrayed any social responsibilities to the tenants.

With only about 2 per cent of its investments in land development and condominiums, Olympia and York weathered the shakedown comfortably. "If you look at all the Canadian and United States' developers," co-owner Paul Reichmann reflected, "those who are doing the major office buildings are not having major problems."

Capital flows out to the most profitable locations as well as the most profitable businesses. The strategy of the Vancouver firm Daon is similar to that of its competitors: to locate operations in what it sees as areas of above-average population and economic growth. This means the southern and western United States, where the blight of economic downturn has not been as extreme as in

Canada and the American northeast. Cadillac-Fairview withdrew from the Canadian housing scene and went south, building the Shannon Mall in Atlanta, the Pacific Gateway centre in Los Angeles and the Shaklee Terraces in San Francisco's business district. Trizec pushed ahead with the Fashion Show Shopping Centre in Las Vegas and the Meadows Town Centre business complex in Denver.

Large development corporations are no longer interested in building housing that is within the financial grasp of most Canadians. But why don't others in the private market meet the need?

A major reason is that the diversified housing market that existed up to the late forties has been crushed under the weight of the developers. From the viewpoint of the market, housing is like any other commodity: a form of merchandise to be produced and sold. So a basic need is turned into an item for sale. What is built matters little, as long as it produces healthy profits. If condominiums priced at $500,000 and trimmed with oak and marble tile promise to sell well, those are what will be built.

Consumers Left Out

As the investment policies of developers, banks, life insurance and trust companies shift towards commercial and luxury buildings, they leave behind a housing situation which reveals a serious failure of the free market. The costs of rental accommodation escalate, as vacancy rates in some major Canadian cities hover below 1 per cent.

Securing a reasonable apartment has become an anxious ritual in cities such as Vancouver, Toronto, Ottawa and Halifax. One tactic is to grab the early edition of the morning paper, scan the classifieds, and rush to be the first prospective tenant to put down a deposit. Another is to buy a list of available apartments from a rental agency, although some agencies are high-priced, unscrupulous outfits that may even sell obsolete listings. The best bet is to find someone who is moving out and make a bid for the place before it goes on the market. There is also the chance of getting into non-profit housing or a co-operative subsidized by the government, but the waiting list can be long. Searching for a place to live can be as frustrating and futile as looking for a job.

The problem is not simply one of supply. There is also the important question of price. Rental units, especially in large cities, tend to be priced beyond the means of those who most desperately need shelter. People on low and fixed incomes cannot even consider the apartments in downtown modern, multi-storey buildings or the older, spacious flats that sometimes become available. They must look for moderate rents, period, and forget about quality, space or location.

Enough affordable or moderately-priced housing is just not being built to keep up with the growing demand. In 1965 five out of ten Canadian families could buy a house and carry the mortgage on 30 per cent of the family income. By the early eighties that proportion had fallen to three out of ten — and only if the family had two incomes. In 1981 a mere 2.3 per cent of Vancouver tenants had the resources to buy their own houses.

The purchase of an average priced house may require an income well above the median. Those who do own a house worry about the economy, keeping one eye on the rate of interest and the other on the calendar, waiting anxiously for the mortgage renewal time. Few people who consider buying a house are able to do what the advertisements urge — "Take flight from the commonplace".

These housing problems are deeply-rooted in the way the industry is organized. Are there any countervailing forces which might promote, or at least protect, the interests of the ordinary housing "consumer" who can no longer afford to consume?

Consumers Write a New Script

The actors — consumers, bankers, developers, governments — have been introduced and the evolution of the housing industry traced. The analysis has come up against one of the limits of a so-called free market in supplying housing. The

> Those who are to be the users of housing must participate in determining the nature of their housing and in the subsequent management thereof. Users of public and other housing must have the freedom to seek improvements without fear of reprisal of any kind. Where urban renewal or rehabilitation is contemplated, it is incumbent that governments, together with the physical and social planners, involve area citizens from the beginning of a project in determining what kind of housing and community will best meet their particular needs, even if this entails changes in current legislation and regulations.
>
> *Lutheran Church in America — Canada Section,* **Towards Adequate Housing for All Canadians,** *1969*

primary reason housing is not being built, in short, is because developers and lending institutions have found other commodities more profitable to build and more secure to invest in.

People naturally wonder about this apparently mysterious system which they cannot directly influence but which nevertheless directly affects them. In trying to understand the housing morass, they are doing social analysis.

Many people are terribly discouraged by the famine in housing. Their failure to find decent space to buy or rent strikes each individual person and family as a very personal, indeed overwhelming problem. How do people transcend their discouragement?

Some have rejected the idea that theirs is only an individual problem. They analyze the drama and identify the various forces at play, in order to take an initiative of their own. Together they develop a collective solution to what once seemed a painful individual dilemma. They are dealing with the concept of housing as a social right.

Since the seventies — as the private housing

market failed — consumers have become more vocal in demanding a housing policy that respects their interests. For example:

- Tenants across the country have formed associations and pressured provincial governments to pass laws limiting rent increases and restricting the reasons for such increases. Tenants have also won the right of protection from arbitrary and unjust eviction.
- Tenants have formed unions to fight proposed rent increases, improve maintenance and push for tenants' rights.
- Homeowners, vulnerable to the fluctuating cost of mortgages, have called on government to set fixed interest rates for housing.
- Tenants have prevented some landlords from selling their buildings for conversion into luxury accommodation by forming co-operatives to buy and run buildings in the interests of the occupants.
- Co-operatives have been organized to buy and renovate existing buildings or to build new ones. Thanks to pressure on the federal government, this programme continues.
- Resident associations of tenants and homeowners alike are being organized to improve their neighbourhoods and protect them from unnecessary redevelopment.

As one solution to the housing shortage, co-ops have enjoyed the sporadic support of local, provincial and federal governments. But the other actors in the housing game are reacting to protect their own interests.

Developers, landlords and lenders are calling for an end to social-housing legislation and programmes designed to provide affordable accommodation. Instead, they want subsidies like the CRSP to assist the private sector — while consumers are thrown back on the mercy of the free market. In this scheme, individual low-income renters would be supplied with a shelter supplement. But a shelter allowance carries with it the feelings of dependence characteristic of the welfare system whereas a co-op helps people to win a sense of dignity and control.

The treatment of shelter as a commodity puts housing beyond the reach of one Canadian family in five. It also renders millions more insecure and vulnerable to anonymous-sounding "free market forces". At the same time old people and single women supporting families end up paying large portions of their already inadequate incomes for shelter.

Stroll through any Canadian city and survey

> In recent years, significant experiences have shown that when citizens group together and decide to establish and carry out a plan, they can change existing conditions. . . . Here and there in Canada, groups have actively engaged in efforts to rejuvenate their run-down districts. Likewise, other groups have set up housing co-operatives enabling average or low-income people to build a decent home for themselves and yet avoid real estate speculation and excessive debts. . . . Those examples show, as do a great many others, that direct participation by citizens in the organization of their area or city helps to improve the social and economic life of the community.
>
> *Canadian Conference of Catholic Bishops,*
> **Decent Housing For All,** *1976*

what is being built: the signs on building sites refer to office towers, sports stadiums, luxury condominiums, shopping malls. Reconsider the roles of the major actors since World War II — financial institutions, developers, various levels of government. Control has increasingly concentrated in the hands of actors who show little interest in affordable housing. Can those with the most power over what gets built be expected to suddenly realign their priorities or voluntarily reduce the cost of accommodation?

Ordinary people have real, lasting interest in decent, reasonably-priced houses or apartment buildings on a human scale in stable, friendly neighbourhoods. As individuals, people do not have much leverage in the housing drama. But once organized, citizens can influence the supply and distribution of housing on the local level. They can continue to pressure the government to channel resources away from private developers and into non-profit housing and other consumer-centred solutions. Such policies would move us closer to an effective respect for everyone's right to adequate, decent shelter... so that everyone might rightfully feel *at home* in Canada.

Questions

- What is your personal experience — and that of others you know — in finding and keeping housing? What arguments are used to blame the consumer for the housing problem?

- Name some of the groups in your community or city who are having the most difficulty in finding decent and affordable accommodation. What efforts are being made to develop solutions to their problems? Individual efforts? Collective efforts?

- "What sort of city, town or village do we want to live in, to preserve, develop or create? For whom do we want to build? How should the manifold resources of our heritage be apportioned for the benefit of the entire community, so that all may be decently housed?"

Resources

- Alexander Laidlaw, *Housing You Can Afford*, Toronto: Green Tree Publishing, 1977. A history of co-op housing in Canada, along with practical suggestions for those interested in starting co-ops. For further information contact the Co-operative Housing Foundation of Canada, 56 Sparks Street, Ottawa, Ont. K1P 5A9, ph. 613-238-4644, and request their bi-monthly newsletter, *From the Roof-tops*.

- James Lorimer, *The Developers*, Toronto: James Lorimer, 1978. A look at Canada's development industry, examining house, apartment, office and commercial construction. Focuses on the major corporations involved.

- James Lorimer and Carolyn MacGregor, eds., *After the Developers*, Toronto: James Lorimer,

Questions (cont'd)

- "Housing for people, or housing for profits? Food for the hungry, or food as a market commodity? Thus, it is not that economic means are lacking; the problem is to find the will to restructure our society and reorder its priorities."

- "Within the next thirty years," according to Barbara Ward, "the human race will have to erect more buildings than it has erected since the beginning of its history. In the underdeveloped countries, the immensity of the task is still more disconcerting: within twenty years, their cities and towns will have to equip themselves with as many houses and working plants as the industrial nations have erected during the last two centuries." Can the analysis of housing in Canada be used to understand the challenge of providing shelter in Third World countries? How do solutions developed there differ from the Canadian approach? Would they be applicable here?

Resources (cont'd)

1981. A collection of articles on urban issues such as the growth of shopping centres and retail chains, city politics and the effects of the development industry on Canada's urban landscape.

- "This Land is Whose Land? The Housing Squeeze", *ISSUE* 26 (April 1982). A critical analysis of the housing industry, in a broadsheet of sixteen pages, with an excellent list of resources. Research in Social Issues, Division of Mission in Canada, United Church of Canada, 85 St. Clair Avenue East, Toronto, Ont. M4T 1M8, ph. 416-925-5931.

- "Castles in the Air", *CBC Fifth Estate,* 1980, 56 minutes. Based on Lorimer's *The Developers:* The Canadian land development industry rises to wealth and power, while millions of Canadians struggle to find and keep affordable housing.

- "Co-op Housing: Getting It Together" and "Co-op Housing: The Best Move We Ever Made", NFB, 16 mm, 23 minutes each. Against the background of the housing crisis in Canada, how co-op housing can be planned and started, presenting an alternative that offers security of tenure and mutual aid.

Chapter Four

Our Planet Earth

Most of us believe that fundamental rights should be guaranteed in our society: the right to free speech, the right to freedom of worship, the right to freedom of assembly. Canada's constitution has a Charter of Rights and Freedoms to provide such guarantees. But a precious right not enshrined in the charter is seriously imperilled: the right to enjoy air and water, without the threat of being poisoned.

Waste and garbage have always accompanied human civilization, but only in recent years has industrial pollution been building up uncontrollably. Menacing new words creep into everyday speech: acid rain, dioxin, PCBs, radioactive wastes and toxic dumps. "Witch's Brew of Chemical Peril" is a typical headline. "Love Canal" is a new synonym for environmental disaster. Can nature continue to provide society with a bottomless garbage pit?

At its best, the environment is a marvelously balanced and self-healing system. Human communities share the world's ecosystem with innumerable other animal and plant communities. The fact that all creatures from the simplest organism to the most complex are linked in an interdependent fashion means that the environment — their home, our home — is very much a social resource. One group or species cannot abuse part of the ecosystem without disturbing an intricate balance and so damaging the whole. Has the damage already gone beyond the point where nature can heal itself?

Some environmental scourges such as acid rain have resulted from the burning over the years of hydrocarbons and the smelting of ores. Other poisons like dioxins and PCBs have been fabricated, accompanying the spread of ever more sophisticated industrial technologies. As these activities proliferated along with the rapid economic growth of the twentieth century, their impact on the environment has become severe enough in the past decade or two to alarm the public. Will the environment itself become a danger to human health?

> Who is not haunted by the "ecological crisis"? Who has not conjured with the desolating thought that [we are] fouling [our] nest, possibly beyond reclamation? Who is not troubled that we are depleting our planet's store of non-renewable resources at an alarming rate?
>
> *United Church of Canada,*
> **27th General Council,** *1977*

Social Costs

Everyone used to assume that there would always be more than enough trees, pure air, fertile soil and clean water. These were regarded as givens — free gifts of nature for society to use and enjoy. According to conventional thinking, something which is "free" has, by definition, no cost or price-tag attached to it.

But in fact there are a whole series of costs, some very tangible and others nearly impossible to quantify, which are incurred by society as a result of pollution. We shall call these *social costs*. When serious pollution occurs, real damage is done. Social costs deprive the community of goods to which it is entitled, and these losses are sustained by all members of society.

Air pollution, for example, causes lung disease and corrodes everything from automobiles to the Parliament Buildings. When a smog descends, some people get sick; the price is paid both by those who suffer and by society in the form of higher healthcare costs. Contaminated lakes and rivers lose their fish and plant life, their aesthetic and recreational value, their ability to sustain tourism, fishing and development. Human illness and suffering, socio-economic losses, and irreparable harm to nature make up the social costs.

Most pollution comes from industrial activity carried on by private corporations or public agencies striving to maximize short-term gains or profit. Industries confine their economic calculations to market values, and fail to include the social costs that cannot be expressed directly in monetary terms or that can be sloughed off onto the public. Damages done to people's health and the environment are treated as "externalities" and not entered on the expense side of the company's ledger.

It is true that, unlike the other costs of doing business — raw materials, labour, energy — social costs are difficult to quantify. But that does not mean that they are unreal or don't exist. The social costs of doing business are directly incurred (but not necessarily measured) by the community or society at large. Yet in return, no part of the product of industry goes back to compensate those whose health has been ruined and environment despoiled.

It is not easy for society to affix a dollar value to sparkling lakes teeming with fish and the crisp fresh air of a spring morning. Sometimes social costs can be expressed in monetary terms: health bills from cancer or silicosis for instance. Sometimes they cannot: What is the cost of a dead lake? Of air that's not fit to breathe? Of a pleasant landscape ruined by a vast open-pit mine? Of a child whose learning abilities are impaired?

If industry is making profits on "free" air, water, soil and resources, how can it be made to stop doing damage? How can it be forced to absorb the costs of the long-term damages which are usually sustained by the public? In the future, how can industry be made to include the long-term potential costs in its estimates, so that it has to make the right decisions from the start?

In dealing with environmental issues, the task of social analysis is to:
• analyze the pollution: what are the damages? the causes? the effects on people and the environment?
• estimate the social costs, and see how they are distributed: who is generating the pollution? who is making the profit? who is sustaining the losses in health, quality of life, environmental harm and so on?
• suggest a more just distribution of the costs and benefits.

This chapter takes a particular pollutant — lead — as an example and tells how one community dealt with the social costs arising from its spread. Other environmental issues will be examined more briefly at the end of the chapter.

Social justice demands that a productive resource base and clean environment be passed on to those coming after us. The decisions made during this decade on land use, forestry, water resources, industrial waste, and energy development will mark the integrity of the stewardship we exercise toward our common heritage.
United Church of Canada,
An Alternative Economic Vision, 1983

Lead Peril

All pollutants are not newfangled threats to human health. Some chemicals have been in common use for many centuries, and lead is one of these. Lead coins were circulating as early as 1000 B.C. Historians speculate that the fall of the Roman Empire could be linked to the poisoning effects of lead, employed by the Romans in cooking utensils and even as a sweetener in food.

Historical Production and Consumption of Lead

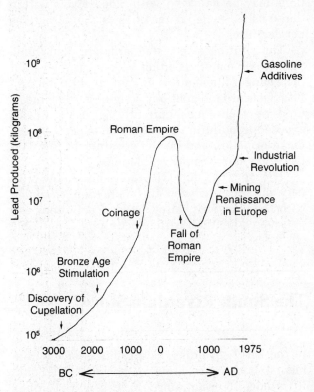

Since ancient times medicine has learned how damaging lead is to the human body. Like some other substances occurring in nature (mercury, cadmium, arsenic), lead is toxic (poisonous) if taken into the body. Small doses of lead inhibit certain cellular processes. Higher levels of expo-

sure can cause infertility, anemia and subtle psychological and behavioural changes. In acute cases, nausea, fever, paralysis and even coma may result.

According to the National Research Council, among "urban children, pregnant women, persons living near busy highways and near smelters without proper emission controls", environmental lead exposure "is high enough to represent an increased and unacceptable risk to health". Young children may suffer learning disabilities, and in 1983 the federal Minister of the Environment declared that lead was "an insidious danger to the health of Canadian children".

Lead can enter the body in a variety of ways. Airborne lead associated with fine particles is absorbed directly into the lungs. Coarser, heavier lead-bearing dust tends to settle locally, accumulating in soil and on vegetation along roadways or near industrial sources, such as smelters. Eating vegetables grown in areas of lead fallout can also bring lead into the body. Leafy vegetables such as lettuce can contain dangerous levels of lead. Lead in the soil poses a particular threat to young children, who may ingest it while playing.

It has been estimated that, all in all, human activities introduce perhaps twenty times more lead into the environment than would occur naturally. Automobile exhaust is the major source of lead emissions in Canada today.

Data on the extent of lead build-up in surface soil from selected Canadian localities are shown in the graph below. If the average value given for Vancouver, namely 205 parts per million (ppm), may be considered typical for residential and light industrial areas, urban lead concentrations

---

Lead Content of Soil (in micrograms per gram of soil)

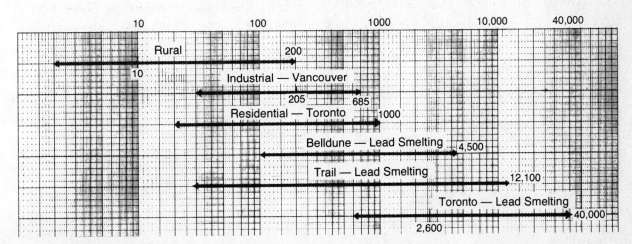

are about twenty times those in uncontaminated rural environments. Most of this urban lead is likely of automotive origin.

Industrial operations involving metal production, and in particular lead smelting, can however contribute significant amounts of additional lead to local soils. The maximum lead values shown for soil near both Cominco's lead-zinc smelter at Trail, B.C., and Brunswick Mining and Smelting's lead plant at Belledune, N.B., (4,500 and 12,100 ppm respectively), are about ten times higher than the maximum concentrations reported for smelter-free urban areas. Even higher lead levels (up to 40,000 ppm) have been detected, prior to soil replacement, around the relatively small secondary-lead smelting facilities of Canada Metal and Toronto Refiners and Smelters in Toronto.

When it comes to measuring pollution things get confusing. Scientists often disagree on what levels of exposure are "safe", "acceptable" or "dangerous". Lay people, who may be directly affected, often feel like strangers in a strange land when they enter the world of statistical subtleties. The nuances of "parts per million" or "toxic threshold" are bewildering.

Lead pollution is a case in point. When children living near a smelter in Toronto first had their blood tested in 1973, the level above which lead was agreed to have toxic effects was 40 micrograms of lead per decilitre of blood. Subsequent research has identified levels above 30 micrograms per decilitre as toxic. But it has also been shown that children's psychological functions may be damaged with blood levels within the so-called "safe" range of 15 to 25 micrograms per decilitre.

The shifting safety standards are disturbing. Some toxic materials either have no safe level, or their danger threshold is unknown, or their harmful effects are too subtle or long-term to be measured by techniques currently in use. Citizens exposed to pollution must rely on expert opinion for information and on the government to establish and enforce safety regulations.

The story of South Riverdale shows how ordinary citizens analyzed their situation, grappled with the questions raised by lead pollution, and persevered in their struggle despite formidable obstacles.

The South Riverdale Story

In the early seventies, as awareness of environmental issues was growing, residents of South Riverdale, a community in east-end Toronto, began to realize their area faced a serious lead pollution problem. Their subsequent battle was long, involving local residents in their community organizations, two levels of government (often opposed to each other), the polluting company, a host of experts and several boards of inquiry. It's a story that shows the strength and limits of community action as people tried to analyze and grapple with social forces affecting their neighbourhood.

South Riverdale is a traditional working-class community. The houses were built closely together early in the century. Residents have only a short walk to the factories that still dot the streets of the area. The neighbourhood is convenient to downtown, so that some affluent, upwardly mobile people have moved into newly sand-blasted houses. In spite of such changes the community has preserved its character. Many factories still remain in South Riverdale at a time when other urban industries have shut their doors and moved to the suburbs.

One of the big plants in the area is a lead smelter run by the Canada Metal Company. For years residents had considered the dust from the smel-

ter simply a nuisance. They did not know about lead with its associated health risks. But concern about the potential hazard was sparked in 1972, when it was learned that the provincial Ministry of the Environment had withheld information on elevated lead levels in dust produced by Toronto Refiners and Smelters on the other side of town. Contamination of soil and vegetation near the plants was the highest in the province. Residents turned to the municipal Board of Health for assistance.

The city health officials conducted blood-lead screening programmes in the residential districts around the two smelters. The tests revealed that between 13 and 28 per cent of children sampled had concentrations of lead in their blood exceeding the level recognized as toxic at that time (40 micrograms per decilitre). The community organizations that had become active on the lead issue and the Board of Health used these findings to pressure the provincial government into forcing Canada Metal and Toronto Refiners and Smelters to control their emissions of lead.

When the Ontario Ministry of the Environment issued its first "stop work" order against Canada Metal, the company challenged the order in court. Prominent scientists retained by the International Lead Zinc Research Organization (an industry association) were brought to Toronto. These expert witnesses testified to the effect that lead in the air was no threat; the danger to health lay in ingesting lead.

The government mounted a weak defence of its control order, failing to bring in as evidence a University of Toronto study identifying industrial emissions as a serious health hazard. The control order was set aside.

The citizens, obviously far from satisfied, continued to pressure the Ontario government, which reluctantly initiated a series of inquiries. Its Working Group on Lead recommended more stringent standards for airborne lead and criticized low-level "fugitive emissions" from the plant. A task force from the provincial health ministry investigated the situation in detail, but its report, instead of making a recommendation, merely summed up the inconclusive opinions of the scientific community regarding lead pollution.

In late 1974 the Environmental Hearing Board was ordered by cabinet to hold public hearings. By this time South Riverdale residents were exasperated at yet another government delay in taking action and frustrated with the legalistic approach of the hearings. They told the board:

We have written briefs, attended numerous meet-ings, signed petitions and tried to co-operate with all levels of government to bring about a solution to this serious situation. We have had our blood tested and retested, our houses have been inspected from basement to attic, and yet not much has changed.

In May 1976 the Environmental Hearing Board concluded that high lead levels in soil probably did contribute to the lead burden in children. But the report, careful not to assign responsibility too specifically, qualified its findings: "Other sources of oral intake such as leaded paints, house dust, contaminated water supplies, etc. could not be conclusively ruled out."

A year after the report was released, city health officials recommended that soil in the vicinity of the Canada Metal plant containing over 2,600 ppm of lead be removed. That summer the bulldozers came in. But removing the soil did not eliminate the issue. Even before the Toronto officials ordered the removal, the provincial environment ministry had concluded that any soil containing more than 1,000 ppm of lead was unacceptable. Much dangerous soil was left behind.

After their small victory, citizens kept up the pressure on the provincial government, which finally imposed a control order in 1980, forcing Canada Metal to install emission control equipment. Airborne lead concentrations near the plant were brought down to a more acceptable range for urban areas. But although the amount of fresh, lead-laden dust settling on the ground was reduced, accumulated lead in the soil remained. Residents of South Riverdale continued to worry about this menace and some still reluctantly tossed out green peppers, lettuce and other produce from their backyard gardens.

In 1982, twelve years after the first complaints, South Riverdale residents persuaded the Department of Health to do a comprehensive blood-lead screening in the community, testing over two thousand people who lived near Canada Metal. It showed that while blood-lead levels in children had declined since 1972, 13.3 per cent of the children under six years old who were tested and who lived within the immediate vicinity of the Canada Metal plant had blood-lead levels greater than 20 micrograms per decilitre. Further tests in the fall of 1983 showed 18.6 per cent of the children tested had these higher levels. Half a year later, city health officials proposed the removal of soil wherever the soil-lead level was more than 1,000 ppm.

The Department of National Health and Welfare has determined that adverse health effects can occur at blood-lead levels of 20 to 30 micrograms per decilitre. A researcher at the California Institute of Technology is convinced that society should "reduce and eventually halt the mining and smelting of lead and the manufacture of lead products". There seems to be no desirable or healthy level of lead in the human body.

Since safe means for disposing of dangerous wastes do not yet exist, small or remote communities are being pressured to live with the dumping of nuclear or chemical wastes, including PCB's and dioxin, and other dangerous substances. Instead of looking out for the welfare of the Canadian public and placing a moratorium on industrial practices that produce dangerous wastes, or even pressing vigorously for solutions to the problem, Canadian governments have simply suspended democratic procedures to meet the demands of its approach to development.

United Church of Canada,
29th General Council, *1983*

"Get the Lead Out!"

That's the catchy slogan used on informative health-education materials published in South Riverdale. Over the years, the neighbourhood residents have learned to answer questions like these:

- What are the facts about pollution, and what are the proper tests?
- What is an acceptable risk: for a worker? for the general public? for children?

- How do government agencies balance opposing interests when standards for community health are set and enforced?
- Many pollutants are connected to illness. Should those who run the risk — for example, workers exposed to dangerous substances — participate in decisions about the amount of chemicals to be used? Or can they legitimately be exposed to dangerous substances without their knowledge and consent? Do they have the right to refuse exposure without threat of job loss?
- Has anyone the right to sacrifice the health of future generations for the sake of current gain or profit?

In 1973 a frustrated doctor at Toronto's Hospital for Sick Children was faced with two apparent cases of lead poisoning. "Sure I have to treat them if those [high lead] levels are confirmed," he said. "But what the hell do I do then? Send them home to the same environment? And then what — wait for two months and treat them again?"

The South Riverdale dispute pitted a community against an industrial polluter. Canada Metal was treating the local environment as if it belonged to the company. By polluting the atmosphere, the company was shifting part of the costs of production to the community, but continuing to appropriate the benefits of production for itself. What the community organizations had to do in effect was to transfer the social costs of lead poisoning, borne until then by the residents, into the legitimate private expenditures of Canada Metal.

When confronted with industry's own experts, government agencies showed reluctance to act with firm resolve in supporting the citizens' concerns versus the industrial interests. The South Riverdalers turned to independent experts for volunteer technical advice, and indeed developed a considerable expertise of their own.

At the South Riverdale Community Health Centre, not far from Canada Metal, residents compiled a library of current research papers on lead pollution and its associated health problems. New information was regularly reported to people in the neighbourhood. The media helped to put the case before the public, even though the company initiated strong legal measures — libel and slander, injunction, and contempt of court proceedings — which pressured journalists from covering the issue.

Independent expertise and public education were necessary to budge a company arguing that

stricter emission controls would force it out of business. This argument — a form of economic blackmail — is frequently made during conflicts over industrial pollution. It may easily intimidate both government agencies and local citizens, especially when unemployment is high.

Another claim often put forward is that the benefits associated with production — jobs, taxes, industrial and consumer goods — somehow strike a balance with the social costs of pollution and disease. In the case of South Riverdale, the people living near the lead smelter, those who paid the incalculable costs, got too few jobs or benefits. Once they realized how seriously the lead was damaging their health and especially the quality of their children's lives, they decided that the trade-off imposed on them by Canada Metal was unacceptable.

Public concern, expressed by the neighbourhood groups and echoed in the media, finally forced a powerful company to take the welfare of the whole community into account. Company executives now point with pride to their new pollution abatement equipment and their much-improved emission record. Their earlier arguments about possible shutdowns proved groundless.

But some executives continue to deny that there ever was a lead problem in South Riverdale. In 1983 the firm's president said he "didn't understand why it took the people so long to be reassured that prolonged exposure to lead is not a health problem". He also claimed that "There has never been a lead problem in Riverdale".

Public scrutiny, at least in part, will make sure that Canada Metal continues to behave like a good corporate citizen. However, in situations where the polluting industry has an economic stranglehold on the entire community and the risks are long range, it is not easy for residents to decide to fight the pollution.

Industry seems to have an ingrained inability to take social costs into consideration. That's understandable when the social costs are high and private corporations face the likelihood of having to pay. Governments, charged as they are with protecting public health, are also committed to maintaining economic growth and industrial expansion. They often exercise insufficient vigour in protecting the environment and health of the community.

It therefore took concerted political action to translate the social costs borne by everyone in South Riverdale into private expenditures for the pollution control devices. This improved form of production, in turn, should prevent unnecessary social costs from being incurred in the future.

Time Bombs

The process of analysis, organization and education illustrated by the example of South Riverdale may be applied to an alarming variety of current environmental "time bombs" ticking away across Canada:

Lead — Despite the introduction of unleaded gasoline in 1975, some 8,000 tonnes of lead are still released into Canadian air by automobile exhaust each year. Mainly because of the risk to children's health, the federal government agreed to reduce the lead content in gasoline by 60 per cent by 1987. While this is a move in the right direction, it still permits a level of lead emissions considerably higher than that allowed in most industrialized countries.

Uranium — Every phase of the "uranium cycle" is perilous: mining, milling, transportation, production of nuclear power, waste disposal, and the ultimate threat of nuclear weapons. The tailings (radioactive wastes) from uranium mines and the spent fuel-rods from nuclear reactors will emit deadly radiation for thousands of years. How can such a hazard possibly be balanced against a

AREAS OF ENVIRONMENTAL CONCERN

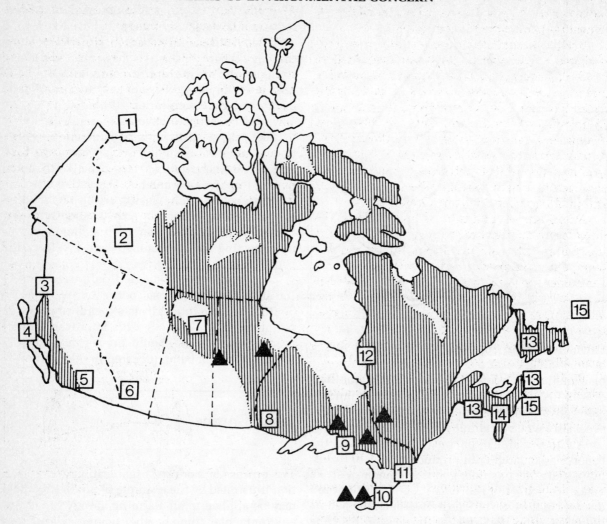

1. Beaufort Sea: development of oil and gas fields

2. Mackenzie Valley: plan to build an oil pipeline along the Mackenzie River Valley

3. Alice Arm: dumping of molybdenum mine tailings into marine inlet

4. West Coast: future development of oil and gas reserves

5. Okanagan Lakes: spraying of herbicide 2,4-D to control water weeds

6. Pincher Creek: acidic emissions from sour gas plants

7. Northern Saskatchewan: pollution from uranium mining

8. English-Wabigoon River System: mercury pollution from a pulp mill

9. Elliot Lake: pollution from uranium mining

10. Niagara River: seepage of toxic chemicals from industrial waste dumps

11. Port Hope: radiation from uranium refining

12. James Bay: flooding associated with dam construction to generate electric power

13. New Brunswick/Nova Scotia/Newfoundland: spraying of herbicides and pesticides to enhance forest production

14. Bay of Fundy: plan to harness tidal power to produce electricity

15. East Coast: development of offshore oil and gas reserves

— Acid Rain: 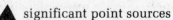 significant point sources

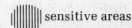 sensitive areas

mine or a plant with a useful lifespan of twenty-five or fifty years? There is no known safe level of radiation; even low-level or trace radiation is damaging to human cells and genes.

Herbicides and *Pesticides* — Some chemicals designed to kill weeds, brush, hardwoods (herbicides), insects (pesticides), fungus (fungicides) and other plant diseases have been insufficiently tested for their effects on human life and nature. Some effects — skin and lung diseases, birth defects and cancers — have been documented. Across Canada, forest management spray programmes (to protect pulpwood from pests and encroaching vegetation) have been meeting with stiff public protest since the mid-seventies.

Acid Rain — Acid rain is caused by sulphur dioxide and oxides of nitrogen produced by burning coal, smelting ore, or refining and using petroleum. These oxides mix with water vapour in the atmosphere to form weak acids. Acid rain damages soil and forests, kills life in lakes, erodes buildings and releases toxic metals that threaten health. Half the acid rain falling on Canada comes from the United States, while Canada causes about 10 per cent of what falls on its neighbour.

PCBs — Polychlorinated biphenyls, once widely used as coolants and insulators in electric transformers, have been linked with birth defects and cancer. Today the safe disposal or storage of PCBs is a major problem.

Asbestos — Quebec is the world's major producer of asbestos, valued as a fireproof fibre in many industrial applications. Now linked with silicosis and lung cancer, asbestos has become an important issue in occupational health and safety. Asbestos-based ceiling materials need to be replaced in many public buildings built before the dangers of asbestos became widely recognized.

Dioxins — Dioxins are a family of chemicals, including the most deadly synthetic materials known today. Dioxins have been leaking out of twenty- and thirty-year-old chemical dumps into the water supply, as well as releasing dangerous gases. Trace quantities are also found in chemical products used in agriculture, forestry and around the house.

All these examples, all the "hot" spots located on the map, and many other potential environmental issues across Canada broaden the scope of the analysis illustrated in the case of South Riverdale. Some issues, such as acid rain, show no respect for national boundaries. Each issue requires new scientific knowledge as well as familiarity with the regulations and agencies governing the particular pollutant or industry.

In each case: how do citizens assess the social costs — ascertain if there are particular victims in the community — and ensure responsible participation in the decision-making?

Canadians need to balance industrial development, which provides much-needed jobs, over and against the health of citizens who are confronted by the dangerous spin-offs of industry. It would be folly to oppose all industrial and technological development. It seems even more foolish to accept those developments whose human and ecological costs are by common consent clearly excessive — or whose long-term costs are still unknown. Some substances are best left alone altogether, because there's no known safe level of human absorption, or no responsible way of handling or storing them.

"Trade-offs are unavoidable," according to environment minister John Roberts. "In the 1980s *we* will have to deal with a balance of evidence and control pollutants according to the concept of acceptable levels of risk." But who are "*we*" in this context:

- an agency of the federal or provincial government?
- the industry that pollutes, or manufactures products of dubious safety?
- the workers who daily handle dangerous substances, and the unions under pressure to preserve jobs?
- the people who live in areas affected by pollution?

"*We*" should include those who bear the costs of environmentally harmful production, and the more directly affected anyone is, the greater should be their participation in the decision. Others should not *decide for* residents of communities like South Riverdale, imposing a trade-off on them without their knowledge or against their will. These residents should have the best possible evidence, balance the risks and benefits, and share in the decision. If they consciously accept a certain danger to their health, at least they do so with dignity.

Could people live in perfect harmony with unspoiled nature? Probably not. In any case, clean air, soil, water, healthy plants, animals and human life are "free" gifts to be cherished and taken good care of, not squandered, on our planet earth.

> In these areas of ecology, we touch deep levels of our being, our habits, and our expectations of the good life. Dealing with environmental issues means dealing deeply with our own selves. It is exceedingly hard work. However necessary and ultimately liberating it may prove to be, the passage to an ecologically responsible life-style is closer to an act of repentance and new birth than to an educational process. It is an engagement with sin in the social order and in ourselves.
>
> *United Church of Canada,*
> **27th General Council,** *1977*

Questions

• Have any environmental issues affected your community? Who participated in the controversy? Have groups formed to fight the pollution? Were they organized around this single issue, or to address several social concerns? Why have they succeeded — or failed — in their efforts?

Explore the economic background of the conflict and the economically-viable alternatives. Very frightening economic threats, once looked into, often prove groundless.

Discuss how to help a community manage an environmental crisis, once it occurs, whereby everyone involved can co-operate to minimize the damage and clean up the mess.

• Do an inventory of environmental hazards. In a rural area, what are the effects of herbicides, insecticides or chemical fertilizers on those who handle them, on the food produced, on wildlife and water supplies?

In an urban neighbourhood, are there industries that endanger worker health and safety, or reduce the quality of the air?

What about smog, or the effects of automobile exhausts? Noise pollution?

Having taken stock of the community's environment, plan to seek information from the municipal board of health, provincial and federal agencies, trade unions, environmental groups, industries.

Resources

• Lloyd Tataryn, *Dying for a Living: Politics of Industrial Death*, Ottawa: Deneau and Greenberg, 1979. Canadians who live and work in the contamination of asbestos, gold and uranium mines analyze their environmental problem.

• Penny Sanger, *Blind Faith: The Nuclear Industry in One Small Town*, Toronto: McGraw Hill Ryerson, 1981. This book deals with the controversy surrounding radioactive waste in the Ontario town of Port Hope in the 1970s, where Eldorado Nuclear is the major employer. The book discusses the community and economic questions raised when a local environmental issue attracts widespread attention.

• Ross Howard, *Poisons in Public*, Toronto: James Lorimer, 1980. An overview of the modern dilemma of industrial wastes — where to put them, the health risks involved, the political controversies surrounding their disposal. Howard treats the lead issue in South Riverdale, as does C.C. Lax, "The Toronto lead-smelter controversy," in William Leiss, ed., *Ecology Versus Politics in Canada*, Toronto: University of Toronto, 1979.

• Phil Weller and OPIRG, *Acid Rain: The Silent Crisis*, Toronto: Between The Lines, 1980. A short, concise analysis of an environmental issue that has won international attention. This book focuses on the sources of acid rain, its

Questions (cont'd)

- What is the source of your community drinking water? Is it tested for contaminants? If it is, are the tests for bacteria alone or do they cover a broader range of potentially hazardous substances?

    If your group knows little about local water, can it develop a plan to better inform itself?

    Keep a record of your phone calls and conversations on the issue. Which officials seemed most helpful? Did some seem ill-informed or defensive? Write to Health and Welfare Canada for "Guidelines for Canadian Drinking Water Quality" and to Environment Canada for "Water Quality Source Book".

- How clean is your community's air? Are there any local industries that may be emitting dangerous pollutants? Are they monitored by the provincial environment ministry? See if your group can track down the records and keep informed of the monitoring.

- Policy-makers and experts in high technology are used to working with obscure reports, intimidating statistics, flow-charts and game plans. This experience can easily lead them to doubt the ability of most citizens to assimilate and understand complex data. But without the facts, how can ordinary people make informed judgements about far-reaching issues, such as low-level lead pollution and the accompanying threat to their health? What responsibility to the public do experts have who are employed by industry or government? What are some alternative sources of expertise, which community groups can rely on?

Resources (cont'd)

effects, and what is and is not being done about the problem.

- "Our Health is Not For Sale", NFB, 1978, 16 mm, 30 minutes. Looks at occupational health hazards and the lack of worker control over the working environment.

- "Pollution Front Line", Walford Hewiston, 1970, 16 mm, 46 minutes. Air and water pollution in Hamilton threatens health and environment.

- For information about local environmental groups or national issues, write to the Jesuit Centre, 947 Queen Street East, Toronto, Ont. M4M 1J9, ph. 416-469-1123.

Chapter Five

Social Analysis Again

Social analysis starts with very normal concerns. Perhaps you are visiting with friends from the United States, and end up chatting about various ailments or the times the kids had to be taken to the doctor. The discussion soon turns to the difference between the healthcare systems in Canada and the United States.

You might never have thought about the advantages of Canadian medicare, but your U.S. friends can't take medical care for granted: They are not assured of good medical care unless they can pay for it out of their own pockets. Their experience might leave you asking whether medicare is all that secure in Canada. You have a question for social analysis.

An environmental concern presented in chapter four began with bothersome dust and noise and a few symptoms in some children. The issue turned out to be lead pollution. The citizens needed to gather detailed information on lead, for two main reasons. First, they wanted to understand the problem for themselves. Secondly, they had to equip themselves to face the intimidating array of experts mobilized by the companies and various government departments.

The citizens of South Riverdale did not quietly bow down before the expertise of recognized specialists with their battery of scientific data. The Riverdalers waded through it all while stubbornly upholding the obvious, that lead in the blood was not good for their children. In the process, they developed their own expertise and regained some control over decisions affecting their own lives.

A conversation, an experience, a book, a dis-

cussion, a personal or family crisis can all serve to bring urgent questions to the forefront. Something familiar and unexamined — doctors' bills or dust — can suddenly require examination. But this is an age that reveres experts and scientists. So, in addition to feeling concerned, people also need to feel they are equipped to do the necessary analysis.

Experts may have an aura of objectivity, but they can be used to support a specific position. They can intimidate citizens and the media or end up by simply confusing the issue. Experts can also have important and precise information to contribute. For example, an economist can analyze the relative costs of medicare, or a geochemist can explain how airborne lead spreads through a neighbourhood. Still, they do not automatically hold a monopoly on correct interpretation, and they should not necessarily be allowed to sit in judgement over an entire issue. That's why social analysis is often a matter of people developing their own expertise as well as learning to identify

experts of their own who can contribute to the solution of the community's problem.

The purpose of this chapter is to pause and reflect: What happens when we do social analysis? What kind of expertise has been acquired?

Learning to Read

Some people never have the opportunity of learning to read. "Functional illiteracy" is defined in Canada as including "that part of the population 15 years of age and older, not attending school full-time and with a level of education less than grade 9." According to the official definition, the 1981 census reveals that Canada has over four million functionally illiterate people.

What is illiteracy like in a country where every adult is presumed to be literate? An Ottawa man spent most of his life unable to read and write: "Going shopping was a pain. I always got someone to go with me because I couldn't read the labels. . . . I thought I was the only one in the world who couldn't read." Reading and writing "are, without question, critical to active participation in any group in our society today". Illiteracy can handicap people from participating fully in life.

There's another, even more common form of illiteracy that also prevents people from participating in Canadian society, and that is *social illiteracy*. For example, given an obvious shortage of affordable housing:
• How did the shortage arise?
• What is its impact?
• Why does it continue?
• What can be done about it?

A person might recognize that the questions are important, but not know where to begin, what to ask or think or say. That's a feeling people may have had before reading or discussing chapter three. Not knowing where to begin is an experience of social illiteracy.

Such illiteracy can be very frustrating, too. Social illiteracy means being unable to read — to interpret — the events that are going on in society. Unfortunately, many institutions do not teach Canadians to read social reality. A good percentage of the population remains unaware of how society works or where it is headed.

There's another interesting parallel between the understanding of language and of society. Once upon a time, people thought of language as something forever fixed and unchanging, "a gift of the gods". But linguistics makes it clear that every word is a *human* creation; language is inherited and it evolves as it is used.

Similarly, people also used to think of human society as something God-given or eternal, as divinely created or the result of an age-old contract. Today nearly everyone agrees that social institutions are totally human creations, the deliberate product of human ideas and the result of habitual human action. As evolving *human* creations, social structures and institutions are something people can learn about and understand — and change.

Learning how to read — whether in a native language or a foreign one — is a somewhat mysterious process. What's involved? Certainly not memorizing a grammar or dictionary. First of all, connecting sounds with letters, pictures with words. The learner grasps individual words, builds up a vocabulary, starts recognizing new words from their context. With time this process develops into *expertise*, which allows the newly literate person to understand the messages communicated by sentences and paragraphs.

In order to read tolerably well, it is not necessary to understand *how* language works, any more than driving a car requires an understanding of motor mechanics. Still, an acquaintance with the workings of language can make the learning more interesting and effective. That which explains the building-blocks (parts of speech) and the workings (rules) of language is *grammar* — the subject nearly everyone remembers as rather dull and forbidding.

Beginning to do social analysis is like learning how to read: You learn by doing. The preceding chapters on health, housing, and environment are three introductory "readings" of social reality. This chapter goes on to present some of the grammar of social literacy, some of the building-blocks and workings of social analysis. Four of these building-blocks are: symptoms; reification/commodification; social costs; and structures. Although these "parts of speech" flow directly out of the discussion of the three previous chapters, they are liable to emerge as well when other Canadian issues are analyzed. Different parts and patterns will also emerge in the remaining chapters of the book — and still others will be found or invented as people further develop their own social analysis.

The signs of the times today compel us as Christians to think about our social responsibilities and to put our words into action. We live in a world that oppresses at least half the human race and this scandal threatens to get worse. Right around us, human suffering of many kinds scars the face of Canada: poverty for many, inflating prices, housing crises, regional disparities, strikes and lock-outs, cultural violations, native land claims, overcrowded cities and rural neglect. With all this comes a growing sense of loneliness, powerlessness and alienation in our society and institutions. So we have cause for deep concern.

Canadian Conference of Catholic Bishops,
From Words to Action, *1976*

Symptoms

Pain or malaise is often all too obvious. Good medical practice begins with a thorough description of the ailment, so as not to merely treat the symptoms with pain-killers, but to discover and remove its cause. Anatomy and physiology provide an ideal picture of the whole body, with which the diagnostician can compare what has broken down and what is functioning properly.

Social malaise is also there on the surface for people to see: Witness Canadians suffering from lack of access to adequate health care, affordable homes or safe clean air. However, sometimes the malady, perfectly obvious to those suffering it, is hidden from those who are well provided for. To note carefully, describe, categorize and finally explore the symptoms — that is one task of social analysis.

Yet another link exists between medical diagnosis and social analysis. Bodily illness itself can be a symptom of social injustice. Infant mortality, reduced life expectancy, malnutrition and many diseases (in addition to cancer, analyzed in chapter two) are often symptoms of a social malaise, economic injustice, political or cultural oppression. Moreover these medical problems can be documented and quantified as proof that people's rights are being violated.

Reification/Commodification

The tendency to reduce a person or relationship to an object of economic value, a commodity to be bought and sold in the marketplace is called reification or commodification. Reification derives from the Latin word *res*, for thing or object; commodification means to turn something into a commodity, an item for sale.

Chapter three, without mentioning the strange-sounding terms, brought them into play. For instance, decent, affordable shelter, which is a basic need and human right, is reified or commodified into a consumer item available to those who can afford it.

An extreme example of this process would be to turn the fire department into a private business. What would citizens think of firemen offering their services to individuals on a pay-as-you-go basis? Obviously, at the moment of crisis everyone (except those who had private insurance) would feel held up to ransom by the fire company. The poor would not have the same access to fire protection as those who could afford the premiums.

Social analysis tries to make clear how basic necessities of life are transformed into commodities. It tries to show where the market is violating people's fundamental rights such as the right to clean air and adequate health care. And it tries to indicate the responsibility of various social groups (government, employers, labour, consumers) to protect these rights.

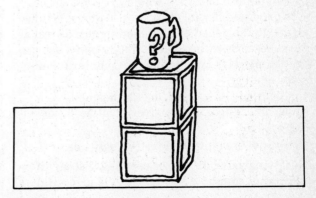

Social Costs

When industry fouls the air, water or soil, the costs often go unrecognized and end up being paid by the community at large. When developers choose to shift their money from housing to more lucrative shopping malls and office towers, their profits are not balanced by any accounting of the losses that Canadian consumers and taxpayers incur through this decision.

Profit-and-loss and other business categories by themselves fail to take long-term questions of health, aesthetics, justice or even jobs into account. Social analysis does take illness, homelessness, pollution and injustice into account. It analyzes them as social costs which otherwise go unreckoned. With this analysis, citizens can see to it that those who profit also repair the damages they cause, or pay for the repair, and that costs are not imposed on workers and communities without their knowledge and consent.

Structures

The word "structure" is familiar with reference to buildings — the Peace Tower, the Regina parliament buildings, the local hockey arena. They become structures because a lot of parts — foundations, stairways, windows, roof-top — get set in a certain pattern to form a whole.

So too with social structures — they are not so visible to the naked eye but they are just as real as the solid mass of the Chateau Frontenac. They can be identified by considering the complex relationships among:

• patient, health worker, doctor, hospital;
• consumer (tenant or buyer), landlord, developer;
• citizen ("breather"), industry, regulator.

Social analysis takes these seemingly straightforward and common relationships and considers them not as a series of separated, isolated units but as a whole, as parts of a structure. It thus unveils the overall structures that define or confine these common relationships, that define the meaning and set the limits of people's daily activities. The structures can be good or bad in their effects on people. Too frequently they favour a few and damage the many. They may be invisible to the eye but they are just as much there and apparently just as much beyond the power of the individual citizen to move as the Halifax Citadel.

There are structures of different kinds — social, economic, cultural, political, religious — and social analysis has to adapt its approach to each, discerning which kinds of structures are most important in a given situation. In the case of the medical profession, financial interests (which are part of certain economic structures) play a decisive role. But cultural and political considerations also serve to determine the nature of the relationship between doctors and patients or the attitude of physicians towards a programme like medicare.

The word "structure", in its social usage, suggests that root causes are not personal but rather institutional; not transitory, but solid and permanent. Social analysis involves discovering, describing, explaining and ultimately changing the structures that define social existence in Canada.

Ways of Reading

Once a subject for analysis has been chosen, there are a number of "grammatical norms" that serve as useful guides to social reading and interpretation.

> **Many people agree that there is something wrong with the present social and economic order. It fails to meet the human needs of the majority of people. The present economic order results in the very uneven distribution of wealth and the control of resources by a small minority. On the global scene, the poor peoples, especially in the Third World, are calling for the creation of a new economic order based on a just distribution of wealth and power. And within this country, in its various regions and communities, there are similar signs that people want to find new approaches now, to make better use of human and material resources, to end waste and want and exploitation.**
>
> *Canadian Conference of Catholic Bishops,*
> **From Words to Action,** *1976*

To Survey Popular Beliefs

The economic and political structures of Canada are primarily — but not exclusively — responsible for giving the country its shape. Patterns of thought and belief also influence the shape of society.

The beliefs that developers have the right to do what they want with their earnings, or that natural resources are simply there for the taking in the name of economic development, lead society in certain directions. Chapter two noted a pattern of an almost unquestioning respect for doctors that most people have, yet many doctors have traditionally opposed one of the country's most popular programmes, medicare.

If popular understanding of issues was always accurate, there would be little need to embark on social analysis. In fact, common notions about society, Canada and the world often tend to be based on scattered bits of information or even misinformation. Erroneous opinions are promoted, at times unwittingly yet quite vigorously, by radio, television, newspapers and magazines (see chapter ten). For a number of reasons the media are more likely to put forward already accepted, official or established points of view than to report on critical or innovative viewpoints. Social analysis is critical. It questions whether *official* truth is really always true. The results of the analysis may well stand in sharp contrast to popular beliefs.

To Trace History

Nearly every social issue has a long history and has been examined before. In an historical analysis, the object is to view the past, not with nostalgia for the good old days, but critically, with an eye for its effect on the present.

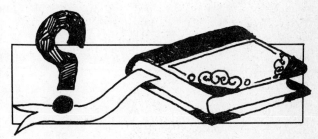

Even in the short lifetime of Canadian medicare there have been periodic crises, with a remarkably consistent pattern of complaints by the medical associations and of responses by people who use the healthcare system. That struggle is an essential thread in the process whereby medicare became part of the Canadian social fabric.

Chapter three looked at the housing boom of the fifties and the changes it brought to the structures of housing development. If, for example, people were not aware of the accumulation and concentration of capital in real estate development and still believed that most landlords were small, independent businessmen, their analysis of this part of Canadian society would be seriously flawed.

If you were analyzing the relationships involved in the production of a cup of coffee, it would be important to consider what happened in the nineteenth century when Indian peasants in Central America had their land taken from them and turned into coffee estates, and what that means to today's coffee growers. Or again, the problems posed by technology today are similar to those which arose nearly two centuries ago (see chapter eight). Most social issues have a history that contributes to — and, if understood, helps to explain — the problem currently at hand.

To Identify Key Actors

In the discussion of housing, the leading question was: "Who are the actors?" It is clear that some actors make decisions and benefit from those choices. Others, namely consumers — and especially people on low incomes — have little say in what happens, even though they are often adversely affected.

Actor analysis is an important method of discovering how society actually divides into those with decision-making power and those who are powerless. Once the groups or classes have been identified, further questions help to sort them out: Who makes the decisions? Who benefits from the decisions? Who pays the cost of the decisions? These questions clarify the social divisions that both surround an issue and are characteristic of society as a whole.

The questions of who the actors are and how evenly the decision-making power is distributed apply easily to many issues besides housing. For example, what are the roles of the medical establishment, the government and the pharmaceutical industry in structuring Canada's healthcare system? Who has a say in the decisions about acceptable pollution levels? Who in fact benefits from pollution?

To Move Back and Forth

There is a strong tendency to see individual problems as requiring individual solutions, and to see social problems as insoluble. In response to this tendency, social analysis moves in two ways:

from the individual case to the social structures in which that case is embedded and back again; and from "someone's" vague problem to "everybody's" concrete social issue. The three preceding chapters all provide examples:

Illness at first appears to be a pre-eminently individual problem. Sick persons usually can't think of anything but their own misery. But going to a doctor would be difficult without medicare, which is a collective, social solution. At the widest social level, if government does not guarantee access to necessary health care or enforce pollution regulations, illness becomes an even more individual, apparently "private" matter.

Housing is also a problem for every individual person or family. People with trouble finding housing they can adequately pay for may feel they just need to get out and hustle for an appropriate apartment or house. Yet the market is not working for many of them. Any real solution to the problem of acquiring decent, affordable lodging must be sought on the social level, for example, by organizing an alternative structure such as a co-op to make housing available.

Environmental hazards concern a community and even the whole society: They are "everyone's" problem in general. They have to be brought home to the individual level. Lead in car-exhaust emissions is not simply a problem for society in general, it can affect any person's health. Acid rain has a devastating general effect, but it is also causing people to lose their livelihoods in fishing or tourism. Once individual citizens see pollution as their own problem, they can band together and tackle it as *our* concrete issue.

Social analysis thus involves agility. It means learning to move back and forth from the individual to the collective aspects, from the social arena to the family and neighbourhood.

To Focus on the System

Many symptoms, many actors, many issues and many structures are interconnected to form a functioning unity. The word "system" suggests how these elements fit together in a set pattern at a particular moment. "System" links apparently quite different issues and shows how very different groups are actually related.

For example, chapter two began by discussing symptoms and ended by looking at particular structures of healthcare delivery. The professional associations, medical and pharmaceutical industries and insurance companies all interconnect. When looked at together, these organizations or institutions, relationships and structures, point toward a system that has to be understood in any effort to strengthen medicare or develop alternate health services.

The analysis in chapter two brings people up against this experience of system. Although the analysis may be partial and tentative and although more analysis would be necessary to provide a comprehensive picture of the healthcare system, still a good beginning can be made.

However, *Getting Started* does not speak much of *the* establishment or *the* system, as if there were a single grand pattern to explain every Canadian problem and injustice. Instead, it acknowledges the complexity of Canadian society, without allowing that complexity to discourage people from beginning to do social analysis.

A clearer focus on the system that ties a whole social issue together provides a greater sense of what makes Canada tick, of how its social, economic, political and cultural structures interweave and overlap.

> We can achieve a new vision of reality by becoming more present with the hungry, the homeless, the jobless, the native person, the poor immigrant and others who may be victims of injustices in our communities. By listening to their problems and sharing in their struggle we can learn much more about the attitudes, activities, and structures that cause human suffering and what can be done about them.
>
> *Canadian Conference of Catholic Bishops,*
> **From Words to Action,** *1976*

Welcome to Part Two

People could learn how to read social reality without pausing to reflect on "social grammar". Similarly, people could continue to do social analysis by moving from one issue to another. Besides better housing, access to health care and a safe environment, other basic needs, such as food, education, culture and recreation, are worth analyzing and could easily have been added.

But eventually it becomes clear that basic issues do not get resolved — or even fully understood — simply as human needs and basic rights. For almost all social problems have economic roots that also need to be analyzed. In fact, all three issues discussed in Part One display important economic aspects, as the elements of reification and social cost suggest.

Part Two considers economic questions, but this is not really economics in the academic, professional or traditional sense. Nor is it a complete introduction to economics. The task of its four chapters is to analyze several economic issues affecting Canadians in important ways — the retail food trade, unemployment, microtechnology and energy — to illustrate some fundamental economic ideas and methods. These elements and techniques, in turn, should enrich our reading of Canada.

> We urge all our brothers and sisters to join us in a continuing process of acting and reflecting.... It is in our local communities that we can best exercise these social and political responsibilities. This calls for our personal and collective participation in local struggles for justice with the jobless, exploited workers, poor or lonely immigrants, small producers, native people, culturally oppressed peoples and others.
>
> *Canadian Conference of Catholic Bishops,*
> **From Words to Action,** *1976*

Chapter Six

Lost in the Supermarket

The economy mystifies many Canadians. Data flood in on us every day: the inflation rate, the Dow Jones Industrial Average, fluctuations in the price of gold, the rise and fall of the Canadian dollar. Neo-Keynesians, monetarists and supply-siders lock in battle over words like fiscal policy, money supply, equilibrium, soft demand, recession and depression.

Statistics Canada produces monthly figures on the state of the economy, while university economists, business executives, union officials and government policymakers appear on TV to chew over the latest "indicators". Our leaders urge us in turn to save, to spend, to invest, to compete, to lower our expectations.

Many Canadians may feel a bit like children overhearing the grown-ups arguing in the next room. While we know that the outcome of the argument affects us, we are left unsure as to what the fight is really about.

Far removed from the realm of complicated financial statistics is economics in its most basic sense: running a household. In fact, "economy" comes from the Greek word for household management. And that definition is still appropriate: People receive payment for their labour and spend those dollars on their personal and household needs and desires. Turning work into money and then exchanging money for what people want — these are two major transactions that the entire system is supposed to help make happen.

The huge world of economics and the more immediate necessities of running a household are not totally unrelated. They come together in an experience that most everyone has regularly: a trip through the supermarket. The social analysis here will use this familiar routine as a way of investigating one small corner of the economy in order to begin understanding how the whole economy works.

Welcome to the Market

One thing that strikes a shopper is the sheer quantity and variety of goods available for the buying.

There are staples like milk, labelled with the precise degree of butterfat, there is bread marked with a certain percentage of whole wheat, there are eggs efficiently graded in size. There is every conceivable cut of meat packaged and, for the busy shopper, precooked and presliced as well.

The products of the world jostle Canadian produce for attention: Mexican strawberries, Honduran bananas, Moroccan oranges, Indian tea. There is coffee from a dozen tropical nations. The fresh, canned and frozen edibles are supplemented by several aisles of non-food items, from toiletries to automotive oil and house paints. At the supermarket, it seems, nothing is out of season — if you can pay the price.

According to many Canadian business and political leaders, the present market system is the best, most efficient way of producing goods, providing services and distributing them throughout the population. One economic theorist, Milton Friedman, together with his wife Rose, wrote a book that at one point compares the activity of the marketplace with the workings of democracy. Though majority rule is seen as a desirable if imperfect system, the Friedmans are satisfied that the market system represents a kind of perfect freedom: "When you vote daily in the supermarket, you get precisely what you voted for and so does everyone else." This is what the market system supposedly means: When people get their wages and spend them on the goods they need, a complex but effective system assures them of getting the most of what they want for their money.

If this were the whole story, if the entire economy were the sum of our free, individual and equal choices, there would be no need to continue the analysis. But both supermarket and economy are more complicated than that.

Who Does the Shopping?

In hard economic times, with stubborn inflation and high unemployment (or both), shoppers have become acutely price conscious. In 1982, the trade publication of the Canadian grocery business reported surveys showing that 80 per cent of consumers viewed price as the most important factor in choosing where to shop. Because of lower prices, nearly half of those surveyed had recently switched to a supermarket they liked less. Obviously, many shoppers are acutely conscious of their limited food budgets.

According to Statistics Canada's "official" poverty levels, one Canadian family in ten lives below the poverty line. But the poverty line is difficult to set and the cut-off point is rather arbitrary. The National Council of Welfare estimated that in 1981 one Canadian family in eight was living below the poverty line. Whatever the figure, it's obvious that poverty in Canada continues to be widespread in spite of the abundance on supermarket shelves.

If the nation's households are divided into five numerically equal groups or quintiles, those in the bottom quintile have access to 4.2 per cent of the national income while those in the top fifth get 42.3 per cent. What's more, if the bottom *two-fifths* are combined, their income share is still only equal to only a *third* of the share of the top fifth.

Percentage Distribution of Total Canadian Income by Household Shares

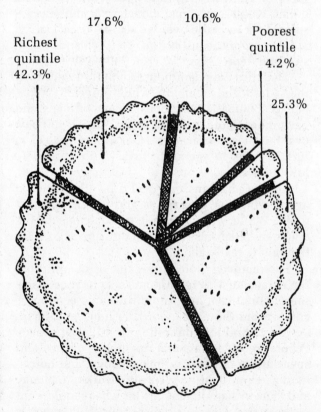

Richest quintile 42.3%
17.6%
10.6%
Poorest quintile 4.2%
25.3%

Those who have the thinnest slice of the national economic pie must struggle to scrape by.

When it comes time for the weekly shopping, some can "save" on specials that offer Tibetan yak filets or succulent Westphalian ham imported from Germany. But the weekly challenge for the working poor, the aged living on fixed incomes, the sole-support mothers and people on welfare is to fill the basket without emptying the wallet. They keep an eye out for good deals on hamburger and macaroni.

Going back to the Friedmans' analogy, if the supermarket is like an election, the voting is rigged: Some have many votes to cast and others (a larger number) are lucky to have one. The "economic votes" are not equally distributed throughout the population.

Is it surprising that at least one-tenth of a supposedly prosperous country lives in *officially defined* poverty — and that actual poverty levels are much higher? The picture of unequal access to food, a most basic human need, may surprise those who believe Canada is an ever more egalitarian society where everyone's basic needs are satisfied.

> The economy is something we share in common.... It is the way we put together human and natural resources for the good of the common life.... It is a vast collective enterprise and the domain of no particular sub-group in society.... It must be marked by justice, participation and sustainability.... It summons us in the time of our stewardship to be good gardeners and partners.
>
> *United Church of Canada,*
> **An Alternative Economic Vision,** *1983*

bigger is better — or at least cheaper. The increased efficiency in running one huge store instead of several smaller ones should be reflected in lower prices. The same reasoning governs many economic decisions made by business and supported by government. But the *size* of stores, and especially of the corporations that control them and most of the economy, raises many a question for social analysis.

Big is Beautiful

In a visit to the supermarket it's also worth considering sheer size. The traditional supermarkets of between five thousand and thirty thousand square feet, which the children of the baby boom remember being wheeled through, are no longer novel. Indeed, retailers like Safeway, Dominion, Loblaw's and Steinberg are abandoning the very stores that revolutionized grocery shopping in the fifties — and put many a neighbourhood store out of business.

Now the neighbourhood branch of the big chain is being replaced by "superstores" and "superwarehouses" of one-hundred thousand square feet. According to the economy of scale,

Survival of the Biggest

Chain stores control about 60 per cent of the retail food market in Canada, up from 46 per cent in 1967. The six largest food companies are George Weston, Provigo, Steinberg, Safeway, Dominion and the Oshawa group. In Edmonton four firms control 93 per cent of the retail food market. In St. John's four firms control 87 per cent and in Winnipeg four firms control 81 per cent.

The major Canadian food chains are large by anyone's standards. Moreover, they are aligned with one another in five volume-buying groups. Together the companies in these groups account for over 85 per cent of all Canadian retail food sales. They buy mainly from the largest food processors and their tremendous turnover enables them to keep the prices they pay to suppliers down. Farmers and food processors who cannot meet the price demands of the big five are at a competitive disadvantage.

Again following the Friedman metaphor, the "free market" system applied to the grocery business is like an election where the smaller and weaker candidates are continually squeezed out of the running.

A good example of small enterprises squeezed out by bigger ones is health food stores. They sprang up in the seventies in response to consumer concern about chemical additives in the increasingly processed food offered by the supermarkets. Accordingly, many supermarkets have borrowed the health food store idea of using bulk displays of products, and now allow shoppers to scoop from the bins the amount of food they want. Some bins contain so-called natural foods, others hold everything from soup mixes to cheese puffs. *Canadian Grocer*, the principal trade magazine of the Canadian supermarket industry, noted in 1982 that the dominant chains are "threatening to do to mom 'n' pop health food stores what they did to mom 'n' pop grocery stores — drive them out of business".

The biggest companies keep on growing because joint purchasing, advertising and sheer size give them an edge over smaller, independent operations. While there may be competition among the supermarket chains, the market is dominated by a few large, powerful chains. Consumers may have a vote, but they still have little or no control over who or what to vote for.

Keep Up the Demand

New supermarkets in new shopping centres opening to serve an increasing number of people with more and more money to spend — this is an accurate image of the postwar economic boom in construction, manufacturing and real estate development across Canada. Of course, there have been downturns and slumps. The recession of the early eighties was notably severe. Still, what accounts for this spiral of growth? Among the most important factors is the growth in *demand*.

In 1945 there were twelve million Canadians, in 1983 twenty-five million. The population has grown not only in numbers but in productivity and buying power. More people have more money to spend. Obviously there would be no point in producing more if people could not buy more. Economic demand has been maintained and made to grow through several effective strategies: Mili-

Canada's Grocery Buying Groups

tary spending, consumer credit and advertising are three examples.

Military spending has been a potent source of demand in the North American economy. Because armaments are made to be destroyed, they keep generating their own new demand. Production for the Korean War ended a mild economic downturn in the late forties, and the escalation of the war in Viet Nam helped to snap a recession in the early sixties (see chapter seven). Weapons systems also become "obsolete", as defence-oriented research and development constantly come up with new technologies of ever greater destructive power.

The problem is that military spending siphons funds away from other needs such as affordable housing, public transportation and social services. Arms production stimulates growth in certain fields (petrochemicals, electronics and aerospace technology, for instance), but leads to a neglect of research and development in other areas. For example, in the early eighties North American automakers required 80 per cent more time to build a car than their Japanese competitors, whose postwar economy has avoided military production. Military spending spurs the economy sporadically, but distorts its overall development.

Demand for consumer goods is also on-again and off-again. The demand used to depend on people saving up for what they wanted. Merchants displayed signs like

No more. The stimulation of consumer credit helps to generate demand. Today virtually every retailer, from the smallest corner hardware to the largest department store, displays a cluster of familiar stickers telling consumers what credit cards are accepted. Supermarkets do not generally take credit cards (yet!), but a similar card allows customers to cash their paycheques when paying

for their groceries. Many Canadians carry a colourful deck of credit cards and "Put it on plastic" is a common phrase. Credit card companies warn us, "Don't leave home without it."

At the same time, *advertising* uses special words and images to create wants and turn wants into needs. In food and supermarket advertising, for example, concern for the quality of food is used both to create and to change demand among the buying population. The demand created can be for a specific brand of a staple such as flour or for a product of dubious nutritional value such as a sugar-laden breakfast cereal.

In the early seventies, federal government authorities found that cereals like Applejacks, Sugar Pops or Count Chocula contained up to 54 per cent sugar by weight. A better choice for breakfast would be a Sara Lee chocolate cake (36 per cent sugar). When the government asked cereal companies to put the amount of sugar on the label voluntarily, the reply was an emphatic no.

Instead, the companies that control Canada's breakfast-food market spend tens of millions of dollars a year on advertisements that offer virtually no useful information — with young children as the principal targets. Apparently the voters in the marketplace need not be well informed.

In the early seventies cereal makers noticed a consumer backlash against sugar-loaded cereals as people began going to health food stores to buy whole cereals, such as granola, made by independent companies. The big four cereal-makers quickly developed their own wholesome brands and advertised them with names and images like "Country Morning" and "Nature Valley".

Taking another leaf from the success story of the health food stores, the big supermarket chains began to advertise bulk-shopping and generic items that had become popular. "No Name" has itself become a registered trade mark. People feel they are saving by avoiding nationally known brands, with their built-in cost of advertising, in favour of similar goods in plain packages. Advertising works even when it seems to go against itself.

Advertising promotes not only products like microwave ovens that promise to save you time, but also others like video games that help you spend the time you save. *Consumer credit* enables people to buy goods now and pay later. And *military spending* is an effective generator of demand that requires virtually no advertising since it has its own demand already built-in, due to the fact that it consumes itself.

Competition or Conglomeration?

Producers and advertisers do everything possible to woo consumers and increase demand. Executives in the retail food sector say theirs is a tough competitive market with very narrow profit margins. Weekly sales, "deep discounts", "super values" and the occasional all-out price war provide consumers with lower prices. Such competition is often cited as proof that the system really supplies the highest quality products at the lowest possible cost.

Let's look at a couple of examples. In the sixties Weston opened a Loblaw's store in Kitchener, Ontario. When it failed to win enough cus-

> **The present market is designed primarily to make profits, not to feed people. The supply and distribution of food is determined mainly by "effective demand", not human need. Effective demand is usually defined in terms of "ability to pay". Food supplies are often controlled in such a way as to drive up prices on the market. Furthermore, some food industries have gone so far as to destroy their produce when they could not get the market price they wanted.**
>
> *Canadian Conference of Catholic Bishops,*
> **Sharing Daily Bread,** *1974*

tomers from locally owned stores, Weston made another attempt to break into the market with a "Busy B" store, but again to no avail. Having failed at competition, Weston bought out Zehr's, a family-owned local chain. Alas, Mr. and Mrs. Friedman, what the consumers vote for is not necessarily what they get.

Del Monte is a familiar name on cans of peaches. By the late seventies Del Monte, only one of about 170 fruit and vegetable canners in Canada, controlled fully one-fifth of the market. It achieved this size through the purchase of Canadian Canners, producer of Aylmer products. Rather than compete with Canadian Canners in classic free-enterprise fashion, the American canning giant used its economic power to grow through acquisition.

The process of sidestepping competition by buying out the competitor tends to concentrate economic power in fewer, but larger, corporations.

The top eight firms in the rubber industry control 81 per cent of sales. The top eight beverage-makers account for 62 per cent of sales in that industry, while in the field of petroleum and coal products the top eight control 85 per cent of sales. The most highly-concentrated industry in this respect is tobacco, where the top eight control 99.8 per cent of sales.

Corporate Assets and Concentration

Top 500:
assets $522.2 billion
73%

Other companies:
assets $193.3 billion
27%

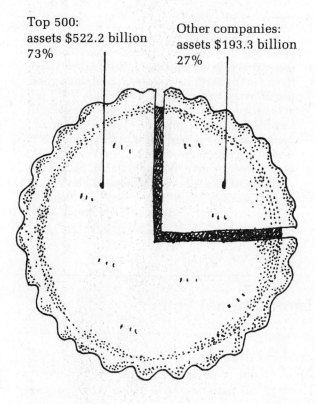

Overall, Canada's economy is very highly concentrated, with a few firms wielding enormous clout. Between 1965 and 1978 the twenty-five largest non-financial enterprises more than doubled their control of all sales from 10 per cent to 22 per cent. In 1978 Canada's top 100 firms controlled 48.6 per cent of all assets while the same number of American corporate giants held 30.6 per cent of assets in the United States. One business magazine concluded:

> In a corporate sense, Canada is reminiscent of a backsliding banana republic. Mouth-watering assets and wealth are densely concentrated and, instead of finding their way onto more plates, they're ending up on fewer. In 1978 ... the 500

largest enterprises in the country controlled almost three-quarters of private sector assets and slightly more than half its income and profits. Unfortunately for defenders of big business, however, the Top 500 didn't manage to generate even a quarter of the nation's employment.

Moreover, the biggest firms in any area of business are not necessarily independent actors. Two of Canada's most powerful supermarket chains are themselves branches of larger corporate empires. Loblaw's is owned by the Weston company, which also has interests in food processing and forest products. Dominion Stores is part of the Argus group, which has interests in oil and gas, financial services, mining and broadcasting.

Companies expand not only horizontally, buying out their competitors and going into other lines of business, but also vertically, controlling all aspects of production and distribution. Take, for example, Safeway (a subsidiary of the U.S. Safeway), which has 60 per cent of Alberta's retail food market. Safeway stocks up to half its retail volume with its own products. Safeway's wholly-owned subsidiaries include MacDonald's Consolidated (wholesale grocery), Lucerne Foods (milk and ice cream, meat processing, eggs and cheese) and Empress Foods (bakeries, fruit and vegetable canning, freezing, coffee roasting, jams and jellies). If you live in Edmonton, it might be difficult to cast your vote for anything but a Safeway product.

The major food companies tend to dominate production and processing and to seek monopoly control over regional markets. As a result, the neighbourhood grocery store, bakery or butcher, the family farmer or small food processor may go under. Competition may still exist between the big chains, but control over the ballot boxes of the economy is becoming concentrated in fewer and fewer hands.

Big is Beautiful II

In the words of Paul Desmarais, one of Canada's most successful businessmen, "You're never too big.... If you put a limit on your growth, then you're dead the minute you reach it." The logic of the economic system dictates that a company that earns enough to survive but not enough to expand is either closed down or reorganized to make more money.

Industry argues that high profits allow new investments, which in turn create new jobs and generate new demand. The prosperity of business is supposed to trickle down to everyone in the society. Therefore profit-making should be appreciated by the public and protected by the government. For when profits rise, companies reinvest and grow, create more jobs and thus more spending power, in turn stimulating demand. The economy expands and everyone eventually prospers.

But when the economic future looks uncertain, corporate profits are more safely used in gobbling up the competition rather than in starting new businesses or increasing the productive capacity of existing ones. Some of the holding companies that control much of Canada's wealth were put together by entrepreneurs who have never started a business from scratch. Paul Desmarais, whose Power Corporation controls over seventy companies selling everything from cardboard to insurance, hardly projects the image of the creative builder of the economy when he says, "I'm in a hurry. Starting something from scratch is too slow a process."

Since the end of World War II, the growth in demand has more or less been matched by a parallel rise in productivity and investment. The table below gives a picture of the major growth indicators.

Between 1946 and 1972 productivity per hour of work jumped by 200 per cent, which means that the average hour of work produced three times as much. Canada's Gross National Product has risen by 22 times since the end of World War II, while investment jumped by roughly 25 times.

Faced with a business slump and falling profits in the early eighties, companies tried to maintain their earnings by raising prices or by lowering costs through investment in new technology. Rising prices cause inflation. New technology, rather than creating jobs, seems to be eliminating them (see chapter eight).

When business and government leaders speak about the economy, recovery becomes synonymous with expansion and growth. This involves creating more needs and fulfilling them with more products, channelling as many natural resources and as much energy as possible into the creation of the highest possible return on investment.

Companies are free, however, to do with their earnings whatever they judge will do most to generate more profits. The growth that makes good sense for investors and corporations, however, may not be the kind of development that Canada needs. Why should one assume that further growth, bigger profits, expansion and conglomeration will reduce inequality, alleviate poverty, and improve the quality of life in Canada?

How responsibly do we use the great wealth in our custody — land, water, technology, food? Do those of us who are believers recognize that "God intended the Earth and all that it contains for the use of every human being and people"? Do we acknowledge that "all other rights whatsoever, including those of property and of free commerce, are to be subordinated to this principle"? And do we accept the implication of this recognition: "Feed the man dying of hunger, because if you have not fed him you have killed him"?
Canadian Conference of Catholic Bishops,
Sharing Daily Bread, *1974*

International Votes

Products like coffee and bananas are available in all Canadian supermarkets. They are produced in the tropical nations of the Third World, some of which have become known as "banana republics". This label implies two things: dependence on one or two cash crops to support the economy; and unstable and oppressive governments.

Such countries are typically poor in comparison to industrial nations like Canada and the United States, reflecting the fact that the world's wealth is even more unequally divided than Canada's.

Growth Indicators

	1946	1952	1962	1972	1982
Productivity (output/person-hour 1971 equals 100)	35.2	47.4	68.9	104.0	118.9
GNP (current $; million)	11,885	24,588	42,927	105,234	264,279
Public and private investment (current $; million)	2,761	7,576	8,715	22,218	75,079

Such divisions are reproduced internally, with small classes of rich landowners and businessmen dominating the vast majority of poor peasants. It is more profitable for rich landowners to produce bananas for the North American market than beans for the domestic market.

Sometimes the landlords in banana republics do not have the foreign-sounding names of Latin American proprietors. The bananas Canadians get in the supermarket, labelled with familiar names such as Chiquita, were likely grown, packed and shipped by one of three firms that control 70 per cent of the world's banana trade. Like local landlords, United Brands, Del Monte and Castle and Cook are not in the business of growing food for hungry peasants who lack the cash to pay for it in the first place. Return on investment is what matters.

Thus, countries where people are literally dying of hunger actually export food. Human need does not count as a vote in the international supermarket, where the laws of profit and growth hold sway.

When returns are threatened by governments that want to redistribute plantation land to the poor, a powerful company can arrange to have the offending government overthrown, as United Fruit did in Guatemala in 1954. Or if banana republics attempt to get more money for their bananas by joining together to impose an export tax, a big firm can try to break up the effort by bribing a local politician. This is what United Brands did in the early seventies when it paid off the president of Honduras.

Unequal access to products of farm and field — poverty in the midst of affluence — doesn't occur only as the poor of Canada manoeuvre their carts down supermarket aisles. Even more gross disparities of income exist on a world scale, where injustices *between* nations are duplicated by terrible inequalities and sufferings *within* them. While Canada and other countries produce surpluses of grain, people in many countries go without food as a matter of course. Yet in every so-called poor country, there are elites who live in conspicuous luxury. The patterns in poor countries and in the world economy are the same — relatively few people get more votes in the marketplace while the poor, who are the majority, get less.

Another important aspect of the global economy is the international movement of capital. "Capital lacks loyalty — capital will go where the returns are most attractive," said an official of the Royal Bank of Canada. Likewise the president of

Distribution of World Income by Quintiles of
World Population
(in billions of 1979 dollars)

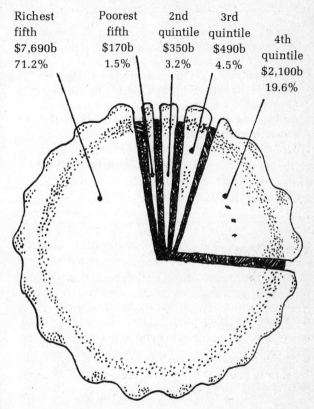

Richest fifth $7,690b 71.2%

Poorest fifth $170b 1.5%

2nd quintile $350b 3.2%

3rd quintile $490b 4.5%

4th quintile $2,100b 19.6%

IBM World Trade Corporation expounded on the nature of free enterprise: "For business purposes, the boundaries that separate one nation from another are no more real than the equator.... Once management understands and accepts this world economy, its view of the marketplace — and its planning — necessarily expand."

Canadian capital and profits tend to leave the country, in part because of the foreign, especially American, control of the economy. Though Canada has a healthy surplus in its exports of *goods* (pulp and paper, minerals, wheat and the like), it exports such large amounts of money in the form of *services* (interest and dividends paid to foreigners, freight and shipping charges and other service payments) that on balance the country is a net exporter of capital. While this has been a trend since 1945, it has recently become acute. Between 1975 and 1982 interest and dividend payments rose from $2.9 billion to $10.7 billion while capital exports in the form of other service payments rose from $4 billion to $13.5 billion.

At the same time the amount Canada earned by exporting its goods also rose, but could not keep pace with the rapid growth of capital exports. So the country's wealth is slowly being siphoned away to other centres of economic power.

> **Among the causes of the worsening food problem, analysts point to climatic disasters, population growth, monetary instability, oil prices and the arms race. Yet the underlying causes are found in the consuming and marketing practices of economic systems — practices which continuously widen the gap between humanity's rich minority and poor majority.**
> *Canadian Conference of Catholic Bishops,*
> **Sharing Daily Bread,** 1974

At the Checkout

The trip through the supermarket nearly over, we reach the checkout counter. Here we might pause to remember the people who used to work the cash register, or the others who boxed the groceries in left-over cardboard cartons. What has happened to these jobs?

When faced with economic stagnation or stiff competition, supermarkets and other companies reduce costs by cutting back the number of employees on the payroll. Labour is often cited as the most costly factor in running a business. So companies replace "labour-intensive" techniques and processes with "capital-intensive" ones, substituting capital in the form of machines for labour in the form of people. This is exactly what the supermarkets did at the check-out counter. This again is the process of "rationalization", noted in chapter three.

First the packer's job was taken over by the cashier, forcing the customer to wait longer in longer lineups. As if to make up for the delay, the store installed electronic scanners to "read" the Universal Product Code (the small patch of stripes that appears on nearly every product sold in Canada) and register the price on the cash receipt. Now the cashiers no longer have to punch in each item, so they can move the customers through more quickly. The electronic scanner reports the sale of each item to a central computer which automatically keeps inventory. Management can change prices instantly by punching a few keys on the computer. This rationalization has reduced the number of people needed to keep stock and

affix price labels to goods before they are put on the shelves.

As for the packing job, at some of the biggest stores it has been transferred to the customers, who pack their own groceries in plastic bags.

Like the supermarkets, the banks are taking full advantage of computerization. Customers often no longer interact with a human teller, but conduct their normal business on a banking machine. Canada's largest bank, the Royal, advertises its electronic service as "Personal Touch Banking" even though one is touching a keyboard, not dealing with a teller. Such rational-

ization cuts costs, increases efficiency and generates more profit. It also puts people out of work, and they come to the supermarket each week with fewer votes.

"The bottom line", one of today's overworked figures of speech, is supposed to express the most important feature or factor in any situation. The expression was borrowed from accounting, where "the bottom line" in a company's statement tells how much profit or loss the firm showed in a given year. Its frequent use suggests that the maximization of profit is a key, maybe *the* key, to the present system.

The fact that profitability is the goal of the most powerful economic actors — and that they're always getting bigger — means that the bottom line has little to do with people's basic needs and issues of economic justice.

In the supermarket case, conventional economic wisdom says that as the big stores compete with one another, customers benefit from lower food prices. There may well be heated competition in this particular sector of the economy, but at the same time the concentration of economic power puts the squeeze on small retailers, processors and farmers.

The supermarkets allegedly provide Canadians with the best quality, cheapest food. But the present system entails several dilemmas:

• to keep smaller merchants and producers in business, but to pay slightly higher prices;
• to provide more jobs, but to enjoy a narrower range of products to choose from;
• to gain efficiency, but at the sacrifice of smaller-scale, independent operations run by their owners.

There is no easy answer to dilemmas like these. They involve painful trade-offs. The choices that are being made — rarely in consultation with the people affected — represent the effective policies, the direction in which Canada is developing, the real "bottom line". To remain lost in the supermarket is to leave such decisions up to others.

> **The possession of money, land and economic power confers heavy responsibility. We do not and cannot *own* them: they are *lent* to us by God. Both individually and collectively we must use our freedoms, powers and resources in ways which help all to come to fullness of life.**
>
> *Anglican Church of Canada,*
> **Poverty in Canada,** *General Synod, 1978*

Questions

• Consumer demand can be created through advertising, but how useful are the products being advertised? Where do worries about "the greasies" or "ring around the collar" come from? How many ads promote the actual merits of a product that is really needed?

By contrast, how many ads create needs artificially by promoting unattainable images or playing on insecurities? Do we really need a further multiplication of sugar-coated breakfast cereals on the supermarket shelves?

Resources

• *Ethical Choices and Political Challenges: Ethical Reflections on the Future of Canada's Socio-Economic Order,* Ottawa: Canadian Conference of Catholic Bishops, 1984. The Catholic Bishops' submission to the Macdonald Commission is published in an illustrated booklet, with discussion starters and resource list. The text summarizes several important principles of social ethics, analyzes the current socio-economic problems in Canada, and presents the challenge of alternative visions and models. Order from Publications Service (CCCB), 90 Parent Avenue, Ottawa, Ont. K1N 7B1.

Questions (cont'd)

- The food store used to serve a particular neighbourhood. Shopping was not just a commercial transaction but a social event, a chat with the owner, clerk or a neighbour. A boy used to help the cashier, carry out the groceries, and — long ago — deliver them to the house on his bicycle. When the independent local store was squeezed out by the supermarket, what was lost? What gained? Is it to our advantage to have fewer and fewer grocery chains with bigger and bigger stores?

- The challenge confronting Canadians can be put quite simply: "Not enough food available for most of humanity: that is the issue. Enough food at reasonable prices for all people: that is the goal." Is the *world* food crisis easier to analyze than the Canadian economy? What are some examples of local action which make people aware of — and do help to alleviate — situations of real starvation?

- Why are corporations driven to expand? When a retail food chain supplies consumers with food and makes a decent profit — should not its managers, owners or shareholders be content?

- Canadians are getting relatively cheap food. But cheap food is not without its social costs. What are the most important characteristics of our economic system? Were they all illustrated in our analysis of the supermarket? Are these the same values which we espouse personally? Which aspects of the economy need further study?

Resources (cont'd)

- G. Baum and D. Cameron, *Ethics and Economics: Canada's Catholic Bishops on the Economic Crisis*, Toronto: James Lorimer, 1984. A commentary on the controversial 1983 statement, *Ethical Reflections on the Economic Crisis*, by a Canadian theologian and political economist. Baum situates the statement within Catholic social teaching, while Cameron analyzes the issues raised by the statement regarding Canadian economic policy.

- *The Poverty Game,* a workshop which immerses participants in the experience of living on a low fixed income in Canada. It covers both the hopelessness and insecurity of subsistence living and some alternate solutions to these problems. The workshop package and further information is available from The Poverty Game, P.O.Box 2294, Dawson Creek, B.C., ph. 604-782-5642.

- "Potatoes," NFB, 1976, 16 mm, 28 minutes. Examines the disappearance of the family farm in the face of the rise of corporate farming, with emphasis on the ensuing problems and personal hardships.

Chapter Seven

The Plague of Unemployment

"What do you do?"

When people meet for the first time, conversation quickly gets around to "What do you do?" The question refers not to their hobbies, of course, but to how they earn a living. "What do you do?" means "What is your job?" Similarly, "How much do you make?" really means "What are you worth?"

In Canada a person's identity is strongly linked to a job, and work is often considered the most important measure of a person's worth. One can have a good job, an important job, or a bad job. Shipping clerks and managing directors are rarely seen to be of equal stature. Yet they are both a cut above someone who has no job at all.

When a person is asked, "What do you do?" and must answer, "Nothing . . . I'm unemployed"

or "I'm on pogey", it's easy to imagine a dark cloud settling on the conversation. Popular opinion sees unemployment as a very negative thing. Active and capable people who have no paid work can feel — or be made to feel — that they are not pulling their weight.

In the distant past the main economic problem used to be not how to employ people, but how to produce enough to meet their needs. Then the industrial revolution multiplied the output of material goods. Now productive capacity has developed to the point where there is more than enough to go around. But access to the abundant goods and services depends mainly on whether one has a job, which is the usual source of income.

A "good" job with high pay promises not only

material comforts but also social status, a sense of personal worth, and the image of success. The question is still, "What do you do?"

"Nothing"

Many Canadians — officially, nearly 1.5 million in 1984 — answer "Nothing". They are the unemployed, and unemployment affects every aspect of their lives. A sudden layoff means the disappearance of a regular paycheque and an obvious decline in material living standards. Families are forced to cut back on both luxuries and the basic necessities of life. Budgets are stretched as incomes shrink and prices rise.

On another level, unemployment has more subtle and — in the long run — more serious effects. It demeans people in their own eyes and in the eyes of others. It carries with it a kind of stigma.

Of course, things are different from the depression of the Hungry Thirties when the unemployed were highly visible, lining up for free meals and riding the rails. Now the net of the welfare state catches many of the unemployed and supports them with unemployment insurance (UIC) for a time, until they become "exhaustees", or welfare payments when UIC does not apply.

But dependence on social security can wear people down just as the bread-lines did. "I don't cut welfare people up, you know, but I have my pride. To me, that's not my type of thing," explained one laid-off worker. "I want to go out and be a useful member of the community and say that I'm working and not freeloading." People find it humiliating not to be able to earn their own living. "I'd like my children to see me as someone who can look after them the way the other guys do. But now they must think of me as a good-for-nothing bum."

"What's your number?"

How many Canadians are confronted with these feelings of purposelessness? It is hard to say, for Statistics Canada gives an incomplete answer. The federal information agency releases data showing how many are "officially unemployed". To be officially unemployed one must be actively seeking work. To these must be added:

- the hidden unemployed, whose frustration has prompted them to abandon the futile search for a job;

- the partially unemployed — those who want full-time work but can only find part-time;
- women who would work if jobs and child care were available;
- people on temporary government training programmes.

To figure out the real rate of unemployment, one can conservatively add 40 per cent again to the official rate. In 1983, for example, when the official rate averaged 11.9 per cent, the real rate hovered around the 16 per cent mark. Though the Statistics Canada estimate was 1.4 million, in fact over two million people out of a work force of 12 million were unemployed if you count those who were out of work but not "officially" unemployed. Over two million Canadians willing to work could find no adequate job.

Unemployment is also regionally uneven. Canadians in some parts of the country find it much more difficult to get a job than others who live in more prosperous areas. Atlantic Canada, many parts of Quebec and northern Canada have always had much higher rates of joblessness than Toronto or Vancouver. In remote parts of Canada, entire communities such as Uranium City, Sask., Pickle Lake, Ont., and Schefferville, Que. attract a workforce for a while and then suddenly turn into virtual ghost towns.

The impact of unemployment is uneven in another way. The numbers have *always* been high for the young, for women and for those living in the poorer areas of the country. For many such people, not having a job is far from temporary. It is not an inconvenience that will go away once a badly-listing economy manages to right itself and surge forward once again.

> Unemployment inflicts much greater harm on the poor than inflation does. The persistence of high rates of unemployment, year in and year out, is in fact an instrument of oppression, whether intended or not.
>
> *Anglican Church of Canada, General Synod,*
> **Poverty in Canada,** *1978*

Unemployment: Here to Stay

People frequently assume that the crushing levels of unemployment of the early eighties will decline with an economic recovery. They like to refer back to the good old days. The roaring twenties, for example, was a period of expansion with a strong job market. Even the fifties and sixties can be fondly remembered as "good old days". Some say that good times will always follow bad as the economic cycle continues.

But on reflection these good times take on a very transient air. The twenties gave way to the doldrums of the thirties: bread-lines, work camps and hard times. The eagerly-awaited recovery was only ushered in by World War II, with its artificial demand based on terrible destruction. Canada has been on an economic roller-coaster ever since.

After the war, returned veterans, refugees, the baby boom and the explosion in housing maintained the economic recovery. When the economy faltered slightly in the late forties, the Korean War ushered in the fabulous fifties. Jobs abounded until, late in the decade, an oft-forgotten downturn drove unemployment up again to then-intolerable levels. Production slackened off and unemployment hit a high of 7 per cent after having hovered around 3 per cent since the end of World War II.

This rise in joblessness was considered alarming enough to merit the establishment of a special Senate Committee to look into the problem. But consumer demand and the war in Viet Nam intervened to produce another boom, so that the soaring sixties are remembered as a time of uninterrupted prosperity.

In the seventies unemployment rose steadily, as intermittent periods of recovery were followed by decline. Government make-work programmes and unemployment insurance sustained most jobless Canadians and kept them out of highly-visible soup kitchens. The eighties have brought talk of a new depression.

Surges in unemployment, then, have been frequent ever since the country became industrialized, ever since the majority of Canadians needed a paying job to help them get by and to lend a sense of purpose to life. There have always been periods when "What do you do?" could only be answered with a shrug or a curse about finding no work.

It has gradually dawned on people that the economy is not organized to provide jobs. Unemployment is not an aberration or a temporary faltering in an otherwise steady march of economic growth. It seems to be a chronic condition that worsens with each backward swing of the economic pendulum.

In 1983 the Canadian Manufacturers Association, poised optimistically at the launching of another presumed economic recovery, polled its members about the job prospects that the expected upswing was likely to offer. The nation's employers responded that they could return to prerecession levels of production with 10 per cent fewer workers. This translated into the permanent loss of 200 thousand jobs. In the same year the Canadian Union of Public Employees, representing public sector office workers, predicted that 1.5 to 2 million clerical jobs would eventually be wiped out through office automation.

Canada is moving towards more — not less — unemployment for reasons that are economic, technological and even political. In the years to come, Canadians may look back on the eighties as the decade during which economists, politicians and business people resigned themselves to unemployment as a fact of life rather than a passing phase.

Who to Blame?

Unemployment, bound up as it is with other complex economic questions, is bewildering. When people cast about for answers, they are actually doing a rough and ready sort of social analysis. Are the following comments typical?

- "Those shiftless young loafers hanging around the shopping malls . . . give them a pick and shovel!"
- "Too many people prefer to live off the government."
- "There's always work for anyone who really wants a job. Just look at the want ads."

> By creating conditions for permanent unemployment, an increasingly large segment of the population is threatened with the loss of human dignity. In effect, there is a tendency for people to be treated as an impersonal force having little or no significance beyond their economic purpose in the system.
>
> *Canadian Conference of Catholic Bishops,*
> **Ethical Reflections on the Economic Crisis,** *1983*

- "The unions have become so strong and greedy they're destroying jobs all the time."
- "People running restaurants just can't keep their dishwashers."
- "Immigrants are keen to work, but Canadians have become soft and lazy and uncompetitive." OR "There are too many immigrants taking jobs away from Canadians."

Such remarks, blaming unemployment on its own victims, are common enough. This analysis sees unemployment as an *individual* problem rather than as primarily a structural problem related to the way society is organized. At the same time these responses are often highly emotional, arising out of feelings of frustration, resentment or powerlessness. Yet there are important economic, technological and political factors at work in creating the plague of unemployment.

Another reaction, similar to blaming the victim, is to place the weight of blame on the shoulders of individual employers. This is understandable, since it is specific bosses who decide to shut down plants or introduce machines to replace workers. These highly-visible people can be painted as the villains, especially in the eyes of those most affected by their decisions. After all, not having to endure the loss of income and the indignity accompanying unemployment, the boss can sometimes appear very callous in laying off workers.

Still, like blaming the unemployed themselves, blaming the immediate employer also fails to get at the basic causes of unemployment. These causes have little to do with the actions of individuals as such, be they bosses or workers. Both the small entrepreneur and the corporation manager operate within a specific system of priorities. The logic of private profit and corporate growth takes priority over job-creation, and this characteristic of the Canadian economic system limits the effective action of the individual. A boss or manager who does not promote this priority is most likely to face bankruptcy or get fired. And so both the laid-off worker and the plant manager are at the mercy of the structures of our economy.

Who (or What) is to Blame?

The economy is organized to generate profits and dividends, to grow and expand, not to provide jobs. This fact was pointed out over two hundred years ago — when the industrial revolution was in its early stages — by Adam Smith, an early analyst of capitalism:

> The consideration of his own private profit is the sole motive which determines the owner of any capital to employ it either in agriculture, in manufactures, or in some particular branch of the wholesale or retail trade. The different quantities of productive labour which it may put into motion never enter his thoughts.

The private profit-motive Adam Smith celebrated spurred capitalists to industrialize manufacturing and to mechanize agriculture. This first Industrial Revolution led to expanding job opportunities in the cities and absorbed most of the labour displaced from the agricultural sector.

After World War II, when industry accelerated the replacement of people with machines and women began to enter the labour force in larger numbers, the increased labour supply was absorbed by job opportunities in an expanding service sector. This area of economic activity does not produce a concrete material product. Rather, it involves processing information and filling important needs such as health care and education. Service work is done by office employees, social service workers, people who work in stores and so on.

The table illustrates the dramatic changes that have taken place since the early postwar years in what Canadians do for a living. While the proportion of workers in agriculture dropped by 77 per cent and manufacturing had its share of the labour force drop by 26.5 per cent, the proportion of people engaged in service work jumped by 39 per cent.

Before the eighties, when employment tailed off in one area of the economy, there always seemed to be a new opening for labour. The unemployment of the eighties, however, is qualitatively different from earlier downturns, recessions and depressions. Jobs are evaporating, with little prospect of broad new horizons opening up.

This is true not only in the manufacturing and resource sectors, where machines have been replacing people for decades, but also in the information and service sectors: Jobs for office workers, bank tellers and cashiers are disappearing. This shrinkage in the service sector has a disproportionate effect on women, whose jobs are concentrated there. The new computerized machinery also includes robots which, unlike the labour-saving innovations of the past, need virtually no workers to operate them. They can almost think for themselves.

Two key question arise: Where are the millions of displaced workers going to find jobs? They do not want to become UIC exhaustees and sign up for welfare.

And what job slots await young Canadians, graduating from school in the expectation that there will be something for them to do for a living? These people want to earn their way and have money to spend. They want to contribute something to society, they want to feel useful.

One railway worker, nearing retirement, reflected on the changes affecting his industry. He foresaw the elimination of two-thirds of the railway workers in Canada and summed up the economy's failure to plan accordingly: "They aren't making any provision for getting young people into the workforce because they don't know what to do with them in that workforce."

The surplus of idle workers represents a further absurdity — countless socially-valuable jobs still need to be done. Many tasks, particularly those in which people serve people, have been cut back severely. Governments seek to curb their deficits by reducing spending on social services. People find it harder and harder to get suitable daycare for their children. The educational system falls victim to spending restraint, class sizes increase, schools and universities scramble for dollars while laying off staff. Scientists cannot

Distribution of Workforce 1951-1981

	1951	1961	1971	1981
Agriculture	18.4%	11.2%	6.3%	4.3%
Forestry	2.3	1.4	0.9	0.8
Fishing and Trapping	0.6	0.3	0.3	0.3
Mining	1.5	1.3	1.6	1.8
Manufacturing	26.5	24.0	22.2	19.5
Construction	6.8	6.2	6.1	6.3
Transportation, Communications, Utilities	8.8	9.3	8.7	8.1
Trade	14.1	16.9	16.5	16.9
Finance, insurance and real estate	3.0	3.9	4.8	5.2
Service	18.0	19.5	26.2	29.4
Public Administration	N/A	5.9	6.4	6.8
TOTAL	100	100	100	100
Total Number Employed in Canada (000's)	5097	6055	8078	11830

(CUPE Facts)

find money for important research. Planned extensions of public transit systems remain on the drawing boards while fares rise. Music, theatre, dance and other artistic endeavours are squeezed for lack of government support.

Some of these services have been called the "social wage", meaning they make benefits available to all members of society. Some of these benefits help to reduce hardship, others make life more pleasant and expand people's horizons.

Obviously daycare, research, culture and so forth are not "productive" activities in the same conventional sense as growing wheat, mining zinc or producing automobiles, refrigerators and weapons. But the latter group of "productive" jobs is becoming much more capital-intensive and less labour-intensive (that is, the proportion of costly machinery increases and at the same time less human labour is needed to produce a given quantity of goods). Since fewer people are needed to provide many goods and services, it would make sense to use the energy and resources freed up in providing the social wage. The notion of productivity, and the manner in which wealth and work are distributed in Canada, need to be rethought.

What kinds of work *should* people be doing? A lot of creative but unemployed energy is being wasted at the same time that human services are being diminished. This is the sort of paradox that some economic ingenuity and political courage could resolve.

Cutbacks in people-oriented spending are even more questionable when considered from a job-creation perspective. The largest job payoffs come from investing in services such as health and education. Far away at the other end of the scale is spending on the military.

Direct and Indirect Jobs Generated by One Billion Dollars	
Military	76,000 jobs
Machinery	86,000 jobs
Government	87,000 jobs
Transportation	92,000 jobs
Construction	100,000 jobs
Health Services	139,000 jobs
Education	187,000 jobs
Tax Cut to Consumers	112,000 jobs

(CUPE Facts)

One argument *against* investing in social services is that they are not really productive activities because nothing sellable or tradeable results. But primary (resource) and secondary (manufacturing) industries need fewer and fewer workers to produce more and more goods. These goods are Canada's wealth. To spend some of this wealth on social services and the social wage is not to "waste" or "squander" but to use it in a socially-conscious way to enhance the quality of life.

Support for social services is by no means the only answer to the country's economic problems. But a human-oriented society would opt for jobs that help people and provide creative opportunities rather than tolerate the tragic waste of unemployment. Otherwise, inevitably the experience of the unemployed will become an increasing, permanent feature of Canadian life.

> The human and social costs of continuing unemployment are themselves staggering. There is the economic strain on family life that comes with the sudden drop in purchasing power and the possibility of indebtedness. There is the psychological strain that comes from a loss of feelings of self-worth coupled with feelings of anxiety, frustration and bitterness. As a result, unemployment has meant lower productivity in the economy, reduction in public revenues and increasing social welfare costs. And these problems, in turn, are further intensified by cut-backs in social services (including unemployment insurance benefits). Today, as unemployment threatens to become a more or less permanent fact of life in our economy, a substantial proportion of our population is in danger of becoming more marginalized and disillusioned.
>
> *Canadian Conference of Catholic Bishops,* **Unemployment: The Human Costs, 1980**

Government Initiatives

"Although the economic recession is near an end, we face a time of social, technological and economic change," cautioned Lloyd Axworthy, in 1983 Ottawa's minister responsible for employment. "Structural alterations in the marketplace have already been to blame for part of today's unacceptably high unemployment rates."

High rates of unemployment make long-term planning difficult not only for government departments but for nearly everyone. People out of work do not have much money to spend on the goods and services that are being produced; this slack demand is a drag on the entire economy. Another financial drain is the increased taxes and UIC premiums which employers and workers still on the job — as well as taxpayers generally — have to pay. Workers who are idle for long periods of time lose job skills.

What's more, a high unemployment rate discourages people from upgrading their skills. Idle young people whose education has yielded nothing in the way of secure employment tend to be disillusioned and cynical.

Clearly, unemployment makes little sense from any human or social perspective. The only group it could be said to benefit, and even that in a restricted sense, is employers. For them a high jobless rate tends to exert downward pressure on the wage demands of the workers who still have jobs. Workers are advised to curtail their demands and reduce their expectations. The advice is reinforced by the fact that there are a lot of unemployed workers out there ready to take any job.

So the labour market becomes a buyer's market, with supply outstripping demand to the point where the price of labour, the commodity in question, declines. In this way the power of unions also declines as management gains an extra advantage at the bargaining table. Yet the paradox of the situation is that, once again, employers who save on wage bills are likely to suffer from the poor demand for goods and services stemming from falling purchasing power due to high rates of joblessness.

Business leaders are always pressuring the government to give the private sector incentives to help revitalize the economy. They argue that the money is better and more productively spent in this way than on the public sector. "Business will get the country back to work", they claim.

But, as Adam Smith pointed out over two centuries ago, the private sector is more committed to profitability and expansion than to job-creation.

Some government money has been allocated to make-work projects as a means of slowing the steady increase in unemployment. There are programmes that provide just enough work so that people can qualify for another period of unemployment insurance. But twenty-week jobs are not very rewarding.

A 1983 make-work project in New Brunswick employed a group of young men to thin trees on woodlots. But the workers did as little as possible and showed little enthusiasm for the job. Asked why they didn't seem to care about the work, they were forthright. "It's just a project", they shrugged. The workers had participated in other such projects before and probably would do so again, since their community has a chronically depressed economy. They were well aware that the programme was designed not to give them productive work or full-time work. It was simply supposed to provide just enough work to put them back on unemployment insurance for another year.

Such short-term measures seem rather aimless. They do not represent any sort of strategy or vision of Canada's future, or show much respect for the unemployed themselves.

Another government initiative has been to give massive subsidies to the aerospace industry for the production of military and civilian aircraft. But the government-financed debts of de Havilland and Canadair provoked a political storm in 1983 and 1984. Ottawa justified the support of the aerospace industry on the grounds of job creation. In 1983 the Air Industries Association of Canada said 1982 sales amounted to $3 billion and the industry employed forty-five thousand people. The Association estimated that sales would jump by 230 per cent to $7 billion by 1986, but employment would rise by a mere 13 per cent. This kind of increasing capital intensity is similar to most modern sectors of the economy.

During the rest of the twentieth century, the Canadian workplace will change still more, and the nature of work itself will be further transformed (see chapter eight). Put simply, less work will need to be done to produce everything people need to live comfortable lives.

But less work may just translate into more unemployment. In that case, it would make little difference for many Canadians whether the economy was in a recession or on an upswing. They would still belong to the standing army of the jobless, with no choice but to live off the government and an occasional, insecure and low-paying job.

Ottawa's employment department responded to the joblessness of the early eighties by instituting a programme of "work-sharing". In this scheme the government uses unemployment insurance to subsidize workers who, due to recession, technological change and industrial restructuring, have had to reduce their hours on the job. This saves the employer money and avoids layoffs. The government also argues that work-sharing allows workers to undergo retraining during their extra time. This assumes that there will be enough jobs for everyone in the future.

Unions have pointed out that work-sharing, which rose in cost from $10 million to $350 million between 1981 and 1983, still failed to save nearly half the participating workers from layoffs. Work-sharing is a kind of pressure valve designed to ease the burden brought on by the unemployment caused by changes in the labour market.

Still, the concept of *sharing* has strong appeal in times of economic hardship. If there is less work around, but just as much — if not more — wealth being generated by that work, why not share both the work and the wealth resulting from it? If less work is needed to produce more wealth, it makes sense to cut the hours each person spends on the job while maintaining rates of pay. Back in the nineteenth century demands for a forty-hour week were resisted by employers with the same vigour they used to argue against the abolition of child labour. But now the forty-hour week is standard. More Canadians have full-time, thirty-five-hour jobs, and part-time jobs are becoming so prevalent that 2.4 million people worked part-time in 1981. By the year 2000, 10 per cent of all workers are expected to be part-timers.

Instead of reducing workers, why not reduce work? Two people doing one job half-time are more productive than one person working full-time. In the not-too-distant future, people might be able to be on the job two and one-half days a week rather than five; or eleven days a month instead of twenty-two; or five and one-half months a year instead of eleven months. If people were adequately paid for this reduced work, they would have time to go back to school, spend more time with their children or pursue creative hobbies.

How will the increasing amounts of non-paid time available to us be handled? — that is the question. Figuring out what people are going to do with their time makes more sense than having them qualify for unemployment insurance and sit idle for the rest of the year.

This reduction in work hours would involve redistributing the national income resulting from work. A twenty-hour week paid at today's forty-hour rate — where would the money come from? Obviously, such an innovation could easily double the cost of labour in this country, leading to a flight of capital as investors sought better returns elsewhere. And Canadian products might rise in price, putting them at a competitive disadvantage in international markets. The Canadian economy does not exist in a vacuum and those who control capital are interested not in the redistribution of that wealth but in the expansion of their own resources.

Yet economic growth by itself, under present circumstances, promises little in the way of economic and social justice for the jobless and the poor. Clearly, the unemployment problem defies simple, straightforward solutions. But it's equally obvious that the pattern thus far — perpetual growth and expansion; the production of more goods by fewer corporations — is hardly leading to more jobs for more people. In fact, it is leading to more, and more permanent, unemployment.

> Indeed, unemployment is not simply a political or economic or social problem. It is a profoundly moral and spiritual problem in our times. As Pope John Paul II reminds us, the "plague of unemployment" is symptomatic of a basic "moral disorder". We are called, therefore, to examine the basic values and attitudes that motivate the economic and political activities which make our society what it is today.
> *Canadian Conference of Catholic Bishops,*
> **Unemployment: The Human Costs,***1980*

Crisis Or Choice

The economy, as currently structured, condemns some two million Canadians to continue knocking in vain on locked doors — for the rest of the decade, if not the century. To maintain such huge human resources in a state of idleness, in a country so generously endowed with natural wealth as well as capital and technology — is it not absurd?

It's also costly. When people think of rising unemployment, they usually think of endless job searches or perhaps the growing need for soup kitchens and other forms of emergency relief. But an American study concluded that the social costs of unemployment are staggering when expressed in the amount of increased dollars spent on hospitals and jails due to rising rates of crime and sickness. For unemployment also means more suicides, more admissions to mental hospitals, more people put into jail, more people with diseases like cirrhosis of the liver. Adapted to Canada, the social cost formula that takes these factors into account revealed that the unemployment rate increase of 3.4 per cent in 1982 cost at least a billion dollars.

The word "*crisis*" is often bandied about whenever people talk about unemployment. But do the state of the economy and the rate of unemployment deserve to be called a crisis? "Crisis" implies a turning-point or a crossroads, a point at which marked change in direction is imminent, where decisive choices are to be made. The present moment does not merit the label "crisis" if unemployment continues to be the inevitable and recurring fate of so many Canadians, a fate which the country's leaders are passively accepting: Politicians talk about levels of unemployment over 10 per cent as being "acceptable".

What is new in this "post-industrial age" is the irreversible displacement of the jobless. Blaming particular workers or managers sheds little light on the tragedy. A better analysis links unemployment to the structures and attitudes governing the decisions that have been routinely made until now. If unemployment is a critical problem to be solved, rather than the price to be paid for a restricted economic recovery, quite different, more creative and human-oriented priorities must guide economic decision-making in Canada from now on.

The fundamental option concerns the use of capital. If the primary motive of economic practice is to generate private profit and foster corporate growth, then by the logic of the present system unemployment will increasingly characterize the economy. But the capital could be used instead primarily to generate jobs and foster people's creativity. The choices to be made could scarcely be more urgent or decisive.

The Canadian Bishops' concern over these options was reflected in their 1983 statement:

> What is required first is a basic shift in values: the goal of serving the human needs of all people must take precedence over the maximization of profits and growth, and priority must be given to the dignity of human labour, not machines.

The energies of Canadians can be set free and used in creative, fulfilling ways rather than restricted by unemployment. But such a path forward demands a break with the ways of the past. It means a redistribution of both wealth and work. It means mobilizing both resources and technology to serve social priorities.

Questions

- Do you think a job is a basic human right? What is the public attitude towards people who are unemployed? Is it their fault or are they simply victims of larger circumstances?

- Is there anyone you know who is unemployed? Is there a family member who cannot find a job? How long have they been looking for work? Have they had to think of relocating or revising their expectations downwards?

- Have there been any industry shutdowns or large layoffs in your community? What were the reasons? How has the community reacted to the firms that have cut back their workforces?

- Is there a group or association of the unemployed in your area? What are they doing? Are there ways of supporting such groups?

- What are your images of the Hungry Thirties? Do they come from direct experience? From the experience of people's parents? From the media? Do you think such levels of unemployment could afflict Canada again? If they threaten to do so, what might be potential remedies to provide jobs? Is it up to government to find a solution? Or should we depend on private enterprise to create jobs? Do ordinary people have the power to do anything about unemployment?

Resources

- Cy Gonick, *Out of Work: Why there's so much unemployment and why it's getting worse*, Toronto: James Lorimer, 1978. A concise economic analysis of unemployment in Canada.

- "Unemployment", *ISSUE* 18 (April 1978) A six-page broadsheet analyzing several of the popular misconceptions about unemployment. Research in Social Issues, Division of Mission in Canada, United Church of Canada, 85 St. Clair Avenue East, Toronto, Ont. M4T 1M8, ph. 416-925-5931.

- "Worlds Without Work: Unemployment in Newfoundland and Latin America," OXFAM-Newfoundland, 1979, slide-tape, 20 minutes. Looks at government planning and corporate development and their impact on the availability of jobs.

- "For Twenty Cents a Day," Jim Munro, DEC Films, 1980, 16 mm, 24 minutes. The plight of the unemployed in British Columbia during the Depression.

- Provincial federations of labour should be able to provide material on unemployment in each province, as well as the names of groups — such as unions of unemployed workers — working actively on the unemployment issue.

- GATT-Fly. An inter-church project on issues of economic justice, GATT-Fly publishes materials on unemployment, energy, trade and other economic issues. 11 Madison Avenue, Toronto, Ont. M5R 2S2, ph. 416-921-4615.

Chapter Eight

Micro-technology and the Future

There is a French expression, commonly used in English, that starts *"Plus ça change..."* Often it's enough to say just that, "The more things change..." and people will know what you mean even if you don't complete the maxim: *"Plus ça change, plus ça reste la même chose — the more things change, the more they stay the same."*

What's changing, and what's staying the same? Microtechnology may be only a tag for the latest fad in expensive consumer goods — or it may be part of the most rapid and significant change to date in Canada's economic life. Indeed, it is important to know what is merely changing superficially in society, and what is changing more profoundly. At the same time, what is failing to change? To grapple with these questions, let's take a look at the microtechnology sprouting up all around us.

Plus ça change

Did you ever expect to see a headline scream out ROBOT JUST DOING ITS JOB: MAN GETS IN THE WAY!? Strange, but true. The headline appeared over a 1983 newspaper article telling how a Canadian auto worker needed several dozen stitches after being lacerated by a robot.

Microtechnology is said to be the greatest innovation since the development of steam power and the spinning-jenny. Although computers have been around since World War II and could process a lot of information, they were large, awkward and very expensive. Thanks to the development of the silicon chip, more recent micro-

processors have been cheap, tiny and versatile, with constantly improving capacities. Every two years, it seems, a new machine offers twice as much computing power for half the price.

The tiny microchip is turning up not only in computers but in everything from wrist-watches to jumbo jets. Robots work on the assembly line in the automobile industry. Word processors replace typewriters, retrieval systems replace filing-cabinets, and both displace office workers. Computerized banking machines receive deposits and dole out cash — just like tellers.

Many jobs are becoming obsolete. People will soon be able to do the shopping via interactive television, without leaving their living rooms. Inventions have already begun to transform the way Canadians work, spend their leisure time and, indeed, live their lives.

Government tells us that high technology industries are the only hope for economic growth. At the same time there are foreboding statistics on job loss. In 1983 a secret federal government study estimated that between one-quarter and one-half of all jobs in manufacturing will be eliminated by the end of the decade. It said similar changes will occur in business and financial services, where a quarter of all present jobs will disappear. The reason? The invasion of the workplace by the silicon microchip.

It is not surprising, then, that many people respond to the new electronic marvels not with excitement, but with fear. The foreign-sounding lingo of "bytes" and "modems", "videotex" and "robotics" leaves us feeling a little stunned. The idea of machines humming along at speeds of ten million operations per second is incomprehensible and disorienting. Children come home with news of the magic they're learning to perform on the computer at school. People yearn for assurance that their lives won't be altered beyond recognition.

The changes in industry, business, government and communications affect everyone — whether people understand them or not. An analysis of these changes, how and why they are coming about, would equip us to both benefit from the advances and help prevent the nightmares from coming true.

Must everyone become a computer expert in order to survive as a worker or consumer or citizen? It doesn't seem so. But technological laypeople do have to become familiar enough with microtechnology so as not to be intimidated or overwhelmed. A basic understanding of the microprocessor's role in Canadian economy and society should enable us to take some part in the changes and avoid having them simply foisted on us.

The social analysis in this chapter is an initial overview of this immense, complex and exciting issue. The first step is to look at technological change in its historical context. The past provides a clue as to what exactly is changing — and what still needs to change.

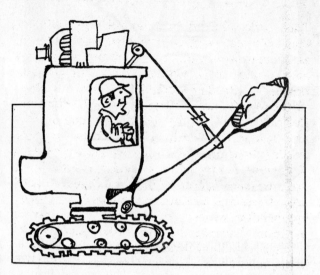

> As long as technology and capital are not harnessed by society to serve basic human needs, they are likely to become an enemy rather than an ally in the development of peoples.
> *Canadian Conference of Catholic Bishops,*
> **Ethical Reflections on the Economic Crisis,** *1983*

The Parable of the Teaspoons

IBM is by far the world's largest manufacturer of computer technology. It is also one of the biggest corporations in the world. In 1982 IBM ran the following advertisement:

> Two men were watching a mechanical excavator on a building site. "If it wasn't for that machine," said one, "twelve men could be doing that job." "Yes," replied the other, "and if it weren't for your twelve shovels, two hundred men with teaspoons could be doing that job."

A business can buy an excavator and hire an operator much more cheaply than employ twelve shovellers or two hundred workers, even if they use their own teaspoons. Given the cost advantages accruing to owners of firms and factories, automation is sure to come and replace more workers. To denounce such innovation without considering its implications and who controls it is of little help. To embrace technological change as the only sensible and inevitable option — because "You can't stand in the way of progress" — seems just as foolish.

In the teaspoon parable, the first man, cast in a pessimistic light, worries about the negative effects of technological change on employment. He hesitates to jump on IBM's technological bandwagon. He seems to doubt the happy times promised by the new technologies. Apparently enough people shared his worries to warrant an expensive ad designed to present technology in a warm, optimistic light.

Doubts and concerns have also been voiced in high places over people being displaced by the new microtechnology. In 1983 the federal employment minister admitted to the Canadian Advanced Technology Association that he was afraid workers might react violently to innovations beyond their control. Too often, he told the employers, workers have been casually informed that they were no longer needed. "That's a fairly harsh system," the minister declared. He worried that if workers in the 1980s and 1990s were replaced by robots and computers, there was a fair chance that they'd become angry and start to smash machines, like the Luddites did in the early nineteenth century.

Story 200 Years Old

Those who seriously question the application of new technology are often labelled with contempt as modern-day Luddites. A group politically active in the early years of the Industrial Revolution in the British Midlands, the Luddites were skilled artisans and craftspeople whose trades and livelihoods were threatened by the looming factory system. They valued their skills and their freedom to control when and where they worked. They did not want to become servants, hired wage-workers subject to the discipline of the factory. In fact, the new machines were often tended by unskilled women and children who laboured in virtual slavery under prison-like conditions.

So the Luddites attacked and destroyed some of the machines threatening to replace them, especially in the textile trade. They were not blindly resisting progress. At various times they pushed for a legal minimum wage, control of the "sweating" of women and children in the factories, the prohibition of shoddy work and the right to form

trade unions. They even demanded that employers be obliged to find work for skilled workers displaced by machinery.

Since workers had no control over the deployment of new technology, the Luddites knew how unlikely they were to benefit from its application. As early casualties of the Industrial Revolution, they would have been sympathetic to the sentiments of a Canadian trade unionist speaking 170 years later: "You cannot stop the new technology, but there's no reason people should suffer from it. We want some of the benefits of technology, not just the adverse effects."

The development of steam-powered machinery and the growth in iron and steel production were two of the driving forces behind the Indus-

trial Revolution of the nineteenth century. With the centralization of production into factories, the jealously guarded skills of artisans and craftspeople — weavers, shoemakers, stockingers and other textile workers — were gradually made obsolete. Although modern industries could produce more goods, the Luddites resisted these changes out of fear that they would turn the world upside down. Displaced workers could either migrate to the growing urban slums to work in the factories, or they could emigrate to the colonies. Given the dilemma they faced, either way the familiar security of their work and lives would be destroyed.

Almost two centuries later, how do people view the resistance of the Luddites? It depends on how they interpret the tremendous mechanical, economic and social changes of the Industrial Revolution. If these are seen as entirely inevitable, "progressive" and of unquestionable advantage to society, the opposition of the Luddites was indeed blind and futile. If some of the costs and consequences are questionable, the Luddites might appear more prophetic than hysterical.

In the 1980s Canadians face a similar, perhaps even greater, revolution in human work. How many people would be permanently unemployed if the Canadian economy failed to adjust to these changes, if industry was slow to embrace the rapid advance of microtechnology? What would have happened if Britain had remained a nation of cottage industries? Similarly, Canada would be bypassed in a frenzy of international competition as other nations captured new markets, including Canada's own. This would lead to more hard economic times.

But what would happen if, following the urging of industry and government, Canada leaped wholeheartedly into the era of microelectronics and competed for the new market opportunities now opening up?

Joining the race or sitting it out, either option seems to lead to similar unemployment problems.

This genuine dilemma sparks a new question for the social analyst. Maybe it is not the technology alone — the steam engine of two centuries ago or the silicon microchip of today — which accounts for the revolution, but also the economic context into which the technology is introduced: the relationships of production and of distribution, the patterns of decision-making, the forms of control over economic life. It is this suspicion which suggests a concrete example, a Canadian industry widely acclaimed as a world leader in new technology.

The introduction of computers and robots in industries and offices has begun to create what may become a new class of people, namely, the so-called "techno-peasants". These are the men and women who are being shut-out or marginalized by their functional illiteracy in the new technologies. The more affected are expected to be workers in manufacturing, agriculture, and resource industries. Indeed, it is the middle classes which are most vulnerable to increasing marginalization, due to the new technologies. The upward social mobility of the post-war years is rapidly giving way to the new trend of downward social mobility for many people. This is likely to contribute to an enlargement of the sectors of poverty and powerlessness in our society.

Canadian Conference of Catholic Bishops,
Ethical Choices and Political Challenges, 1984

Look Ma, No Hands

Canada's telephone industry is regarded as a model of efficiency. The country's fourth largest corporation as ranked by both sales and assets, as well as one of its most profitable firms, Bell Canada provides phone service to central Canada and sells equipment to phone companies in other provinces and around the world. Northern Telecom, an affiliate of Bell, is a leader in the design and manufacture of the electronic operator consoles, switching equipment and computerized components that form the basis of a modern telecommunications network.

The telephone operator has long been the most readily-identifiable representative of the phone company. This position has almost always been held by women. In the old days, sitting shoulder-to-shoulder, they used to plug in jacks whenever a light on the switchboard flashed. They would connect the customers and follow through on their requests. As technology evolved, local calls were switched automatically, and now long distance and overseas calls can be handled without operator assistance.

Of course as telephone communication became faster, more efficient and convenient, the phone company needed fewer workers and some jobs disappeared. In the eighties all but the smallest human functions have been eliminated. Operators mainly handle directory assistance, person-to-person, collect and credit-card calls.

Northern Telecom has designed its switching equipment in such a way that each operator now has her own work station with keyboard, video-display terminal and headset. According to the company, the job has improved tremendously. The firm emphasizes the "personal preference" that operators have of plugging in the headset on either the left or the right. The new workplace also features "freedom of movement" along with a "fully-adjustable anti-glare monitor" and an upholstered chair.

Northern Telecom calls its work station TOPS, short for Traffic Operator Position System. The computer-controlled switching system allows management to monitor the detailed performance of each worker, counting the number of calls handled or the number of keyboard strokes per minute. Thus the employer can pressure operators who fail to keep up with company-established norms of productivity.

A customer call used to be answered when the operator plugged into the switchboard. This setup allowed her a bit of discretion as to when to respond. Now the operator is plugged into the machine at all times, with calls fed into the headset automatically, one after the other. Moreover, the individualized consoles make communication between fellow-operators difficult if not impossi-

ble. The nature of the work has changed, depriving the operators of what little control they had over their jobs. It is easy to see that the digital switching equipment provides more than simply customer convenience.

The operators serve the machine, under conditions dictated by the company owning the machine. Perhaps it is surprising that the operators do not respond like the Luddites of old and smash the equipment that so totally subsumes their work to the needs of the technology.

Nevertheless, management at Northern Telecom and Bell Canada wax enthusiastically about the benefits of TOPS. "Extensive research led to a position that offered a new prestige and in turn, greater job satisfaction and greater efficiency." Yet what looks like efficiency to management looks to workers like the loss of what minimal control they used to enjoy over their jobs. Workers in a host of other fields, from typesetting to the production of machine tools, have suffered a similar loss of control over even the most minute details of their jobs.

Although switchboard jobs could be very routine and boring, some operators took great pride in the quality of their work. Still, few people would want to return to the days of the party line. We all benefit in some way from more efficient telephone service. Moreover, technological change gives enormous cost advantages to owners of firms and factories. They are scarcely considering the possibility of *not* automating, for the competition both at home and abroad is rushing to keep up with the latest technological developments.

Technological innovation is most often introduced unilaterally by management. The phrase

> We are not taking a stand against progress or technology *per se*. **On the contrary, modern advances in the development of capital and technology could be used to greatly enhance the development of peoples here in Canada and throughout the world. The critical question, however, is who controls these instruments and how will they be used.**
>
> *Canadian Conference of Catholic Bishops,* **Ethical Choices and Political Challenges,** *1984*

"top-down insertion" describes the introduction of new technologies into the workplace without participation by the workers affected. Upper-level management makes the decisions and by the time the workers hear about it the equipment has already been purchased and is ready to be installed.

In some cases new machines are designed so that workers need only monitor a few gauges on a control panel. Along the way, skills that were previously highly valued are replaced. Even if it does not result in direct layoffs, this *de-skilling* is frustrating for people who have taken pride in the expertise they have developed and their ability to conceive and carry out a task. When this experience is replaced by a preprogrammed machine, the "need to know" disappears. The most efficient systems aim to reduce the human factor to a minimum. The fewer human decisions or choices on a switchboard, the more smoothly the calls will flow.

The introduction of computers also raises health problems, chiefly for the workers — overwhelmingly women — who assemble and operate them. Silicon chips are so tiny that in order to wire them to circuit boards workers must peer through microscopes all day. This task is usually done in low-wage countries in Asia, where eyestrain limits the working lives of the women in the electronics industry to a few short years. When their eyesight has deteriorated to the point that they can no longer do the job, these workers are simply replaced by new recruits.

In Canada, operators of video display terminals (VDTs) who must gaze at a small screen all day complain of eyestrain, headaches and fatigue. The radiation emitted by the VDTs also exposes pregnant women to the dangers of miscarriages and birth defects.

> In 1981, the Communications Workers of Canada won a landmark agreement endorsing the right of pregnant equipment operators to refuse to work on VDTs. The concession resulted from Labour Canada's investigation of the VDTs used by Bell Canada for possible radiation. It was launched after four pregnant operators refused to work on the equipment on the grounds that doing so constituted an imminent danger to their health — grounds sanctioned under the Canada Labour Code.

While there is no definite scientific link between radiation from VDTs and health problems, there is also no definite proof that the machines are safe. Most frequently, it has been up to the workers involved to push for safe conditions, *after* the machines have been introduced.

In other cases new technologies such as robots, word processors and electronic scanners in stores simply cut down on the labour required to do a given job. In 1982 a Canadian study of computers on the job speculated, "With the automation potential currently available, all the existing goods and services of our society could be produced by a mere 10 per cent of the labour force." Hundreds of studies of the impact of microtechnology on employment have been conducted, and they all point to a reduction in the number of jobs people will have to do in the future. With so many jobs likely to disappear forever, some very normal expectations about economy and society in Canada need to be questioned and revised.

During the first industrial revolution, it took the strenuous efforts of labour and unions to change the situation so that workers could gain a partial share in the benefits of industrialization. Now the new industrial revolution is gathering momentum. Will the owners of the new technology appropriate all the benefits, leaving the costs to the workers? Are workers being asked to make all the economic sacrifices? Will they be consulted at all? Canadians seem to have reached a new threshold.

The labour movement is worried about the effects of technological change on its members. It has urged more consultation between labour and management *before* changes are introduced. Unions are looking for job guarantees, retraining schemes and early retirement programmes. Just like the Luddites of days gone by, labour wants some guarantee of work for those displaced by machines. And workers have also been pushing for specific clauses in their contracts to provide notification and consultation when their employers are considering the introduction of new technology.

A huge number of office and service workers — primarily women — do not even have the protection of unions. The work these women do is likely to be most seriously affected as the office of the future — "the paperless office" — will need fewer people to handle information through jobs such as typing, filing and mailing. In 1969 Bell Canada employed about twelve thousand telephone operators, in 1983 around six thousand.

The impact of technological change was a major issue when the telephone operators at Bell Canada organized themselves into a union in the late seventies. Unions *may* help their members fend off some of the ill effects of technological change. But they will find it far more difficult to hold their ground in the face of layoffs and plant closures. And there are no significant institutions to effectively protect the unorganized and the already-unemployed (see chapter seven).

Two comments shed further light on the nature of the problems of the application of technology. The first is from a TOPS manager at Bell Canada:

> Operators represent expense, and any company would have to look at it the same way. And in order to cut costs in any organization, perhaps part of the way you do that is by reducing expense.... With our telephone company and our business, we're very, very careful, I think, when we go into any technological change, to ensure that there is a payoff within a reasonable period of time.

According to a TOPS operator:

> In an sense, the villain is not really the technology. It is the employer who does not recognize that the people sitting on the machines are not just a piece of technology or a commodity, but that they are working to help maintain the profit level, and that they therefore do have some basic rights to say how they wish to perform their job.

The Bell/Northern case is a classic example of what often happens when new technologies are introduced. Profits are based on productivity, productivity means microtechnology, and microtechnology displaces workers. The technology is labour-saving, efficient and profitable. There is no reason why its introduction should cause hardship, unless the economic and political structures into which it is introduced are unjust.

> Unless communities and working people have effective control over both capital and technology, the tendency is for them to become "destructive forces" rather than "constructive instruments" in economic development. Under these conditions, the human person becomes more and more redundant and a victim of impersonal economic forces. This is the central problem of our times. It is first, and foremost, a moral or ethical problem in the structural order of our economy and society.
>
> *Canadian Conference of Catholic Bishops,*
> **Ethical Choices and Political Challenges, 1984**

A Change for the Better?

Will microtechnology benefit ordinary Canadians? Or will it work against them? A study conducted for the United Automobile Workers suggests that an industrial society like Canada can expect 80 per cent of manual work to have been eliminated by the year 2000. The Luddites faced almost the same challenge nearly two hundred years ago. Steam mills may seem a far cry from the silicon chip, yet the threat of rapid technological change without adequate social support is very similar. "*Plus ça change....*"

Still, nothing is ever exactly the same. In the nineteenth century, labourers displaced by the factory system moved into the growing urban centres or emigrated out to the colonies. There was still room for them somewhere. By contrast, companies are introducing TOPS, computers and robots at a time when the economy does not seem to have room for "surplus" workers.

As capital is invested in the new microtechnologies, the productivity of those still employed rises. The gains in their productivity translate into higher profits. These are reinvested in the most profitable endeavours, that is, capital-intensive rather than labour-intensive ones. More goods are produced — including more new microtechnology — more services provided, more money made, and fewer people are earning a salary. Many who work find their tasks dehumanized, and many others face unemployment.

Microtechnology *can* help to eliminate some of the most dangerous, dirty and boring jobs. But it can never really be termed *progress* if the resulting "free" time is spent by the unemployed trying to survive.

This analysis has uncovered the paradox of combining ever-increasing productivity with ever-decreasing numbers of workers needed. At the same time that this happens, the remaining routine jobs are broken down into the tiniest possible parts. Pride and a sense of accomplishment in work decline as the work is de-skilled.

In the simplest terms: More people have less and less to do while work itself is increasingly mediated by machines. The fantastic changes resulting from the introduction of new technologies have brought society to a crossroads where the choices seem clear.

If the future is to mirror the past — *Plus ça change, plus ça reste la même chose* — unemployment will continue to rise along with dissatisfaction with work. Already youth unemployment is high. But this road is attractive to companies who have the power to introduce and benefit from technological change. Employers do not necessarily see unemployment as a problem, for it has a disciplinary effect, reminding workers to moderate their demands and accept new technology in an unquestioning fashion lest they be replaced by one of the many who are eager for work.

There is another, less depressing choice. This would involve making a new social distinction between the right to have a decent income and the right to have a paid job. This would not mean more people experiencing the permanent insecurity of welfare and unemployment insurance. Rather, it would mean an end to the power of a few large employers to offer people the opportunity of selling their labour in return for a wage.

The link between wage labour and survival would be broken. People would have more of *their own* time to pursue hobbies, to care for each other, the elderly, the young, to work at tasks they find fulfilling and socially productive.

But can the basic meaning of work and income change? To a large degree this depends on the *kind* of society into which the technology is introduced. The existing structures are not equitable in their distribution of work, costs, benefits, responsibility and control. To transform the meaning of work and income will be far from easy. Do people have a say?

If technological change meant a life freer from hardship and insecurity, with more leisure time for everyone, that would be progress. *Plus ça change . . . ?* Then things will have really changed — for a change.

> **Ways must be found for people to exercise more effective control over both capital and technology so that they may become constructive instruments of creation by serving the basic needs of people and communities.**
> *Canadian Conference of Catholic Bishops,*
> **Ethical Choices and Political Challenges, 1984**

Questions

- How have you and other people you know been affected by new technology? Have its effects been felt at home, in the workplace?

- Do you feel that microtechnology offers the hope for a better world? Or do you think it will create as many problems as it solves?

- Experts can easily forget how intimidating computer lingo can be, not to mention the equipment itself. Experts can also fail to question the fundamental economic and social changes that accompany microtechnology. What role does expertise play when new equipment is introduced into a factory or office? Does automation have to be introduced in a top-down manner?

- People often assume that the economic system will remain fundamentally the same, whether Canada adopts microtechnology or not. How does the revolution in technology relate to economic and social change? Does an alternative way of organizing the economy necessarily put a halt to technological progress? How would you suggest that the increased productivity be used? What obstacles built into society prevent microtechnology from benefiting people and representing true progress?

Resources

- H. Dominic Covvey and Neil Harding McAlister, *Computer Consciousness: Surviving the Automated 80s*, Don Mills: Addison-Wesley, 1980. From among the many primers on the microelectronic revolution, this is a particularly good introduction to computer technology.

- Joan Kuyek, *The Phone Book: Working at the Bell*, Toronto: Between the Lines, 1979. A well-documented case study of what happened with the introduction of the new Northern Telecom equipment, written by a woman who spent three years as a service representative for Bell Canada. Kuyek examines the effect of technology on the quality of both work and the service provided.

- Boris Mather et al., *The Implications of Microelectronics for Canadian Workers*, Ottawa: Canadian Centre for Policy Alternatives, 1981. A brief paper treating the same topics analyzed in this chapter.

- Heather Menzies, *Computers on the Job: Surviving Canada's Microcomputer Revolution*, Toronto: James Lorimer, 1982. A good introduction to microtechnology as it is affecting office work, the service industries, blue-collar jobs and the information industry. Education and

Resources (cont'd)

re-training are options for individual workers, while unions need to look at collective bargaining and legislative measures to deal with the new technology.

- Brian O'Neill, *Work and Technological Change: Case Studies of Longshoremen and Postal Workers in St. John's,* St John's: Jefferson Printing, 1980. With an historical focus, this study explores ways of dealing with technological change.

- "New Technology," Education Media, 1980, 3/4" videotape. Part I, "Whose Progress?" 46 minutes, gives the background of the microchip revolution and assesses its social impact; Part II, "Another Way," 33 minutes, documents the response of workers and communities to the new technology.

- "Chips," *CBC-TV Fifth Estate,* videotape, 21 minutes. An examination of microtechnology and its effects on people's lives.

- For further information on microtechnology, contact the Technology Committee, Canadian Labour Congress, 2841 Riverside Drive, Ottawa, Ont. K1V 8X7, ph. 613-521-3400.

Chapter Nine

Energy to Burn

Assume for a minute that you could have equal economic benefits by relying primarily on either nuclear energy or solar energy. Which would you prefer? In 1981 nine out of ten Canadians who were polled chose the solar over the nuclear option. That poll asked about "equal economic benefits", but the important debates over energy in Canada are not only economic.

Until over a decade ago, cheap, abundant fuel supplies — based on exploiting underdeveloped countries — used to be taken for granted. Then in the early seventies OPEC (Organization of Petroleum Exporting Countries) flexed its muscles and petroleum prices began to escalate steadily, along with oil shock, lineups at the gas pump, brownouts, fears of freezing in the dark and astronomical profits for the multinational oil companies.

This was the energy crisis.

Canada tried to respond quickly to gain some independence from the volatile international market and move towards energy self-sufficiency; it hoped to turn the crisis to advantage by producing energy for export. The plan? To tap Canada's rich lode of natural resources — oil and gas, hydroelectric power, coal, uranium — in a series of massive "megaprojects" valued at $100 million or more each:

- the extraction of petroleum on $5-billion artificial islands located closer to the North Pole than to central Canadian markets;
- the construction of pipelines stretching several thousand miles across the country;
- the diversion of entire northern river systems to produce hydroelectric power;
- the exploitation of enormous beds of tar/oil sands lying beneath the northern Alberta muskeg;

- the mining and processing of uranium for the generation of electricity from nuclear power.

Since then some of these projects have been put on hold until there's a clearer picture of future demand. Others have been scrapped altogether. If there is a long-term energy crisis, such ventures may solve it, and they may not.

Either way, they spark a whole series of additional crises. Important issues — the use of natural resources, environmental impact, economic viability, the effects of exports and foreign debt, control over decision-making and the distribution of power in society — come into play. The conflict is not just solar versus nuclear, a billion dollars here or there. What is at stake, rather, is the future shape of Canadian society.

> Our energy choices affect inflation, employment, the environment, health, leisure, mobility, the cost of goods, services and information. Energy choices affect the options that remain open to us in the future.
>
> *Presbyterian Church,*
> **109th General Assembly,** *1983*

Energy shapes society. Coal fuelled the industrial age of the nineteenth and early twentieth century. After World War II, cheap and abundant oil ushered in the transportation age. Now, at the threshold of the microelectronic age, the resources chosen for energy development will stamp the character of Canada. What kind of society do Canadians want?

Obviously we would want energy development to benefit the country's population and improve our living and working conditions; to make Canada as self-reliant as possible, and more independent; to have resources not only more evenly distributed now but available for future generations. These broad objectives have been summed up in the ideal of a *just, participatory,*

and *sustainable* society by the World Council of Churches and reiterated in Canada by the Presbyterian Church and the United Church.

Thinking about a society that is *just, participatory,* and *sustainable* will help to focus this analysis of the energy issue in Canada. They are three *explicit* values that can be used to question the *implicit* values contained in the decisions being made about energy in Canada. Such analysis questions values; it is an ethical reflection on economic policy. This kind of reflection is another useful technique of social analysis.

Just

> Justice requires a fair distribution of energy between rich and poor, the marginalized and the powerful, within countries and between them.
>
> *Presbyterian Church,*
> **109th General Assembly,** *1983*
> *United Church of Canada,*
> **29th General Council,** *1982*

How are energy and its benefits currently distributed in Canada? At the same time, how are the costs and risks distributed? Conventional economic wisdom tends to answer by speaking of dollars and short-run profits. This analysis looks at the megaprojects policy — nuclear development in New Brunswick is the example — and asks two questions, "Is it profitable?" *and* "Is it just?"

In 1976 the New Brunswick Electric Power Commission (N.B. Power) began constructing its first nuclear generating plant at Point Lepreau on the Bay of Fundy thirty kilometres from Saint John. The plant started generating power in September 1982, several years later than planned. The cost had risen from an initial budget of $466 million to a final estimate in excess of $1.3 billion.

In order to understand this kind of investment, recall the real estate market (see chapter three) where the actors are the builders or developers, the lenders of money, the government and the house buyers. The final guarantee of financial security for both the developers and the moneylenders is the ability of people to buy the houses.

Corporations undertaking energy developments are like house builders. As in the real estate business, the energy megaprojects carry with them certain "mortgage" payments. The mortgages are held by the domestic and foreign bankers who lend the money for the megaprojects. The government backs up the loans. But the final guarantee of financial security for the builders and lenders is the ability of Canadians to pay for the increased costs of gasoline, heating oil or electricity.

Upping the Ante

Even the biggest purchases of an individual or family cannot compare with damming the rivers flowing into James Bay or building a reactor on the Fundy Shore. The costs, rather than in the tens of thousands, can run in the billions and tens of billions of dollars. In 1981 the federal government foresaw a potential $500 billion to be spent in megaproject investment — 90 per cent of it energy-related — between then and the year 2000.

The developers of megaprojects are some of the largest, most profitable companies operating in Canada. Of the country's top twenty-five corporations, nine are in the energy business, and their net income topped $2.6 billion in 1983. Electric power projects like Ontario Hydro's Darlington nuclear scheme or Hydro Quebec's James Bay development are undertaken by publicly-controlled utilities whose assets make them the two largest corporations in the land. Like N.B. Power's Point Lepreau, these projects also enjoy the backing of their provincial government owners.

The banks and energy giants are content to have their future profits and growth assured by government. The private sector will develop large energy projects only with government guarantees of "adequate" profits in the 15 to 20 per cent range. These guarantees often take the form of incentive payments and lower taxes.

The biggest private energy corporation in Canada, Imperial Oil, has repeatedly told Canadians that ensuring future energy supplies is "a big, tough, expensive job". By 1982 Ottawa had paid Imperial Oil, Gulf and Dome Petroleum $1.4 billion to search for oil in a single area, the Beaufort Sea. It *is* a risky venture! Let's have another look at Point Lepreau.

The Cost of Lepreau

Delays and cost over-runs were not the only problems at Point Lepreau. Labour conflicts regularly stopped the work. Community groups protested the cost to consumers and the danger to the environment. The provincial Liberal opposition accused N.B. Power of mismanagement, while Nova Scotia and Prince Edward Island withdrew their support.

The choice of nuclear power was made in anticipation of high growth rates in the consumption of electricity and because New Brunswick's geographic location allows it to sell excess power to U.S. markets. While the government of British Columbia placed a moratorium on uranium mining in 1980 because of public concern about the health effects of a nuclear future, both N.B. Power and Ontario Hydro were proceeding full speed ahead with the construction of nuclear power stations. And this for power that would be surplus to the needs of the people paying for it. From 1976 to 1980 New Brunswick electricity rates shot up by 179 per cent, an increase critics blamed on the costs of Point Lepreau.

Point Lepreau was originally justified because electrical shortages were expected in New Brunswick by 1978. But when the nuclear plant began operating in 1982, the province was still a net exporter of electricity. Consumption grew at the very low rate of 0.4 per cent per year, even though N.B. Power was not encouraging conservation. It preferred its billion-dollar nuclear investment.

Consumers were still supposed to benefit, however, through a decreased reliance on the foreign oil that fuels New Brunswick's thermal generators. But once Point Lepreau came on stream, the nuclear electricity had to be exported in order to help cover the costs and risks of Point Lepreau. N.B. Power was reluctant to phase out its oil-fired generators.

The customers and the lenders are foreign. It is estimated that between one-third and one-half of the money to be spent on energy projects in Canada will have to be raised from foreign sources. Half of N.B. Power's debt is in foreign currency. The money is borrowed to produce energy, but the energy must be exported to earn the foreign exchange needed to pay the high interest and immense principal.

As energy and money flow out of the country, foreign indebtedness rises. Meanwhile Canada is "spending" its non-renewable resources and shouldering all the environmental and social costs of megaprojects that serve interests in the United States.

What About Jobs?

Any large investment, particularly in the billion-dollar range, should provide much-needed employment. The backers of energy megaprojects claim that these developments are a powerful motor force for economic growth and job creation. It's true that a lot of transient construction workers keep moving, now west, now north, following the road to the latest temporary workplace. But once built, the capital-intensive energy projects create relatively little permanent employment, and in fact job creation does not seem to be an important aspect of such projects.

Investment in oil, gas and hydroelectricity is a very expensive way of going about the task of providing people with work. The following table shows the relative costs of job-creation in various fields of economic endeavour.

Capital Cost per Person-Year of Employment for
Various Energy Options

Methanol Production:	$16,667
Wind Power:	$17,027
Residential Conservation:	$23,730
Solar Heating:	$30,882
Electricity Related:	$37,500
Oil and Gas Related:	$53,600

This table is drawn from a 1978 study of the capital investment required to create one year of employment for one person, in a variety of energy industries.

Investing in residential conservation is apparently twice as cost-effective for job creation as putting money into oil and gas projects. Moreover, the jobs created in conservation tend to be located where people already live, not in remote frontier areas.

If the billions of dollars earmarked for Point Lepreau, Darlington or Alberta's tar sands were loaned to homeowners to improve heating efficiency in existing houses, the loans could be paid back through utility billing systems and, once repaid, the consumers would see their heating bills plummet. This type of energy plan could be completed within seven years — a shorter time period than is necessary to complete an energy megaproject. The money would be paid back, energy consumption would fall and consumers would be saving money on heat *before* the large, highly centralized projects even produced any energy. At the same time, the money invested would be spread out more evenly in the economy than if it were poured into a few megaprojects.

For every billion dollars Ontario Hydro spends on its Darlington nuclear power project, it will create 8,550 jobs. The same amount of money could create more than 52,000 jobs if it were spent on co-op housing units, senior citizen housing, renovation of existing housing, daycare and hospital construction.

Who Are The Big Gamblers?

Energy megaprojects are attractive for lenders and investors because they are backed by government guarantees. But when the energy giants are offered lower tax rates, someone has to pick up the slack. And when Dome Petroleum's massive plans to strike it rich in the far north go awry or prove overly-optimistic, the taxpayers pick up the tab as part of a government "bail-out".

Megaprojects need analysis in terms not only of dollars, profits and exports, but also of their long-range effects on Canadian society. These long-range costs and risks seem steep. They are not borne by the energy corporations or the corporate consumers either here or in the United States. The price of domestic energy will continue to escalate, as will the environmental and social risks. It is the people of Canada who are the big gamblers, risking much and winning little. The next section, *Participatory*, asks whether *we* ever chose to gamble in this way.

Participatory

Participation demands justice in the process of decision-making, review, access to necessary information, comprehensiveness of viewpoints solicited and empowerment of the formerly marginalized.

Presbyterian Church,
109th General Assembly, *1983*
United Church of Canada,
29th General Council, *1982*

People want to participate in shaping the future of their society. Access to energy and the way it is provided need to be discussed as widely and frankly as possible. Does everyone have a say?

The very size and scale of megaprojects make them difficult to grasp. They are the products of creative engineering, the collaboration of highly-skilled physicists, geologists and chemists. Notices of bond issues appear in the financial press containing the names of dozens of international banks that get together to lend money for energy-related projects.

The impact of megaprojects on society involves other complexities. For example, the search for new, large-scale energy in remote areas threatens the traditional culture, economy and livelihood of the people living there. Native people, realizing how little say they will have over megaprojects on their traditional lands, have repeatedly stated their opposition to pipelines and oil and gas developments planned from the outside. An elderly Dene woman told the Mackenzie Valley Pipeline Inquiry, "If we must make some changes, we don't want it through someone pushing us into it. We must be given time to think and do it our own way." Otherwise northern natives foresee control over their own lives slipping away (see chapter twelve).

On the provincial level, electricity rates have increased throughout the Maritimes. Both Nova Scotia and Prince Edward Island are pursuing non-nuclear policies and have so far refused to buy power from Point Lepreau. Prince Edward Island's greatest problem is the high cost of electricity transmission. Nova Scotia wanted to promote its local coal industry and avoid playing second-fiddle to New Brunswick. The residents of New Brunswick have had the nuclear option imposed on them.

Projects on such a megascale rarely leave room for input from ordinary people who live and work nearby, who pay taxes and utility bills and are looking for jobs. Why? The issues are usually deemed too complicated. Supposedly, only the financiers, politicians and engineers have access to the data and are able to handle the facts. They make the most efficient, profitable decisions within the very narrow terms of their perspectives. Human, social and environmental costs which may become evident only in the long term are downplayed or ignored.

In fact, participation is something which people have to work to achieve. One approach has been to win autonomy from outside forces — be they foreign governments, transnational oil companies or provincial utilities — through conservation and the use of renewable resources. For example, many people have insulated and redesigned their own houses to save energy. In rural areas and small centres people have turned back to wood as their primary source of home heat. Not only does wood provide good heat but it is also possible to supply it on your own. The disadvantages are that it is bulky, costly to transport and does not burn clean. Besides, the forests could never supply all the country's energy needs.

Approaches that emphasize conservation and renewable energy tend to be small scale and decentralized. It is far easier for people to exercise control over a comprehensive district heating plan, local conservation programmes or a small hydroelectric generator than to have input into a drilling programme up in the Beaufort Sea. Government energy policy favours tax breaks and depletion allowances that encourage multibillion dollar corporations to search for non-renewable resources. Far less support is given to small-scale conservation programmes that would benefit millions of households and at the same time save non-renewable resources.

Non-participation has almost become "normal" and acceptable. Citizens are usually

excluded from decision-making about major energy policies. Should they have the chance to consider the full range of risks and benefits of each option? The idea is not to shirk all risks or damn all development, but to prevent costly decisions from being imposed without people having a say.

Participation is a key towards assuring energy policies that are more just and sustainable. Participation is also at the heart of the democratic ideal. It is an end or a value in itself.

Sustainable

> **Sustainability demands our consideration for future generations and measures our sense of maintaining a trust.**
>
> *Presbyterian Church,*
> **109th General Assembly,** *1983*
> *United Church of Canada,*
> **29th General Council,** *1982*

Is the Canadian energy strategy *sustainable* for this country and its people? What dangers lie ahead — or already surround us? Are there better alternatives?

The Canadian Medical Association passed the

following resolution at its 111th annual meeting in 1978:

> The Canadian Medical Association considers it irresponsible for the Government of Canada to allow the further development of uranium mining and reactor construction until a safe, proven, permanent disposal technology is developed for the wastes that have already been generated.

No safe method exists for the disposal of the deadly radioactive waste from nuclear power plants. The spent fuel remains in temporary storage. If social institutions seem unable to plan adequately for energy needs over the next ten years, how can we expect them to take care of cancer-causing garbage which lasts for *two hundred thousand* years? If no institution known to humanity can undertake this task, then what right does anyone have to produce such unimaginably damaging materials?

Burning coal without anti-pollution equipment contributes to the acid rain now destroying forests, lakes and rivers. Oil spills and leaking seabed wells, having wreaked havoc with marine life in temperate climates, pose a major threat to the Atlantic fishery and the fragile ecosystems of the high Arctic. A severe blowout might threaten the arctic ice cap itself. Massive hydroelectric projects destroy both nature and native culture. How much longer can the earth tolerate this abuse?

The Dangers of Lepreau

Vociferous and anxious protests emerged many times during the building of Point Lepreau. At one point, miniscule cracks appeared in the interior wall of the reactor. The Atomic Energy Control Board (AECB) reprimanded N.B. Power for not following proper procedure in repairs. An earth tremor shook New Brunswick and reminded people about an inactive fault-line near Point Lepreau. While N.B. Power assured residents that the building was designed to withstand a certain amount of seismic stress, one engineer resigned over the issue.

Since the reactor began functioning, there have been heavy-water leaks on at least five occasions, involving thousands of gallons. There have been occasional conflicting reports from N.B. Power and AECB about the radioactivity of the water. So far these incidents have caused no perceptible damage to the environment. But they do point to the practical inevitability of human error and the confusion surrounding emergency procedures. The potential social cost of accidents involving radioactive materials is incalculable.

In the light of all the costs and dangers, why has N.B. Power pursued a nuclear strategy? Among its motives were: to meet the growing need for electricity, to gain independence from imported oil, and to project the image of a progressive province. But the utility's legal mandate is to provide cheap power for the residents of New Brunswick.

Another key motive was to help out the Canadian nuclear industry. As foreign sales of Candu reactors falter, the federal government is encouraging the construction of nuclear plants solely for the export of electricity, in order to carry the nuclear industry through its slump and create a Candu manufacturing industry to export reactors. With the support of the federal government, N.B. Power introduced plans to build a second reactor on the Point Lepreau site as soon as American buyers could be found for the electricity. One reason for the ready U.S. market for Lepreau's power is that the American anti-nuclear movement has made the construction of nuclear reactors in New England politically impossible. More than half of the first Point Lepreau reactor's power is already being exported to New England.

Ironically, it is the hard economic times that have consigned many megaprojects to the waste bin. Two Alberta tar sands plants are on indefinite hold because they cannot be justified in financial terms. Dozens of nuclear power schemes in the United States have been scrapped as economically unfeasible. The Darlington nuclear development proceeds only because of Ontario Hydro's willingness to sink further into debt, hoping for U.S. markets and using the ability of electricity consumers to pay more as collateral. The same thinking lies behind plans for Point Lepreau II.

Canadians obviously need to look elsewhere for signs of a sustainable energy policy.

"A Penny Saved is a Penny Earned!"

The old maxim applies to energy. Conservation is often the same as producing new energy, for non-renewable fuels like gas, oil and coal can be kept in reserve until they are needed at some future time.

The energy crisis opened everyone's eyes to the necessity of conservation. As oil became more expensive, smaller fuel-efficient cars appeared on the market. People began to patch the cracks in leaky houses and the insulation business boomed. Sawmills that choked the air with sawdust fumes from teepee-shaped burners were modified to use this "waste" to power the saws and conveyor belts.

Most Canadian households spend over a thousand dollars annually for home heat. Conserving energy means saving some of these costs. Many owners have taken advantage of government incentives to convert from oil to natural gas or to insulate attics and walls, while new housing is better designed to conserve heating fuel.

Despite its northern climate, the heavily populated areas of Canada around latitude 45 have more energy fall on them than homeowners buy. Of course much of the heat is "wasted" during the summer months. Yet technology does exist to take advantage of solar energy even during the winter.

The energy produced on a daily basis by the sun — in the form of direct heat or photosynthesized plant material — is free and can be captured with a relatively small investment. Wood is a form of stored solar energy and can be burned for heat. Other organic materials like jerusalem artichokes, poplar trees or even garbage can be used to produce ethanol, methanol or methane as fuel; these are called biomass fuels. Passive solar designs take advantage of the sun's heat at the time it is generated, to produce hot water or keep a building warm.

The Soft Path

The effort to insulate buildings, the new popularity of passive solar design and wood heat, experiments with biomass fuels and solar energy are all part of the so-called "soft" energy strategy, in contrast with the traditional "hard" strategy based on oil, gas, coal, hydro and uranium.

The soft approach relies on cheaper, renewable resources instead of non-renewable ones and has the effect of diversifying sources of energy. It has the potential to generate more jobs with far less debt, avoiding the major environmental damage caused by large-scale projects.

So far many of the experiments with "soft" energy have been undertaken by small entrepreneurs or industrious individuals. Labour-intensive, modest in scale, adaptable to community control — these attractive features of the soft approach make it unattractive to the energy giants. The conflict of values over participation and sustainability is well illustrated in the energy industry's rejection of a conserving, smaller-scale, soft approach.

According to a spokesman for the mammoth Syncrude tar sands project in northern Alberta:

The bottom line is that no one has suggested a way that we can actually reduce our consumption of energy very significantly without reducing our economic growth. And if we don't want economic growth, we'd better be prepared for the sort of social dislocations that go with a lack of economic growth.

The assumption hidden in this argument is that a certain kind of economic growth is necessary — with it, there will be prosperity, without it, "social dislocations". If the argument were valid, then megaprojects like Point Lepreau would make sense. But Canadians are consuming less energy than the planners foresaw; economic growth accompanied by high unemployment is unjust; and "soft" solutions provide the same amenities while using less non-renewable energy. The real "bottom line", it seems, consists of important choices that Canadians need to make about energy policy.

Just, Participatory and Sustainable

> Energy is the primary means by which our world is ordered, and . . . decisions on how it will be produced and used will determine the future shape of our society. Because energy questions are interrelated with other dimensions of social concern affecting such areas as inflation, health, employment and the environment, the energy policies adopted by our government become in effect a means of social engineering.
>
> *United Church of Canada,*
> **29th General Council,** *1982*

Is Canadian energy policy helping Canada develop into a just, participatory and sustainable society?

With a reputation for being a cautious lot, Canadians boast the world's highest rates of personal savings. They usually investigate before making major purchases. But when it comes to energy, they're being told to "buy" systems that are dangerous, expensive, short-sighted, wasteful and unfair.

Would it not make more sense to use the most benign non-renewable resources as a short-term transition to dependence on a soft, renewable, sustainable energy path in the long run?

It is hard to believe that, if we had a say, we would voluntarily choose a high-cost, low-employment approach that exhausts our resources, devastates the environment, and threatens human health for untold generations to come.

The choices to be made regarding energy policy in Canada are both short-term and long-term. They are usually posed as merely technical issues. But the analysis shows that they are really economic, social, political and ethical — and that asking if society will be *just, participatory* and *sustainable* raises the kinds of questions that Canadians want to ask about Canada's energy path.

Questions

- Are there soft-energy experiments going on in your area or neighbourhood? Invite the people involved to meet with you and some friends, to discuss the advantages and obstacles to this way of supplying heat or electricity. Make up an inventory of local sources of energy that could be tapped. How could other projects be launched? Do they pose a challenge to traditional hard suppliers of electricity or fuel?

- Inquire into the utilities supplying electricity and natural gas to your community. Find out how the rates are set. Is there evidence of injustice in the distribution of energy in your area? What is each utility's policy regarding energy development? Is your electricity nuclear-powered? Try to uncover the reasons — perhaps by meeting with a local group that has already begun work on this question. Make your views known to the utility.

- John Lynn, president of Syncrude, argues that Canadians should stick to what we know best by restoring megaprojects to their proper role as "a fundamental part of Canada's economic development strategy for the rest of the century". From what points of view is this a reasonable proposal? Why would you argue against it? What can you do to encourage a soft path?

Resources

- Paul McKay, *Electric Empire: The Inside Story of Ontario Hydro*, Toronto: Between The Lines, 1983. Examines the uncontrolled expansion of North America's second-largest public utility. Deals in detail with nuclear energy, the financial costs and health hazards associated with nuclear power.

- GATT-Fly, *Power To Choose: Canada's Energy Options*, Toronto: Between The Lines, 1981. An economic critique of megaprojects, presenting the soft energy path as the reasonable alternative.

- Robert Bott, David Brooks and and John Robinson, *Life After Oil: A Renewable Energy Policy for Canada*, Edmonton: Hurtig, 1983. A statistically-based study showing that a soft energy policy would work — and work well — in Canada. Argues for the efficient use of renewable resources.

- "Energy and Environment" is the theme of *CONNEXIONS* 9:1 (Spring 1984), reviewing over thirty Canadian resources — books, groups, newsletters and audiovisuals — on Canadian energy policy and alternatives to the "hard energy path". Write to CONNEXIONS, 427 Bloor Street West, Toronto, Ont. M5S 1X7, ph. 416-960-3903.

Questions (cont'd)

- Oil shock is the realization, brought on by the rapid rise of prices and artificial shortages, that oil is not a limitless commodity. The oil companies profited greatly from the OPEC-enforced escalation in world oil prices. OPEC oil is priced just a bit higher than competitive sources of energy. The 1983 drop in oil prices is due in part to the "discovery" of conservation in the industrial world. What is the real energy crisis? How does it affect us, at work, at home, in our community? Is there any way in which we can have an effect on it?

- After discussing energy, do an ethical reflection on another economic issue. Apply the three ideas — just, participatory and sustainable — to an issue treated elsewhere in this book, for example, housing. Then do the necessary reading to discuss, for example, banking in Canada, and its role in shaping our society.

Resources (cont'd)

- "A Matter of Choice: Nuclear Energy in Ontario," Tetra Media (Filmmakers Distribution Centre), 1975, 16 mm, 28 minutes. Looks at the impact of nuclear energy on residents of Ontario and poses some of the questions, both scientific and moral, connected with the nuclear industry.

- For further information or for the name of a local group involved in the energy issue, write to Energy Probe, 100 College Street, Toronto, Ont. M5G 1L5, ph. 416-978-7014.

Chapter Ten

Media and Ideology

There is an old saying about looking at the world through rose-coloured glasses. It brings to mind someone whose outlook is overly optimistic. It also suggests that everyone looks at the world through glasses of one hue or another.

The media provide a very important pair of glasses through which we view the world. And those particular glasses affect the understanding of every issue treated in *Getting Started*. The first part of this chapter focuses on one aspect of the media, the news industry, to see how its corporate structures and market approach affect the news we consume.

Glasses, as we've seen, also carry a tint — darkened or rose or some other hue. That tint colouring our world view is akin to a rather difficult word, "ideology". The second part of this chapter reflects on ideology, looking back over the basic and economic issues analyzed in Parts One and Two and identifying some of the ideological factors shaping Canadian society. This discovery prepares for the analysis in Part Three.

The Information Industry

In the world of information, Canada holds a respectable position. We have "freedom of the press", which is not as easily gained as it ought to be. High levels of education enable Canadians to consume a wealth of information served up by a variety of outlets.

Canada has two newspapers that claim to be national, *The Globe and Mail* and *Le Devoir*, one in each official language. A public broadcasting system, the CBC, provides news, current affairs, sports and entertainment on both radio and television.

The CBC competes with the privately-owned CTV network and a few other broadcasters — as well as with U.S. networks and stations broadcast into Canada. In addition there are hundreds of newspapers, magazines and radio stations. Sophisticated communications technology gives

citizens everywhere, in Inuvik or downtown Vancouver, access to the news as it happens.

Despite this seeming abundance, the Canadian information industry consists mostly of a few large corporations. Ownership is very highly concentrated in the media, a fact documented by two royal commissions (Davey Committee, 1970 and Kent Commission, 1981) formed solely to examine media ownership.

In 1970 there were 108 daily newspapers in Canada. Of these, forty-three were independent while sixty-five were owned by companies running newspaper chains. By 1980 the number of dailies had risen to 117. But by then there were only twenty-eight independents remaining and eighty-nine papers owned by chains. Sixty-five of these eighty-nine chain-owned papers were owned by just three firms.

Similar levels of concentration are evident in the broadcast media. By the mid-seventies, about twenty-five years after the advent of television in Canada, 56 per cent of private commercial stations were group-owned. And 81 per cent of private radio stations were group-owned by that time.

Just as super-warehouse stores have made an anachronism of little corner groceries (see chapter six), so the large media chains have virtually done away with the crusty newspaper editors who own their papers and print the news as they see fit. Instead, there are two cross-country newspaper chains, Thomson and Southam. There used to be a third — F.P. Publications, owners of *The Globe and Mail*, Winnipeg *Free Press* and other dailies — until Thomson bought it out in 1980. There are smaller chains with provincial monopolies, such as the K.C. Irving group, which controls all five of New Brunswick's daily newspapers.

Besides the high percentage of group ownership, there is also a great deal of cross-media ownership, so that certain chains often control more than one outlet for news. Maclean Hunter, in addition to owning Canada's weekly national newsmagazine and dozens of other consumer and business publications, also has television and radio stations across the country. The Irving interests own all the private television stations in New Brunswick as well as all the province's dailies. A single family in London, Ont., owns the paper, the television station and the major AM and FM radio stations.

Moreover, information outlets are often merely a part of a conglomerate's many interests. Thomson holdings include Hudson's Bay Company, Zellers, Simpsons and interests in North Sea oil.

Southam controls various publishing companies and the largest book retailer in Canada, Coles. The Irving conglomerate includes interests in more than eighty companies in the maritime provinces.

The corporate world is also involved in media through advertising. In the newspaper industry, for example, advertising accounts for an average of 50 to 60 per cent — sometimes up to 70 per cent — of content.

Thus the pattern of corporate concentration in the news media is similar to the pattern in the housing, food and energy industries. Perhaps news is not often suppressed outright, but it is often distorted or downplayed, thanks to the normal, daily relationships between editors, producers and reporters with newspaper owners and other members of the business community. Papers controlled by the large chains are not known for their zeal in unearthing hard-to-get stories that run contrary to their interests.

One would have to go a long way to find an approving or even a balanced editorial on the 1981 Kent Commission Report, or on the proposed 1983 Daily Newspaper Act, both of which criticized the lack of competition among Canadian dailies and threatened the control that non-news business interests have over the papers.

The Kent Commission itself was appointed in 1980 amidst the furor that ensued when the Southam chain closed its Winnipeg *Tribune* on the same day that the Thomson chain closed its Ottawa *Journal*. As a result Southam was left with the *Citizen* and a newspaper monopoly in Ottawa while Thomson came to enjoy the same advantage with its *Free Press* in Winnipeg. Both companies profited from the deal because advertisers then had but one paper to do business with in each city. The public was forced to rely on a single newspaper outlet for information about current events.

The Thomson empire, with its control of both newspapers and major department stores, provides an example of the dangers of having corporate connections between advertising and the media. The Bay, Simpsons and Zellers are major newspaper advertisers, whose displays of the latest fashion and sale items adorn many a page. Can a newspaper with those business connections be expected to report comprehensively or critically on the retail trade industry?

The goals of these companies were well articulated by Lord Thomson of Fleet, founder of the Thomson chain: "I buy newspapers to make money to buy more newspapers to make more money." Testifying before the Kent Commission, Kenneth Thomson reiterated: "I believe in growing. I believe in growing in the newspaper business.... I like to invest. I like my family's investments to grow.... Newspapers I like very, very much."

The concentrated private ownership may be good for owners and stockholders, but it is hard to claim that the consumers of news benefit thereby.

News For Sale

"You can't believe everything you hear" is true of neighbourhood gossip, and it would seem best to apply the same scepticism to the news broadcasts, major papers and magazines. But still, the daily barrage of information has an inevitable influence. The media remain our primary source of information about a very complex world. The matter-of-fact prose of *Maclean's* magazine and the familiar, earnest tones of CBC-News readers exude credibility. The CTV network got to the heart of the matter when it advertised its national news as "Trust and Tradition".

In 1925, the editor of the *Wall Street Journal* said:

> A newspaper is a private enterprise, owing nothing to the public which grants it no franchise. It is therefore affected with no public interest. It is emphatically the property of its owner, who is selling a manufactured product at his own risk.

The media are structured and controlled like a typical Canadian industry. One of the products they manufacture is news. Events are skilfully refined before they are served up with our morning coffee or broadcast into our living room. The news cannot deviate too much from the values built into the corporate structures which own, operate and advertise in the media.

Each day thousands of raw events are readied for Canadians to consume as news. What happens to the events covered in this "manufacturing" process? They get turned into items which are *intense, unambiguous, familiar* and *marketable*. Let's consider these four criteria, in order to interpret better the news that's produced.

Who would pretend that any one of us has been completely freed from ignorance and misjudgements? . . . The media of social communications frequently despoil truth by offering consumers biased information and false propaganda.
Canadian Conference of Catholic Bishops,
Liberation in a Christian Perspective, *1970*

"Intense"

For an audience fed on high-speed car chases and prime-time thrillers, intensity needs to be an ingredient of the news. Either events are chosen for their drama or there is a selective focus within items on dramatic elements. Thus protest marches often win some coverage (they make good pictures), but if there are any scuffles or arrests the news will concentrate on that to the virtual exclusion of all other aspects, including the issue involved. One analyst of media treatment of social movements noted that "Editors take arrests as a sign that something significant has taken place — something 'out of the ordinary.' "

The most dramatic aspect of an event need not be the most important, but it usually gets featured for the sake of intensity. When E.B. Eddy spilled chemicals into the Spanish River in northern Ontario in 1983, the news focused on the irate residents who had responded to Eddy by dumping thousands of dead fish on the factory doorstep. Eddy's history of pollution, the long-term effects of the spill and the assigning of responsibility were all neglected or treated as afterthoughts to the "real story".

Stories pop into the news, evolve at alarming speed and — scarcely digested by the public — pop out again to make room for fresh events. Fresh, novel items are always being served up, but often at the cost of missing the truth behind them. Intense coverage is usually too brief to give much idea of what led up to events or caused them, or what may flow from them in the long run.

"Unambiguous"

Another criterion establishing newsworthiness is that the information be as cut and dried as possible, not ambiguous in any way.

The battles over the Falklands/Malvinas were presented in a simplified, good guys/bad guys form: An incompetent Third World dictatorship made an outrageous assault upon democracy and the British nation. Such foggy elements as the legitimacy of Argentina's claims and the U.S. commitment to protect the Americas from European attack tended not to make the front-page stories selected by the editors. Meanwhile, the press in Latin America, even in countries hostile to Argentina, took it for granted that the British were the bad guys.

Coincidentally, a few days before Argentina invaded the Falklands, Britain concluded a deal with the former residents of another of its small island dependencies. Only after a ten-year struggle did the former inhabitants of Diego Garcia in the Indian Ocean receive financial compensation for a forced expulsion from their homes. The British government had handed the island over to the United States for use as a naval base.

The Diego Garcia expulsion was every bit as arbitrary as Argentina grabbing (or recovering) the Malvinas. It too was a complex affair. Still the British government could easily have been fingered as the "bad guy" in the same way that the English-language press labelled Argentina the villain — and Margaret Thatcher the champion — of the Falklands invasion. In any case the story of Diego Garcia received nowhere near the same amount of media attention.

Strikes in Poland receive sympathetic coverage because they fit into a world view that stresses struggle against Communist oppression. Strikes in Canada, however, are a different matter. They are frequently portrayed as disrupting the economy or threatening the public interest. "Holding the public to ransom" is a favourite media phrase. Strikes in Poland and Canada are thus treated differently. In both cases the treatment glosses over the ambiguities and complexities.

"Familiar"

In order to become news, an event must be culturally and socially familiar.

In the newsroom there's a kind of story called "The Bus Plunge". The event can occur anywhere in the Third World: a bus (sometimes a train) goes off the road (or track) and over a cliff, killing dozens of passengers. The story gets a brief mention because it is intense and uncomplicated. The far-away event is familiar because it fits in with common notions about poor roads, faulty equipment and incompetent drivers in underdeveloped countries.

Bus-plunge stories have a cumulative effect, reinforcing the prejudices many Canadians already have. The media usually neglect to provide background stories explaining what's happening "over there" where bus plunges are all too common.

In the Middle East "warring factions" tend to "overrun" each other's positions. In Africa and Latin America coups and counter-coups, sometimes "bloodless" and sometimes violent, are regularly reported without much explanation or analysis. A 1983 coup in Nigeria, Africa's most populous country and indeed one of the biggest in the world in population, received scant attention in the Canadian press.

Most Canadians have only the vaguest idea about Nigeria, because the last time the country was in the spotlight was during its civil war in the late sixties. Around that time "starving Biafrans" became a popular phrase, applied to any Third World group suffering from acute hunger. This kind of intense but momentary coverage, then, distorts rather than informs. Catchy images become familiar *stereotypes* that do not inform, much less provide a critical point of view.

Familiarity is an important criterion for domestic news, too. The Canadian Union of Postal Workers, for example, is nearly always presented as an unruly, unreasonable and disruptive organization. Businessmen and doctors, by contrast, usually come across as reasonable. In other words, the news industry uses certain familiar (racial, sexual, economic and political) stereotypes again and again and, with each use, reinforces them.

"Marketable"

News has to be made intense, unambiguous and familiar in order to sell. Just as the TV networks produce prime-time soaps to attract a large audience, so too is the news geared to consumer taste. This may mean something as apparently innocuous as pampering Canadians' sweet tooth for royalty. It has also resulted in the Sun tabloids, with their emphasis on sensational and violent stories, neatly packaged with Sunshine Girls and Boys.

Invasions always make good copy. In recent years Canadians have been treated to detailed accounts of incursions into such formerly obscure places as Cambodia, Afghanistan, the Falklands, Grenada and Lebanon. The mere threat of an invasion of Poland won excited front-page coverage.

There are exceptions, however. When Indonesia launched a full-scale invasion of East Timor in 1975, there was scarcely any news of the event. Later there were estimates of as many as 200 thousand people killed in the invasion. Canada voted in 1980 *against* a UN resolution supporting East Timor's right to self-determination. The first in-depth newspaper account only appeared in 1981, when a reporter from the Kingston *Whig-Standard* took the initiative to examine what had happened in East Timor and Ottawa's weak response to events there. By any standards, the slaughter of one-quarter of a country's population ought to have been newsworthy. Yet the East Timor massacre remains practically unknown in Canada. An invasion carried out by a stalwart Western ally in an out-of-the-way country does not seem to be a marketable item.

Analysis

Events are always being refined and made intense, unambiguous, familiar and marketable. A most successful example of this process is *The Reader's Digest*. Over a thirteen-year period, it ran forty-nine articles critical of the labour movement. It ran only five that could be classified as neutral, and eight favourable. There were nine articles criticizing medicare, and none supporting it. Over twenty years, there was not one article supporting government social welfare policy.

Contrary facts, prior conditions, long-term causes and underlying structures that explain events tend to be downplayed or crowded out, not because of ill will, but because of bias built into the manufacturing process. Given the ownership and structure of the news industry, this conclusion should be no surprise. One would expect the media to push the big-business values that maintain the Canadian economy and the social order based on it.

The media are the glasses, and as we've seen they take on a certain tint. They promote a particular view of things that in a hidden but effective way helps to give its actual shape to Canadian society.

A woeful system has been constructed on the new conditions of society, a system "which considers profit as the key motive for economic progress, competition as the supreme law of economics, and private ownership of the means of production as an absolute right that has no limits and carries no corresponding social obligation".
Canadian Conference of Catholic Bishops,
A Society to be Transformed, 1977

Up Against the Wall

How would you react if a mentally-handicapped man lurched into your kitchen, dug his hand into your supper and wolfed down a generous portion? Your emotions might well run through shock, fear and outrage before you called the police to haul the intruder away. But in this incident from *The Tree of Wooden Clogs*, a movie about an Italian peasant family, the mother in question welcomed the person as a guest, let him help himself to the food, and snapped at her kids to be polite. She believed that the mentally handicapped, because of their simplicity, were especially close to God. Her belief, right or wrong, guided her reaction.

Many of our reactions to daily happenings and circumstances — using these glasses of ours — do not represent a deliberate position or well thought-out theory, but rather reflect semiconscious beliefs and values. These built-in attitudes largely shape the way we see ourselves, society, the world, and they point to what is called ideology.

The scene from *The Tree of Wooden Clogs* raises certain questions: Why do people in different societies react differently to similar situations? Where do our social attitudes and responses come from? In the first instance our attitudes are formed through the influence on us of our parents, friends and peers, teachers at school, religious upbringing, neighbourhoods and communities. These attitudes — about what's worthwhile, how society works, who the real heroes are — continue to be moulded by the people and institutions around us. The mass media — newspapers, advertising, radio and television — are another very important influence in Canadian society. These factors are all sources and reinforcers of ideology and they deserve careful analysis.

Ideology is a complex topic. Webster's defines it as "the doctrines, opinions, or way of thinking of an individual, class, etc.; specif., the body of ideas on which a particular political, economic, or social system is based". One student of the word found over a dozen different meanings given to it. This chapter touches on ideology in an introductory way, by describing it rather than defining it, and in particular looks at the role of ideology in everyday experience.

People who confront the kinds of problems analyzed in this book often find themselves at a total impasse. They're "up against the wall", as the phrase goes. What is "the wall"? The word refers at first to the mass of problems (for instance, unemployment, occupational illness, inadequate food and substandard housing) that people face. As social analysis sorts out the problems, "the wall" begins to refer to the issues, structures and systems that are gradually uncovered. "The wall" exists, however, not just out there in society, but also inside our own heads.

Ideology is the word that describes the interaction between what goes on in our heads and what is going on outside, in society. It refers to a whole complex of dominant *ideas* that both form the basis of an economic and political system and shape the manner of thinking of groups or classes of people within that system.

Ideology can be *blinding*. People's blind spots are based on their class, race, sex, language, ethnic and regional origin, education and work experience. Ideology also *conserves* structures and systems by making them appear legitimate, normal, age-old and unchangeable.

People are usually unaware of their own ideological assumptions. At the same time, they make statements like these:

- "The unemployed should get off their butts and find a job."
- "Government should stick to governing and stay out of the economy."
- "Those damn unions won't be satisfied until they bankrupt the country."
- "Ideology and propaganda are what Communists have — here we have freedom of thought."

Everyone has ideological beliefs that govern their opinions and judgements about the world around them. Those who deny their own bias are, like the TV character Archie Bunker, apt to accept wholesale the dominant values of their society.

The role of ideology has been a concern of the analysis in *Getting Started* right from the first. In Part One, the analysis of housing, health care and pollution hinted at sharp differences in attitudes and values. These differences permeated each basic issue. In Part Two, the analysis kept uncovering economic structures and, entangled amongst them, other very fundamental, ideological patterns. For example:

- "Lost in the Supermarket" — Corporate expansion and concentration, along with often astonishing rates of profit, count more in the economy than meeting basic human, social needs. The ideological assumption is that economic growth yields a greater degree of well-being.
- "The Plague of Unemployment" — There is the tendency to focus on individual people and to blame the victim rather than search for the roots of unemployment. The ideological assumption is that unemployment is the fault of the unemployed.
- "Microtechnology and the Future" — Progress in the form of rapid technological change is almost an end in itself. Those who stand in its way are branded as Luddites. These are, again, the assumptions of a certain ideology.
- "Energy to Burn" — The bigger, more centralized and more capital-intensive the better seems to be the law governing the development of energy resources in Canada: another ideological assumption.

Ideological elements are not just personal preferences or private points of view. They are social, in the sense that they are socially generated and widely shared and therefore serve to support the dominant structures of a society.

Ideology is more serious than a matter of individual idiosyncrasies or private points of view. The maintenance of an existing social order depends on the majority of people within it subscribing to the tenets of the dominant ideology.

Who advocates these ideas? Why does an often unjust economic system enjoy people's support? How do short-sighted policies and unreasonable decisions avoid strong popular protest? What factors shape current attitudes and values?

Liberal Capitalism

The prevailing ideology in Canada — what we will call liberal capitalism — is so taken for granted that many people unconsciously accept it as the norm, rather than as one specific ideological option. For many Canadians it is entangled with what makes up "common sense" and its features are not often called into question.

Liberal capitalism has evolved over several hundred years. It is capitalist because it organizes the economy around the private accumulation of capital, and liberal because its bias is against restraints on individual liberty and initiative. It stresses limited or constitutional reform, and emphasizes the maintenance of justice by the state.

Most Canadians cherish freedom and equality, perhaps ahead of any other values. They believe that everyone should be free and enjoy equal opportunity. Up to this point, those who uphold liberal capitalism and those who criticize it are in agreement.

According to the dominant ideology in Canada, however, the fundamental meaning of "freedom and equality" is the equal right for entrepreneurs to invest their money however, whenever and wherever they choose. In practice this belief favours those who already enjoy wealth and power. They are the only ones able to make wide-ranging decisions on what happens to their money. Wealth and power — the ability to pay for what you get — also affects many other rights, for example, freedom of expression and equality before the law. George Orwell's apparently self-contradictory line from *Animal Farm*, "All animals are equal, but some are more equal than others," highlights the practical contradiction within the ideology of liberal capitalism. Though Orwell was parodying the dominant ideology of the Soviet Union, his wry comment can just as easily be applied to Canada.

Originally, those who controlled capital demanded unhampered freedom. Anything that interfered with this uncontrolled freedom was condemned as unnatural and contrary to common sense; for example, laws against child labour and regulations setting minimum wages. The most notable examples perhaps were "the robber barons" of the nineteenth century. At that time, they were an accepted feature of capitalist society; now they are condemned.

Free competition in the business world is another one of the original basic tenets of liberal capitalism. But as the examples in chapter six showed, more and more economic power tends to concentrate in fewer and fewer hands. Government in Canada has even legislated measures to ensure more equitable competition. When the Thomson and Southam newspaper chains divided up the Winnipeg and Ottawa newspaper markets they were charged with violating the Combines Investigation Act. But this legislation proved ineffective in curbing the companies. Vigorous lobbying by large businesses has defeated all attempts to enhance competition and protect both small business and consumers.

Paradoxically, although they have this belief in freedom of competition, entrepreneurs also want to be free from government interference that would restrict or "equalize" them. They want to

be free to invest as they see fit, which means dealing from financial strength and political power, not from the equality they laud.

But liberal capitalism in Canada has evolved and adapted. Structures did change to promote orderly (if often still unjust) relations between those who sold their labour and those who had the capital to buy it. Trade unions, once seen as an obstacle to the freedom of business, were legalized and gradually won improvements for their members. Government outlawed child labour and instituted the minimum wage, plus pensions and social welfare programmes such as medicare and unemployment insurance.

The pure tenets of free enterprise, exemplified in the British and American industrial revolutions, took somewhat different forms in Canada and have been modified, perhaps most significantly by welfare measures like UIC, CPP and medicare, which together are called the social wage. Although the history and experience of capitalism in Canada differs in significant ways from U.S. capitalism, a ruggedly individualistic, free-enterprise form of rhetoric sometimes gets imported into Canada, in no small part because of U.S. influence on Canadian media.

The media disseminate the ideology of liberal capitalism in both subtle and obvious ways. For example, the news only occasionally paints sympathetic portraits of people who are unemployed, and rarely questions the priorities of corporations whose exclusive concentration on growth, profits and protecting their investments may result in payroll cutbacks and therefore unemployment.

The analysis in *Getting Started* often conflicts with the media viewpoint which, for example, might favour cut-backs in "unproductive" social services, uncritically laud the wonders of microtechnology, or assume that unfettered but subsidized free enterprise will get the country back on its feet.

Social analysis gets at ideological assumptions such as these, not so much by talking about ideology, as by asking further questions and pushing beyond what is "normal" or what makes common sense. For example, the values of a just, sustainable and participatory society promise to serve the interests of workers, consumers and citizens better, but these ideals are often pitted against the conventional wisdom of business and government decision-makers.

The structures that buttress society, the values of private enterprise and private profit, corporate growth and progress are constantly assumed and positively reinforced. The ideology itself is hardly ever questioned. The idea of ordering the Canadian economy according to any norms other than those of liberal capitalism would seem absurd to many citizens, especially those who control the command posts over the economy.

Our country is still profoundly marked by the founders of liberal capitalism. We carry forward many of the consequences of their lives, for their ideas have become our institutions. Their values shape much of today's economic system which, in turn, gives rise to materialistic aspirations that are the idols that millions worship today. Those values constitute an economic religion that inhibits the development of an ethic of sharing. While people have worked hard to plant the seeds of human solidarity and love, the dominant economic and social structures of our times have become the rocky ground of self-service and self-aggrandizement.

Canadian Conference of Catholic Bishops, **A Society to be Transformed,** *1977*

Questions

- What are other mechanisms, besides the media, for communicating the dominant ideology? How do they work? Who controls them? Identify some sources of alternative, competing viewpoints.

- The media usually defend their selection of events and editing of stories by claiming that they are giving the consumers what they want. Do they in fact give us what we want? Does the news industry have any responsibility to society beyond catering to its taste? What is the role of the media in creating taste? Should the news industry be allowed to consider itself "a private enterprise owing nothing to the public"?

- Significant numbers of radio and TV outlets in Canada are not owned by large private conglomerates, but are publicly owned. What difference does this fact make? Does the CBC promote an ideology that is distinct from the dominant liberal capitalism? If so, in whose interests? If not, then how does the business establishment exercise corporate, political and ideological pressures upon media which it does not directly own?

- Check the news source of an important event: If it's an international story, does it come from a

Resources

- Eleanor MacLean, *Between The Lines: How to Detect Bias and Propaganda in the News and Everyday Life,* Montreal: Black Rose Books, 1981. A book exploring methods of decoding the newspapers and radio and television news. It also provides a critical examination of the predominant sources of information.

- Walter Stewart, ed., *Canadian Newspapers: The Inside Story,* Edmonton: Hurtig, 1980. An inside look at eleven of Canada's daily papers by the people who write for them. This book examines the growing influence of advertising and multimedia chains on the everyday workings of the newspaper industry.

- *CONNEXIONS* is a quarterly annotated bibliography of alternative sources of information. Each issue focuses on a different theme. Canadian groups, local projects, and resources, both printed and audio-visual, are helpfully presented. Write to Connexions, 427 Bloor Street West, Toronto, Ont. M5S 1X7, ph. 416-960-3903.

- "Between the Lines," Edmonton Learner Centre, slide-tape, 18 minutes. Describes and analyzes four ways in which the news is distorted.

Questions (cont'd)

Western-based, Western-oriented wire service such as Associated Press (AP), United Press International (UPI), Reuters or Agence France-Presse (AFP)? Does the local paper have *any* correspondents outside of town or does it rely on wire services for all of its non-local news? If it's a domestic story, does it come from the Canadian Press, owned by its member papers across the country?

• Look for quotations: Whom did the reporter talk to — government officials, recognized experts, "usually reliable sources" or anonymous "informants"? If quotes come from a prepared press release, does the paper usually say so? What are the interests and motives of the people quoted? Do their opinions represent conventional wisdom?

• Review the story: Do you feel you understand the conflict? Are some participants in the event absent from the story? Have credible witnesses been neglected or presented in a dim light? Comparing two or more reports, does the situation seem to have been confused by a particular news outlet, and might there be a reason? Are there clues about where to look for more reliable information?

• Evaluate your sources of information on one of the issues in this book. Do you rely on the major networks, newspapers and newsmagazines? Are you familiar with alternate sources, such as church, labour or special-interest publications? Compare an alternate source with a major news outlet, with an eye on the selection of stories, the depth of coverage and the viewpoint of the journalist.

Welcome to Part Three

Elements of Canada's dominant ideology are lodged within our heads. This book, in its efforts to analyze, interpret and judge Canadian reality, tries to shed light on our ideological blind-spots. What might have been taken for common sense before now deserves to be questioned and — very often — changed.

Part Three deals with social issues (though not exclusively social, any more than previous chapters were exclusively economic). It analyzes the experience of three groups of people: the aged, native people and women in Canada. In different ways, these three groups are kept out on the edge of society; the reality of their lives clashes with the dominant ideology of Canadian society. They are often presented in an unfavourable light or in an incomprehensible way. But at the same time they are struggling for freedom and equality.

The fourth chapter in Part Three looks at Canadian foreign policy to ask about the policies — and the values behind them — that the Canadian government, acting in the name of the Canadian people, extends to people in the Third World.

In a sense the groups in the next four chapters face the same basic issues and economic issues that have already been analyzed. But how do they look from *their* point of view? If the media usually give a distorted picture of their needs, rights and demands, is it possible to break through the stereotypes and hear from *them*?

The next four chapters together hold up a mirror to Canadian society: This is how Canada looks to people whose voice is heard too rarely in the land.

> We can achieve a new vision of reality by becoming more present with the hungry, the homeless, the jobless, the native person, the poor immigrant and others who may be victims of injustices in our communities. By listening to their problems and sharing in their struggle we can learn much more about the attitudes, activities, and structures that cause human suffering and what can be done about them.
>
> *Canadian Conference of Catholic Bishops,*
> **From Words to Action,** *1976*

Chapter Eleven

Aging — Out of Sight

"I must be getting old."

An offhand remark that any of us might mutter, breathless after running up a flight of stairs, having forgotten someone's name, or being unable to do something as we used to . . . an offhand remark that speaks volumes about our feelings towards aging, our image of old people, and our self-image as we age.

The idea of aging seldom suggests an improvement in a person's general situation. On the contrary. "Aunt Jane just doesn't seem able to cope anymore." Old people are frequently viewed as frail, forgetful, confused, infirm — perhaps even dangerous to themselves. Above all, old people are people in need of help.

The analysis in this chapter touches on several ideas about old people common in Canada:

- *Useless* — Old people have no useful purpose and are a drain on society's resources. In a way they're seen as useless, and often feel pretty useless themselves.
- *Dependent* — The fact that the aging may be in need of some help can mean they lose any right to their independence. Old people become dependent on others.
- *Separate* — Old age is a distinct period of life separate from one's earlier years; old people are a special group whose unique problems separate them from the rest of society.
- *Hidden* — The experience and plight of the elderly, far from being taken into account by society, somehow remain "out of sight" and hidden from view.

Social analysis looks into the experience of growing old in Canada and finds a whole host of important issues. We find that aging is not just a matter of "they" and "them". Aging affects everyone. We will all be old someday, unless we die young, and more people than ever are living longer. *How* we grow old is determined partly by society's assumptions about what it means to be old, and in large measure by our prosperity in the younger years.

"The Golden Years"

As it has become industrialized and urbanized, less agricultural and rural, North American society has changed in a curious way. The curious change is that of having people "retire". It is a pattern that has emerged only since the turn of the century.

In earlier times — and still today in certain societies — people continued to perform productive work for as long as they were physically able. Canada's Inuit people, like many other traditional societies, continue to look to their elders as a rich source of wisdom and advice. The Inuit have no word for "senior citizen". Mainstream Canadian society, however, has begun to think of the old as a separate group who, at some predetermined point, suddenly stop working for a living.

In industrialized countries in the 1930s between 40 and 70 per cent of all men over the age of sixty-five had paid work. In Canada around the same time over 60 per cent of men aged sixty-five and over were working. By the mid-1960s the proportion of aged men at work had declined markedly, to between 10 and 40 per cent in industrial nations. In Canada this segment had shrunk to less than 25 per cent by 1971. In the twenties and thirties, one elderly woman in five was working for a wage but by the 1970s this had shrunk to less than one in ten.

Compulsory retirement at age sixty-five has become routine in many occupations. Retirement is supposed to be a well-deserved rest after several decades on the job. Many employers have quarter-century or forty-year clubs to honour workers of long service who will soon be retiring. At the retirement party a gold watch serves as the traditional gift and testimonial to a long and loyal career, a career now over. At this point the so-called golden years begin.

How people react to retirement often depends on their previous work. Those who spent their working lives in jobs that were boring or frustrating, dirty or dangerous, are more likely to embrace retirement eagerly. Some workers do not want to wait until sixty-five to retire; with the slogan "thirty and out", certain unions have won contract clauses permitting employees to take their pensions after thirty years' service, no matter what their age. But since only a minority of workers are even unionized, few enjoy this option.

On the other hand, people who have found their work challenging, enjoyable and satisfying are likely to be dissatisfied with sudden joblessness. "Father can't seem to get used to the lack of a routine," is a common worry among children of recently-retired workers. In a society where a job is so intimately bound up with individual status and personal dignity (see chapter seven), the sudden termination of work can easily lead people to feel useless and lacking in purpose.

Society has come to define mandatory retirement and old age as the end of a certain part of life — the useful part. This is especially true in a period when old skills are quickly being replaced with new ones. As both public and private institutions become ever-larger and more remote, feelings of obligation between employer and employee evaporate. The labour market is often biased against the older worker, especially in times of high unemployment. When large numbers of employees are threatened with layoffs, older workers are often pressured to take early retirement so that jobs can be kept open for younger people.

All of a sudden, people are less valuable to society than they were before. This "fact" is driven home when retirement suddenly and dramatically drives down an income level. In a society dominated by the exchange of goods and services for money, people who lose the ability to sell the only asset they possess — their labour power — often face a sharp reduction in income and standard of living. When you are over sixty-five and have no job, they say you are retired. At a younger age, you would be unemployed.

Advertisers favour images of fun-loving groups of smiling, attractive people in their twenties and thirties. This imagery links positive feelings about youth with particular products. When was the last time you saw elderly people in a beer or soft drink commercial? "Think young — have a Pepsi!" used to be a sales pitch. Vigour, imagination, energy and purpose are frequently associated with youth. This assumption is not only faulty in itself, but leads to negative attitudes about old age.

Getting old and being retired acquire a kind of stigma: not really the golden but the declining years in which old people now have to deal with age discrimination and lack of choice in many aspects of their lives, including work and/or retirement.

Many people are reluctant to end their working lives because they are afraid of losing both their sense of purpose and much of their income. But there are various pension plans to support people when they leave the labour market, to protect them from the ill effects of unemployment, to guarantee material security in their later years. These are the safety nets designed to protect people from poverty when their active participation in the labour force ends. Unfortunately, for over half of Canada's elderly citizens, the "golden years" are all too often tarnished by poverty and insecurity.

> The plight of elderly women and men on pensions isn't simply a matter of whether there is enough money in the pension pot to spread around, but rather a matter of how we will guarantee to the elderly enough money that they will have a fair share of the goods and services we produce. We could offer that guarantee if we chose to. Right now, Canada seems to live out other priorities.
>
> *United Church of Canada,*
> **The Quest for the Shalom Kingdom,** *1982*

Pensions . . .

In 1907 the federal government introduced a scheme whereby people could purchase an annuity with government assistance. "I doubt extremely the expediency of having recourse to a system of old age pensions," said one senator:

> But I do believe there is great opportunity for the state to avail itself of the machinery at its disposal for the purpose of placing within the grasp of every industrious man in Canada the opportunity, at an easy rate and at a very small cost to the state, of providing a reasonable annuity for his support at an advanced period of life.

The emphasis was on individual thrift, and at that time pensions were a long way off. But today discussions of pension reform still tend to reflect this individualist perspective.

When the idea of Canadians receiving an old age pension was discussed in the 1920s, some politicians opposed the idea on the principle that it would place a premium on laziness. However, as compulsory retirement spread and fewer people remained economically active in their later years, pensions became widely accepted. By 1951 everyone seventy and over was entitled to an old age pension. The qualifying age for old age pensions was later lowered to sixty-five.

Old Age Security, as it was named, falls far short of providing sufficient income for a retiree. Today it is but one of several sources of income Canadians can draw upon to support themselves in their old age:

- The oldest form of income security is individual savings. Workers are expected to squirrel some money away to support themselves when they can no longer work. Government uses a tax incentive to encourage personal saving for retirement through Registered Retirement Savings Plans (RRSP).
- Job-related pension schemes. People who work for government agencies and large firms contribute a portion of their salary to a pension plan. Such plans cover two out of every five working Canadians, 48 per cent of men and 32 per cent of women.
- Old Age Security (OAS), the oldest form of government pension. The federal government provides all senior Canadians with a basic pension and pays for it out of general revenues.

- Guaranteed Income Supplement (GIS). The government "tops up" the OAS with this means-tested supplement for those with no other source of income over and above the basic pension. Each province also has a system of payments to supplement the OAS.
- The Canada Pension Plan (CPP). Begun in 1966, the national CPP is similar to private plans in that employees contribute through their wages, and the employers also contribute. CPP is a portable fund which workers carry with them as they move from job to job.

This list of programmes protecting people against old age poverty seems comprehensive. But RRSPs and private savings obviously exclude those who cannot afford to save for retirement because they need all their income to get by in their earlier years. What's more, 65 per cent of elderly Canadians have either no investment or pension income at all or an income from these sources that is under $1,000. Except for the OAS/ GIS combination — which by itself fails to keep the recipient above the poverty line — all pensions are geared to previous peiformance in the labour market. Those who were paid higher wages will have bigger pensions while low-income people will receive less. People who were frequently unemployed and women who have taken time off work for childbearing and child care are left out.

Those without a good track record in the labour market are condemned to continuing poverty in their later years. Thus the inequalities characteristic of economic life in Canada are reproduced in old age. In fact, despite all the programmes, each person has the primary responsibility for his or her own well-being in old age. The guiding principle of an individualist ethic remains unchanged. The social system scarcely guarantees economic security to retired Canadians.

... or Poverty?

The combined income from both the OAS and the GIS falls short of the official Statistics Canada poverty line, which itself may be inadequate (see chapter six). In March, 1979, a single person receiving the basic pension plus supplement had an annual income of $3,783 and the official poverty level was $5,280. The combined income for a

couple was $6,991 while the poverty line was $7,742.

Large numbers of aged Canadians have incomes so low that they are eligible for the Guaranteed Income Supplement. Fully 53 per cent of all Canadians over sixty-five fall into this unenviable category. In only two provinces, Ontario and British Columbia, do more than half of the pensioners have enough income *not* to qualify for the GIS. Many of these people are still in the group that the statisticians call the "near-poor" — often a worse situation financially than those designated as poor, because the "near-poor" do not qualify even for the meagre services available for the officially "poor". In Newfoundland four out of five pensioners depend on the supplement to get by, while in Nova Scotia and New Brunswick two out of three are eligible for the GIS.

Why should most Canadians anticipate their old age with foreboding, wondering whether they will be living in poverty? Since the individually-oriented pension system is geared to making the highest retirement incomes available to people who earned the highest incomes, those who held dead-end, low-paying jobs — or who only worked sporadically because they had trouble finding secure employment — get less money to support themselves in their old age. Once retired, their entire incomes must come exclusively from the government, and hence are subject to shifting government commitments.

Women are particularly vulnerable in this respect.

In Canada over half of all women now hold paying jobs, and many raise children at the same time, often alone. But when women stop working to care for the children, they stop earning. Not only are they unable to save for the future, but these long periods without a paycheque may also interrupt their pension plan contributions. In fact, for the first seventeen years of its existence, from 1966 until 1983, the publicly-run CPP discriminated against women who took time off work for child care. On average, women dedicate a total of ten years outside of paid employment for child care but still spend twenty-five years in the workforce

Since women are paid less than men for similar work (see chapter thirteen), their pensions reflect this discrimination. Those contributing to private pension plans receive lower pensions than their male colleagues because of interrupted earnings and lower wages.

As a result, the retirement income of a mother and homemaker is usually dependent on her husband's pension and savings. Without such support, or if the husband dies without leaving any survivor's benefits, a woman is condemned to poverty, dependent on the inadequate OAS/GIS combination.

In essence, the pension system penalizes women for being what society wants them to be — housewives and mothers.

Older Canadians who live out their lives in poverty must struggle to find housing that is not too cramped, dirty and draughty. The press occasionally features stories of pensioners forced to subsist on pet food. Towards the end of the month, when the pension runs out, there is nothing left for the barest necessities of life.

Material poverty also eliminates many other, seemingly smaller things that contribute to daily life. An older woman describes the constant grind:

> You can mend or remake your clothes; you can stop going places that cost money; you can stop the daily paper; you can put off the doctor as long as possible. But if an emergency arises the only place the money can come from is your food allowance. Perhaps at first it's a game but as the dreary days drag on, the clothes wear out, the spartan diet becomes monotonous and you wonder why you ever lived this long to come to this.

The smaller things — newspapers, trips downtown, a new item of clothing — many people take for granted. But reading a newspaper and getting

around town are important because they give one the sense of participating in the day-to-day life of society. When old people are deprived of these "little things", they are denied the opportunity to participate. They feel excluded, no longer part of the busy life they once knew, and *separate* from what is happening around them.

"Homes" for the Aged

Poverty in old age is unlikely to disappear of its own accord. People over sixty-five *are* a fast-growing part of society. The table shows that by 2031 — when the Baby Boom generation will have become part of the "graying" of Canada — the percentage of people sixty-five and older will have more than doubled.

Now and then the media intone darkly on the subject of the so-called demographic bulge, with ominous images of a future crowded with grandparents in the hundreds of thousands. Pension plans and social resources, they report, will be stretched to the limit. According to Simone de Beauvoir, "In society's eyes the aged person is no more than a corpse under suspended sentence." What a chilling assessment! What becomes of people who are sentenced in this way?

Some people live in their own homes until they die. Others stay with relatives who provide whatever assistance is required. Still others live out their years in places established to care for the elderly.

A glance through the nursing homes listings in the Yellow Pages turns up an array of institutions with comfortable-sounding names: Green Gables Manor, Eventide Home, Leisure World, Country Place, Heather Lodge. Some of these places are run by companies whose business it is to look after the old, and their names are also intended to sound comforting: Extendicare Ltd., Diversicare Corporation, The Carewell Corporation.

Of course, older people are more susceptible to disease than the young. But the tendency towards putting people into special homes treats old age itself as a disease instead of as a part of life. Hospital-like environments foster a kind of "medicalization", and those in charge have often been trained in hospital administration courses. The equation "*to be old* equals *to be sick*" is so strong, especially in homes for the aged, that old people themselves begin to believe it.

If present trends continue, more and more of Canada's health care dollars will be spent on the elderly. In Ontario by the year 2000, fifty cents out of every health dollar will be funnelled into care for the elderly. What kind of care is being provided? Where are the dollars being spent? Are the benefits going to old people?

In Ontario nine out of every ten people over sixty-five live in their own homes or with family. But in 1980 the provincial government spent only $40 million on community support services for the elderly while at the same time spending $445 million on institutional care.

Keeping people in institutions, even if they are called homes, is very expensive. With better community care facilities, more old people could remain in their own homes and, indeed, get out more. Those living at home would also feel less separated from society. If they had a choice, most old people, like the young and middle-aged, would choose an autonomous life where they make their own decisions. Many elderly are shut in through no choice of their own, and even the label "shut-in" evokes the pejorative image of prison.

Institutions like nursing homes are designed to *care for* people, not to provide them the wherewithal to look after themselves. Besides contributing to the medicalization of old age, nursing homes, residences for the elderly and the like have a way of robbing people of their self-sufficiency. If, all of a sudden, everything is done *for* you, chances are your interest in doing things for yourself is going to wane sooner or later.

One administrator of a modern old people's home recalls a woman who was admitted just after she had finished canning the produce from her backyard garden.

> She owned her own house and had cut her finger quite badly the day before while doing her preserves. I'm sure it was because she was upset about coming in. Within one week that woman was as confused as can be and couldn't dress herself. And I remember a man who had lived in the district and knew people all around. Every day he would wander through the halls asking "Why don't people talk in here?"

People who have little to do can easily be convinced that they are feeble and infirm.

Britain has a lower rate of institutionalization of the elderly than Canada. Its publicly-funded National Health Service has provided financial support for all types of care — including home care services — right from the start.

	Canadian Population Projections by Age (population in thousands)								
Year	Total Population	Age 0-17	%	Age 18-59	%	Age 60-64	%	Age 65+	%
1976	22,993	7,312	31.8	12,774	55.6	905	3.9	2,002	8.7
1981	24,330	6,933	28.5	14,134	58.1	963	4.0	2,310	9.5
1986	25,713	6,833	26.6	15,159	58.9	1,110	4.3	2,615	10.2
1991	26,975	6,966	25.8	15,918	59.0	1,114	4.1	2,980	11.0
1996	27,993	6,993	25.0	16,640	59.4	1,115	4.0	3,248	11.6
2001	28,794	6,805	23.6	17,401	60.4	1,165	4.0	3,425	11.9
2011	30,068	6,411	21.3	17,968	59.8	1,764	5.9	3,924	13.1
2021	30,877	6,378	20.7	17,255	55.9	2,151	7.0	5,093	16.5
2031	30,935	6,162	19.9	16,715	54.0	1,817	5.9	6,240	20.2

(Statistics Canada)

Not so in Canada. Public money supported institutional care in the early days of medicare. Thus institutionalization got a running start and developed a momentum of its own. People were forced to opt for institutions because only those costs were insured. A whole industry has grown up to maintain, expand and profit from "homes for the aged". Companies are in the business of running chains of homes. As one newspaper report put it, "Private enterprise has been making inroads into the healthcare field in recent years — particularly in the delivery of geriatric services — as governments have found themselves strapped for both capital and operating funds." Health professionals earn their living through work in these institutional settings and thus support their continuation.

Support for home care continues to lag far behind. Moreover, changes in the family have also altered the position of older people in society. Daughters and daughters-in-law — formerly full-time housewives in a position to help out aging relatives — have moved out of the home and are now often full-time workers. As family size has declined, so has the ability of families to assist their elderly members. The table facing shows that Canada will have proportionately fewer young people and more old people in the years to come. Apparently many more older Canadians will be consigned to institutions.

It is important to reflect on whether or not senior citizens are better off living in their own homes. A home, more than just a place to live, is a personal space, a place to belong (see chapter three). At home, people are more likely to feel they have some control over what they do. These are intangibles that all of us — old and young — cherish. Living in a building designed to look after them and controlled by others, people are likely to become isolated from society, dependent on others and estranged from themselves. Rarely indeed is an institution really a home.

> **To the Older Members of our Society:**
> **Although your outlook on things may have changed with the years, the change should mean not a lessening but a deepening appreciation of life. Indeed, your present situation gives you** *time* **for leisure, for creativity and new activities — a time in which each individual can live life with a sense of fullness and accomplishment....**
> *Canadian Catholic Conference of Bishops,*
> **Pastoral Message,** *1980*

The End of Separatism

Even if we are not in our own later years, most of us have accompanied parents or grandparents through old age — or will have to do so in the future. We cannot help but wonder what will become of us when we get old ourselves. Perhaps the most important discovery is that we all share the problems of the old, not simply because we will one day be old ourselves, but because the problems of the old are closely linked with other social problems.

The level of material comfort in old age is a function of class and sex. If you are a middle-class man who had a steady job with a pension plan during your working life, your retirement is likely to be materially secure. But if you are a working-class woman who spent part of your life at home looking after the kids and part in paid work, you will likely be one out of every two senior Canadians who depends on an inadequate government pension.

If you were poor in your earlier years, chances are you will be poor in your old age. If you fail to save enough, the state will dole out some charity, but this small stipend condemns you to poverty. In Canada, it seems, a comfortable and secure old age is a privilege to be earned, not a right that is guaranteed. According to this do-it-yourself attitude towards retirement, each person is responsible for his or her own income, through private savings or a private pension plan.

How people live in retirement is a function of what they were "worth" on the labour market, not necessarily what they contributed to society over the course of their lives.

Society has come to treat aging as something that is *done to* people who happen to be in the later years of life. With institutionalization, the ability of old people to take care of themselves declines, just as it has declined with the rise of compulsory retirement and the reduced ability to earn an income. While the old face so much hardship and uncertainty in Canada, we do not hear or see much of them, because they are hidden away. People are also separated mentally and spiritually, because they get the sense that society considers them useless and unproductive. This separatism makes no sense for old people and ignores the skills and accumulated experience they have to offer in helping to solve the many problems society faces.

Institutionalization imposes a heavy financial burden on everyone, and the load will become more onerous as the demographic bulge grows older. The practical issues of pensions and enabling old people to be autonomous citizens cannot be tackled simply by providing more community care and adjusting pensions upward.

The tendency to treat the graying of society as a disaster is a socially-imposed and self-fulfilling verdict in Canada. The attitudes of looking at old people as a group apart, and using retirement as a form of waste disposal, are institutionally supported. Aging has to be redefined so that old people are not hidden but seen, not impoverished but living with dignity, neither useless nor dependent but playing a useful, independent and participatory role in society.

Any new approaches to aging need to emphasize *power* — making sure that old people have the power to provide for themselves, to use their skills to help each other, to be active subjects in their own lives rather than passive objects of institutional policy. Power is a most important attribute not provided, at present, by those who work with old people.

Here are some suggestions for different approaches to aging:

• Rather than force everyone to retire at an arbitrary age like sixty-five, take a more flexible approach to retirement. This would enable those who wanted to retire to do so and allow others to stay on the job as long as they were capable of working and still wanted to do so.

• Many families could and would assist their elderly members if subsidies were available to them instead of only to institutions.

• A service as simple as meals-on-wheels enables "shut-ins" to have regular, hot meals of good quality in their own homes. Given the poverty of so many old people, this meal is frequently the only source of decent sustenance each day, a break from diets of tea and toast. Services like meals-on-wheels are frequently underfunded and constantly short of volunteer drivers.

• Day hospitals and visiting healthcare workers could meet many of the medical needs of old people at much less than the current cost of chronic care.

• Special transit services providing, for instance, vehicles designed for wheelchairs can bring transportation to the homes of those who have trouble getting out. Old people could live at home and still have access to many services they need.

• Multi-service community centres can meet a variety of old people's needs: food, health care, companionship, things to do, legal aid and recreational facilities.

"Change, not charity!" is what many older Canadians are demanding: programmes that would provide them with whatever support they may need to care for themselves. To stop separating old people from society and to reintegrate them means to change society itself.

Alternatives to the degradation and institutionalization of old age do exist. Putting an end to the problems of the elderly requires, in the most basic terms, ending the equation of old age with poverty. It also involves putting an end to the conception of old age as a problem. Old people need both more autonomy as well as facilities and services to allow them to participate more actively in their own lives.

The way Canada is organized, the social and economic forces at play have worked on old people in the same way they have worked on the rest of us. But they have done so for longer, with more extreme — and final — consequences. Is it any wonder that older people want the separation and dependency to end?

Questions

- Does old age *have* to be a period of decline? Like health, aging is an issue from which no one can be exempt. Do you look forward to growing old or is it something you put out of your mind as soon as you think about it, thus revealing some apprehension?

- Mandatory retirement: How have your parents or friends reacted to retirement? Has it been an enjoyable time or have they had trouble adjusting to different routines? Do people actually *want* to retire? Should retirement at a set age be mandatory?

- Your chances of having a materially-secure old age improve if you are male, worsen if you are female. Similarly, they vary with social position and economic track record. Does this have to be so? Can it be justified?

Resources

- Edna Alford, *A Sleep Full of Dreams,* Lantzville, B.C.: Oolichan Books, 1981. This collection of stories chronicles the lives of a group of old people who live in a nursing home. A provocative revelation of the solitary and enclosing world of the aged.

- Morden Lazarus, *Looking Forward: A Guide for Retirement,* Canadian Council of Retirees (CLC) Ontario Section, 1983. A very useful guide, written from a labour point of view, to the various social and economic problems faced by the elderly, and to available programmes.

- *Sixty-five and older,* A Report by the National Council of Welfare on the Incomes of the Aged, February 1984. An excellent source for current statistics, analyzed in a clear and useful way.

- Leah Cohen, *Small Expectations: Society's Betrayal of the Older Woman,* Toronto: McClelland and Stewart, 1984. This is a critique, based on interviews, of society's denial of women's needs and its failure to honour their basic rights. Cohen analyzes the political remedies that are available and gives examples of older women who have struggled against their status as second-class citizens.

- Canadian Association on Gerontology, *Newsletter* and *Canadian Journal on Aging.* Published six times a year, the newsletter gives information on upcoming events dealing with aging in each province, as well as lists of current publications. P.O. Box 1859, Winnipeg, Man. R3C 3R1.

Resources (cont'd)

- "Tales of Tomorrow," DEC Films, 1983, 16 mm, 22 minutes. Weaving together the stories of two very different old people, this film gives a voice to spokespersons too rarely heard.

- "The Battle of Beech Hall," Cinemagic Productions, Kinetic Films, 1981, 16 mm, 27 minutes. Toronto senior citizens oppose a decision by municipal councillors to evict them from their subsidized housing.

- "A New Age for the Old," Altana Films, Kinetic Films, 1979, 16 mm, 27 minutes. Challenges several durable misconceptions about the old and portrays various options for living longer.

- "In Our Own Homes", slide-tape montage, 1979, 28 minutes. This montage was produced by a group of old people. It explores how and why old people in Canada have been isolated from the rest of society. The emphasis is on the need for more choices in retirement and work, services, income and living arrangements. A good statement of the need for a contribution to society by old people themselves. Available from Development Education in Action, 427 Bloor Street West, Toronto, Ont. M5S 1X7, ph. 416-484-8421.

- For further information, contact the National Advisory Council on Aging, Jeanne Mance Building, Room 1264, Tunney's Pasture, Ottawa, Ont. K1A 0K9, ph. 613-996-6522.

Chapter Twelve

A Home and Native Land

Realtors think of land as real estate, a commodity to be parcelled and sold on the market. Municipal planners distribute land according to various uses — commercial, industrial, residential. Farmers work the land. It is the source of their livelihood and the country's vital food supplies.

Canada's native peoples have a different view. According to their traditions, land is not something separable from human life, as if people could live apart from the land, over and above nature. Rather, land is *the* basis of the one natural family, to which humans also belong. They are one with the land, and from the land springs their relationship with everything, with all aspects of the natural world that come from the Creator.

These two differing conceptions of land and indeed of society are eloquently described by Walter Currie, an Ojibwa from Chatham, Ontario:

> In the yesterdays of my people, we were three major groups — those who lived between the Rockies and the Pacific, those who moved across the plains and those of the forests and streams. The nations had their varied languages, their customs, their beliefs, their ways of living. Unlike the arriving white man with his peasant ethos, the Indians of North America followed a hunter ethos. He lived — and lives — within his environment; he was part of the land and what it yields. He took only what he needed. He had no need either to command or to obey another's wishes. Time and work had not been invented; acquisition of property was unknown. Group interest was paramount to self interest: When I eat you eat; when you go hungry I go hungry.

The concept of being "part of the land" is telling, especially when the land base is shrinking, when toxic wastes imperil human life, when the rain itself has become a threat as well as a bles-

sing, and when the primacy of property rights and self interest have resulted in the treatment of native people as an obstacle to development. Most alarming to Canada's native people has been their own diminishing access to the land from which they once drew their material and spiritual nourishment.

Well over half of Canada's native people live in the southern part of the country, many of them in major cities far from reserve lands. The problems they confront are complex and increasingly urgent. But the roots of these difficulties can be traced back to three central points — *the land, colonialism* and *development.*

The Early Years

Noble Savage or Hapless Victim?

The conquest of the land and its original inhabitants came in stops and starts with varying effects on the sporadically conquered people. Epidemics of previously unknown illnesses decimated native societies; smallpox, for example, killed off Indians and Inuit by the thousands. The European settlers constantly pushed back the frontier, often betraying, bribing and coercing the Indians into signing treaties and ceding their land. Native people gradually retreated from the onslaught of white society.

Tribes that once depended on the co-operative activity of hunting switched to the more competitive work of trapping. They became dependent on the fur trade for their sustenance. When trade in furs declined, around the turn of this century, the Indians became outcasts within what had formerly been their own world. In fact, their societies simply ceased to exist as they had known them.

By the early 1900s many of Canada's Indians had been relegated to reserve lands. The treaties they signed with the authorities ceded their traditional rights to the land in exchange for tiny cash annuities, schooling and small tracts of reserve land. The rest of the land — for centuries the life support of the indigenous societies and an integral part of their very lives — became "Crown Land". But other native peoples, principally in the Yukon, the Northwest Territories and British Columbia, never signed any treaties. The precise legal status of much of the land in Canada as a whole was and remains unclear to this day.

As the European population increased its pressure on the native people and their land, the indigenous population dwindled. One colonial politician, Sir Francis Bond Head of Upper Canada, saw the Indians as a doomed race who were "melting like snow before the sun". He wanted to consign all Indians in Ontario to Manitoulin Island where they would eventually die out.

As a matter of fact this failed to happen, and by 1900 the trend began to reverse itself. Since the 1950s the Indian population has been increasing at a faster rate than the Canadian population as a whole. At the beginning of the eighties in Canada there were about 300 thousand status Indians (people officially covered by treaty), 500 thousand non-status Indians, and 500 thousand Métis (people of mixed blood).

The images of native people held by many Canadians have their roots in classrooms across the country. A 1925 primary school reader, part of the Dent Company's Canadian History Readers series, describes what for many young minds became a typical Indian band.

The Indians were led by War Hawk, a "great chief" and veteran of many battles, who remembered how the Indians lived before the coming of the white man. War Hawk is pictured as a tall, distinguished man adorned with a long feathered head-dress. His tribe, wrapped in abundant furs and with plenty to eat, lived contented lives in their teepees. It was the portrayal of a noble people.

But as a reminder that Indian ways were still quaintly primitive, rather than bustling and up-to-date, the young students learned about an Indian sawmill. The device the Indians used, according to the Reader, was a frame holding a tree trunk well above the ground with one Indian on top of the log and the other below, moving an ordinary hand-saw up and down between them to slice the log. "It takes a long time to cut logs this way," the book stated. "But Indians have plenty of time."

Another common impression in Canada is the stereotype of a destitute, drunken Indian. One resident of Kenora in northern Ontario was so alarmed by overt drunkenness on the streets of the town and so threatened by a group of militant Indians who had occupied a local park that she wrote a pamphlet blaming the victims for their own plight.

Claiming that the white population was "fed up" with Indians openly drinking wine and sprawling on the streets of Kenora, Eleanor Jacobson characterized native people as a charge on the public purse: "The only way the Indian pays taxes now is when he buys a bottle of booze." The picture sketched by this observer of the bleak side of native conditions depicts a group of dissipated, shiftless derelicts with no one but themselves to blame.

Yet this pamphleteer failed to see the connection between the symptoms and their social causes, just as the textbook failed to explain how native people really lived — much less why. War Hawk's people and the down-and-out Kenora alcoholics are both racial stereotypes. Rather than repeat the stereotype uncritically, this social analysis looks for some of the underlying facts and reasons. A first question could be: Why is the native population of Canada so dramatically different from the non-native?

> For the Native Peoples the land is more than simply a source of food or cash. The land itself constitutes a permanent sense of security, well-being and identity. For generations, this land has defined the basis of what the natives are as a people. In their own words, "Our land is our life."
>
> *Canadian Conference of Catholic Bishops,* **Northern Development: At What Cost,** *1975*

Native Conditions

Statistics and charts may seem impersonal, but they can communicate very real human suffering. Among Canadian native people, the infant mortality rate (deaths below one year of age) is nearly double the national average. Above one year, as the chart illustrates, the Indian death rate ranges from two to four times the national average.

Mortality
Deaths per 1,000 Population in Each Age Group
1973-1976 Average

	Indian	Non-Indian
1-4 yrs.	3.1	0.8
5-19 yrs.	1.9	0.7
20-44 yrs.	6.0	1.5
45-64 yrs.	15.7	9.0
65 and over	57.0	55.0

Life Expectancy
Average Additional Years of Life

	1961		1971	
	Male	Female	Male	Female
At 1 year:				
National	68.5	74.3	69.3	76.3
Indian	59.7	63.5	60.2	66.2
At 50 years:				
National	24.3	28.5	24.5	29.9
Indian	25.1	26.2	24.8	27.6
At 80 years:				
National	6.3	7.0	6.4	7.9
Indian	6.0	6.6	8.0	8.9

Violent Deaths (Age Specific)
Accidents, Poisoning and Violence per 100,000 Population at Each Age Level

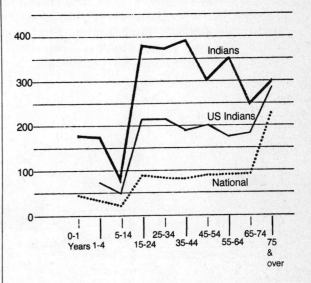

Suicides
Per 100,000 Population at Each Age Level, 1977

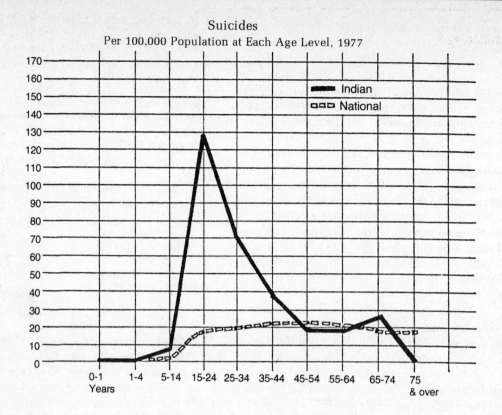

At one year of age, natives have a life expectancy about ten years lower than other Canadians.

Native people are vulnerable to diseases that reflect inadequate housing, lack of safe drinking water and proper sewage disposal, poor access to medical care, chronic unemployment, and racial and social discrimination.

Adolescence, usually a time of turmoil, is often a traumatic period on the reserves. The rate of native suicides is almost three times the national rate; amongst fifteen- to twenty-four year olds, there is even greater disparity: The national rate is 20, the native rate is 130 per 100,000.

The generation aged fifteen to thirty-five should be the energy and strength of their communities. Their conspicuous absence is a puzzlement. Young native people, sufficiently educated to know there's something very wrong but lacking the means to take action, seem to suffer a gnawing despair whose unhappy expression is suicide.

Some of the above facts reveal conditions we usually associate with the plight of the poor in countries of the Third World, yet we find them here in Canada, published by our own federal government. What are the roots of these conditions?

Colonialism

In 1981 a United Nations meeting of indigenous people from around the world analyzed the scandal of native living conditions. Their explanation had much to do with foreign occupation of the land and the imposition of colonial rule:

> The integral relationship of the spiritual life of indigenous peoples . . . with the Mother Earth has many profound implications. It means for example, that the separation of the Indian people from the land — even when replaced by money payments — is a concrete form of ethnocide and genocide. . . . When Indians become rootless, experience has shown that they suffer a loss of identity, of national existence, and become subject, in addition, to symptoms of social psychological annihilation such as alcoholism.

Colonialism usually begins with military occupation by an outside power, but essentially it means that the economically and politically powerful impose their will and their ways on a less powerful people. In Canada, the key to the colonizing process was the gradual but inexorable destruction of the indigenous people's relationship with the land. One band after another was removed from its ancestral territory and usually confined to reserves "for their own good". The bands had no choice in the matter.

Colonialism disrupted the evolution of native societies which, like any other, were complex. They had both shortcomings and strengths. A way of life that had been developing in its own autonomous way for centuries was effectively undermined.

The Europeans infected the native people with more than physical disease. They also promoted feelings of intellectual, cultural and religious inferiority. They defined the world, and the Indians were forced to accept the definition along with the whole colonial package.

What was formerly Indian land became Crown land, available for forestry, mining and the exploitation of energy resources. At the present time, timber licences, new mines, potential gas and oil fields and a pipeline corridor are the uses planned for native lands in Canada. The backers of such projects speak of exploring resource hinterlands, evaluating investment opportunities, conducting cost/benefit analyses. According to one mining group:

> It is our indisputable view that the cornerstone of northern development is the exploitation and dis-

covery of new mineral resources. The exploitation of natural resources provides the major source of new wealth for our country and accounts to a large extent for the high standard of living of all Canadians.

But the exploitation of natural resources does not promise to be of nearly as much benefit to native people and most other Canadians as it does to corporations such as Imperial Oil, Dome Petroleum, Brascan and Canadian Pacific. Certainly the living standards of the shareholders of these companies cannot be compared to those of most of the country's native people. Moreover, the hardnosed, dollars-and-cents approach to investment betrays a drastically different understanding of the land from the human, integrated, spiritual conception of its original inhabitants.

Giant resource projects, many based on access to lands currently occupied by native people, are supposed to revitalize the Canadian economy and provide beneficial spinoffs for northern native societies. The historical evidence suggests they do neither. Only after megaprojects secure supplies of energy and encourage industry in the south, might there be any attempt to accommodate the northern people.

The people affected by major decisions should obviously have some say in the making of those decisions. The failure to consult them and take their interests into account runs contrary to Canada's professed ideals of democracy and equality. In this light the very name of the federal government department dealing with native people seems rather paradoxical — the Department of Indian Affairs and Northern Development.

The Only Way?

An Indian band on the shore of Hudson Bay once took time to study a proposal by a consortium of energy companies. The proposal was for a pipeline to bring natural gas from the high Arctic to markets in eastern Canada and the northeastern United States. The pipeline would cut through their lands. The band expressed skepticism: "We are opposed to being offered the so-called choice between massive development schemes which will ruin our land and our lifestyle, or the equally unacceptable choice of welfare dependence. This is like being asked which method of suicide we prefer."

Organizations such as the Council of Yukon Indians, the Dene Nation, the Inuit Tapirisat and the Nishga Tribal Council are extremely wary of the corrosive effects of industrial penetration on indigenous societies and their traditional ways of life. These and other groups that have never ceded their land to Canada by treaty believe there must surely be a saner way of developing natural resources. They are attempting to chart their own autonomous course of development rooted in their own traditions and based on their own priorities. Otherwise the future will continue to reproduce the errors of the past.

> **Native peoples in the far North have made it clear that they are looking for more than the right to sit on a small piece of real estate. They want to develop a new social contract with the rest of Canadian society, to ensure that the North is developed in such a way that their political, economic, and cultural institutions will be preserved and new ones developed that are consistent with their understanding of development.**
> *United Church of Canada,*
> **29th General Council, 1982**

Native Development

The members of the Bearskin Lake band live near the northern edge of the boreal forest of northwestern Ontario. This beautiful wild area of lakes, rivers and coniferous forests is inaccessible by road. The people depend in part upon government transfer payments but they also live from the land by fishing, hunting and trapping. Their activities generate some cash income as well as provide "country food" — moose, trout, pickerel, berries — an important part of their diet. These woodland Indians are Ojibwa people, whose artwork is esteemed by collectors throughout North America.

The silence of the boreal forest is likely to be shattered by the whine of the chain saw, or the rattle of the rock drill as logging and mining companies push northward in search of raw material. The people of Bearskin Lake belong to the Nishnawbe-Aski Nation, the Indians who signed Treaty No. 9, a treaty covering much of the area in Northern Ontario whose rivers drain into Hudson Bay. The people of the Bearskin Lake Band have responded to the impending penetration of their territory in a clear and forthright way:

> It has been said many times, nevertheless we wish to say it again. We are not against development. [But] development as it is proposed by these huge corporations is being imposed on us. We do not want imminent over-night developments to destroy so much of our environment, so much of our land — the land which means so much to us. We want development which will not create shock or hurt the people of the Nishnawbe-Aski. What we want is to play a part in the development of our land the way we want to keep it.

What is this concept of development? Development is a relative idea, reflecting the priorities of whoever controls the process. For resource corporations it is primarily a commercial proposition, a catch-word for growth and expansion. For native peoples it takes on a different meaning. In French the verb "to develop" is frequently expressed in the reflexive form — *se développer* — *to develop oneself* rather than to be developed by someone else. *Se développer* suggests autonomy, dignity, having a say in what happens. It suggests a kind of power. In this sense development offers native people the opportunity to define their own priorities in the light of their own past experiences. It is quite the opposite of colonialism, in which others have the power —

they make all the decisions and impose them by force.

A member of one of the five aboriginal tribes in the Northwest Territories, the Dogrib, voiced his people's fears of development as imposed from without:

> Why does the government want to assimilate my people? Because where our faith in the Great Spirit was nourished is where the white man has found minerals and oil. The government is giving us everything that money can buy. Yet, it is taking from us the only thing we demand, our identity which includes our home and native land. Many of us have tried to be assimilated, but we are incapable of taking up the white culture and way of life. Generations of suffering have proven this. Have you ever seen white people living like the Dogrib? I would laugh at them if they tried. They wouldn't know how. Yet, that is what is expected of us: to live as a white man, and to accept the projects, programmes and laws he imposes upon us.

Native groups are not digging in their heels. The simple questions — what kind of development? for whom? directed by whom? — open up far deeper issues than merely economic ones. Many native people have decided that cultural assimilation is an unacceptable price to pay for industrial megaprojects. In shaping the future of their societies, they want development to be the product of conscious choices. Their struggle is contributing in a unique way to changing what the word "progress" means in Canada.

Land Claims

In seeking some control over development, one strategy native people have adopted is to make land claims. These claims represent the native people's efforts to have their rights to use and live off their traditional land legally acknowledged by the government. The claims often are based on aboriginal title, and seek the right to control the exploitation of the resource wealth such as timber, minerals, oil and gas, of the lands being claimed.

The bands begin by researching how the land has actually been used. Band members interview elders, and record what they all — young and old alike — know about the history of their people. They make maps of traditional hunting and fishing grounds and trap lines, as well as of the locations of ancient rock paintings. They canvas members of the band to determine how much livelihood is generated from the land.

All this evidence helps to prove that the fruits of the land have been supporting the band for many generations. Basing their argument on these age-old patterns, the native people then try to negotiate a settlement with the government.

It is important to remember that the native conception of the land has very little similarity with the conventional view of property. Private ownership of a piece of land is an entirely foreign idea to Indians. The land and the rest of the natural world are inseparable from the people. Canada's indigenous people find it difficult to "claim" something that so deeply grounds their spiritual conception of the world.

The Dene of the Northwest Territories developed what has become the most widely-known initiative in the country, and stated their claim in the Dene Declaration of 1975. They clarified their claim, documenting it exhaustively, in the long struggle to make submissions to the Berger Inquiry, which ultimately recommended that the Mackenzie Valley pipeline not be built.

"It is not unusual for some Dene to demand of their own leaders that they explain 'what land claims is'," observes a white Canadian who has been close to the Dene struggle for self-determination.

> The people who ask such advice are not unable to define their own positions, but are unable to understand and "own" someone else's definition. What could be more natural? This is, in a nutshell, the essence of colonialism — a relationship which leaves one side dependent on the other to define the world.

Land claims provoke scepticism in some segments of Canadian society. Business leaders believe that resource megaprojects are key to the economic recovery of the whole country — allegedly standing in the way are intransigent

Indians and their unreasonable land claims. Journalists express incredulity when Indian leaders inform them that self-determination, political control and self-government are serious demands.

These ideas often raise the spectre of "separatism". Some Canadians feel threatened and react defensively. Eleanor Jacobson, claiming to speak for the white population of Kenora, typifies such a response. "Ottawa is spending up to $7.5 million to help the Indians research their land claims in Canada. Now why the hell should we be discriminated against by our own tax dollars? Why should we pay for these Indians to search these lands?"

Such resentment seems to betray deep feelings of insecurity and powerlessness that often underlie overt expressions of hostility against a particular racial group. Some people are justifiably edgy about losing their jobs, incomes, homes and so forth. They easily transfer feelings of political impotence and insecurity to readily-identifiable groups with even less power than themselves: welfare recipients, immigrants, racial minorities, or in this case the Indians. Yet the Indians are struggling for something many Canadians would like: greater control over the forces shaping their own lives.

Towards Autonomous Development

Large numbers of non-native Canadians have of course responded sympathetically to the efforts of native people to rectify the patterns of the past and find their own solutions. In 1975 the Canadian Catholic Bishops published *Northern Development: At What Cost?*, which compared "the struggle for justice and responsible stewardship in the North today" with "that in distant Third World countries," and called on all Canadians to become involved in these struggles. Many southern Canadians have participated in campaigns to mobilize popular support for native rights and land claims.

Canadian society has much to borrow from the native conception of nature, the land, and development. The land and all it contains — air, water and soil, plants and animals — are gifts to be tended with an eye to the future. But there is much to learn, too, from the native people's experience of colonialism. In fact their historic resistance to colonialism has continued to the present day, to the point where many native people are now asking to be recognized as politically distinct.

The idea of native self-government raises certain problems. While the Canadian government officially encourages a policy of multiculturalism, for instance, can the country as a whole allow independent political, economic, and social structures within its own boundaries? The answers to this question, far from easy to work out, may help to shape the future of both the indigenous peoples and the other citizens who make this land their home.

Questions

- How do you see the land? How is your idea different from the traditional indigenous idea? What kind of "property" should the land be: personal (like one's own toothbrush), or family (a place to live), or private (controlled by an individual or group for the exploitation of resources), or communal (to be used, shared, and cared for by people)? How can these different ideas of property be fitted together?

- What are people's racial prejudices? How are they formed? How are Indians portrayed in movies and on TV? Has their image improved, in the media, over the past ten or twenty years?

- Looking at the huge tracts of land covered by the land claims, people ask, "How can the native minority want to control so much land?" Is this a legitimate question? Or is it based on a misunderstanding of what the native people are claiming? The Ojibwa at Bearskin Lake insisted, "We are not against development." What kind of northern development would be best — for native people? for the majority of Canadians? Is the best path that of megaprojects to exploit energy and resources for export? Or should native lands just be left alone? In struggling for their own rights, are native people contributing to the good of the whole country?

Resources

- Harold Cardinal, *The Unjust Society: The Tragedy of Canada's Indians,* Edmonton: Hurtig, 1969. A widely-read account of the plight of native people in Canada. Cardinal speaks of racial discrimination as a "buckskin curtain of indifference, ignorance and . . . plain bigotry."

- J.E. Chamberlin, *The Harrowing of Eden: White Attitudes toward North American Natives,* Toronto: Fitzhenry and Whiteside, 1975. This very readable work examines the relationships between "whites" and Indians, as well as the crucial land question. Differences between the Canadian and U.S. situations are pointed out.

- René Fumoleau, *As Long as This Land Shall Last,* Toronto: McClelland and Stewart, 1973. This is a comprehensive historical analysis of native land claims in the Mackenzie Valley, covering treaties 8 and 11 (1870-1939).

- P. Petrone, *First People, First Voices,* Toronto: University of Toronto, 1983. Covering the time of first contact up to the present, this is a collection of speeches and writings by native people themselves.

- "The Land is the Culture," Fred Cawsey, Keith Bradbury, Gundar Lipsbergs, 1975, 16 mm, 28 minutes. Made by the B.C. Union of Indian Chiefs, the film interviews Indians from different parts of British Columbia faced with the destruction of their way of life.

Resources (cont'd)

- "I Was Born Here," Marlin Motion Pictures for Department of Indian Affairs and Northern Development, 1977, 16 mm, 22 minutes. The Dene of the MacKenzie River Valley express their love for the land and their fears of development.

- Project North is an ecumenical coalition of the major Christian Churches, which supports native self-determination and aboriginal rights in the north, and encourages the Churches and the public in southern parts of Canada to support the native people in their struggles. Project North's work of research and advocacy has often helped to mobilize southern and non-native campaigns in support of native rights. 80 Sackville Street, Toronto, Ont. M5A 3E5, ph. 416-366-6493.

Chapter Thirteen

"A Woman's Place . . ."

Simone de Beauvoir's classic book *The Second Sex* describes the role of women in society from the earliest times. Its short title suggests the stigma that women — half of humanity — have borne in many societies. Wherever men monopolize the dominant positions, women exist merely to complement and serve "the first sex".

Many Canadians believe that a woman's proper place is at home, raising children and doing domestic work, while her husband — the head of the household — goes out to win the daily bread. They believe that the words "housewife" and "homemaker" describe exactly what women are and should do.

These beliefs, often held with deep conviction, are not merely personal, private opinions. Rather, they are assumptions widely accepted as normal and built into nearly all of society's major institutions. In fact, the pattern of husband on the job and wife at home emerged less than a century ago. Maybe it is really not so "normal" after all.

Their Proper Place

Nineteenth-century Canada was a largely rural society, with an economy based on agriculture. At that time the family unit was the centre of production. Men, women and children all contributed to the family's survival, helping the land yield its bounty. Women maintained the household, made the clothing, grew the garden, milked the cows and did dozens of other tasks. They bore and nursed the infants, but the children grew up living and working with both their parents.

A poem that appeared in the *Farmer's Advocate and Home Journal* in 1910 sums up the facts of life for women in 19th and early 20th century Canada:

She rose before daylight made crimson the east
For duties that never diminished.
And never the sun when it sank in the west
Looked down upon work that was finished.

She cooked an unending procession of meals,
Preserving and canning and baking.
She swept and she dusted,
She washed and she scrubbed,
With never a rest from it taking.

A family of children she brought in the world.
Raised them and trained them and taught them.
She made all the clothes and patched, mended
  and darned
'Til miracles seemed to have wrought them.

She watched by the bedside of sickness and pain
Her hand cooled the raging of fever.
Carpentered, painted, upholstered and scrapped
And worked just as hard as a beaver.

And yet as a lady-of-leisure, it seems,
The Government looks on her station
For now, by the rules of the census report
It enters her — No Occupation.

With ironic humour, this poem celebrates women's pivotal role in production and indispensable role in reproduction — roles no less important than men's. Without their labour the farm could not have functioned. Yet at the time when the poem was written, women could neither own a farm nor vote. Economically and legally, socially and politically, they were second-class citizens. Like children, they did not exist as persons in the public sphere.

The discrimination had its expression in laws but its basis was in beliefs about the nature of women, about their capacity and place in society.

In 1856 the Reverend Robert Sedgewick addressed an audience at the Halifax YMCA on the very question of women's "proper" place. The talk began with a short disclaimer. "In the economy of nature or rather in the design of God, *woman is the complement of man*. In defining her sphere and describing her influence, this fact is fundamental." The matter seemed so commonplace as to hardly merit discussion.

Still, as Rev. Sedgewick went on to explain, it was only in domestic pursuits that women could truly complement men. Some might dabble in other endeavours like biology, astrology, entomology or geology. But no woman could afford to remain ignorant of "the sublime science of washology and its sister bakeology. There is darnology and scrubology. There is mendology and cookology. . . ."

For this lecturer, domestic work was not a job anyone might choose, but a pre-ordained role inextricably connected with "natural" feminine characteristics. In fact, the limited access that women had to formal education was the main thing condemning them to "the sublime sciences" listed above.

With industrialization the factory began replacing the farm as the main arena of production. Men, women and even children who had left the farm now worked for wages in towns and cities, selling their labour to others rather than contributing as before to a family-based enterprise.

By the turn of the century, child-labour laws and other improvements won through early trade union struggles eliminated some of the worst injustices of the factory system. But the pattern of family life had changed. Husbands now spent the day away from home earning money while wives stayed behind and looked after the house, cared for the children and provided emotional support. Women worked as hard as ever, but "domestic" work was separated from "productive" labour.

During both world wars, when men enlisted in the armed forces by the tens of thousands, women filled many of the jobs they left behind. Women did the same work men had been doing on assembly lines and in the mills and smelters. Government advertising extolled their role in war production, picturing women marching to the plant in overalls, lunch bucket in hand. Women proved they could do "non-traditional" jobs. But when the men came back from the war, women were once again told that their place was in the home.

Job Ghettos

Since World War II, the number of clerical and service jobs in Canada has mushroomed, and women have been entering the salaried workforce in steadily increasing proportions. By the eighties over half of all women in this country were working for a wage. If present trends continue, women and men will be more or less equally represented in the workforce by the year 2000.

Women's paid work usually involves tasks like answering the telephone, typing and filing, ringing up sales, looking after the sick, caring for children, washing hair and waiting on tables. By

and large women fill clerical and service jobs, which are often seen as less important than production jobs and, of course, inferior to management.

At the same time men in Canada occupy nearly all the positions of authority and responsibility. They dominate the prestigious professions, the executive and managerial levels of business, and the world of politics. In other words, sex usually determines the kinds of jobs available to men and women.

According to this sexual division of labour, women are largely confined to "job ghettos" at the bottom of the employment hierarchy. Those jobs offer less control, less satisfaction — and less pay. A person's worth is all too often identified with the work they do, and the value of their work is measured by their pay (see chapter six).

According to the latest census data, women working full-time earn 64 per cent of the average man's salary. This is up from 49 per cent ten years earlier, reflecting increased unionization among women workers. But if *all* women workers — including those who cannot find full-time work

due to lack of child-care — are counted into the statistical picture, they were still earning just less than half (49.7 per cent) of what men earned at the beginning of the eighties.

Of course, not all women confront the same obstacles in the workforce. Those from middle class families are more likely to get the "proper" education, to have the right connections and experience that enable them to develop professional qualifications and rise to administrative positions in industry or government. It is women from working-class and poor backgrounds who tend to occupy the job ghettos. They begin with even more limited opportunities to "make it" onto an equal footing with male workers. But as the chart makes clear, in no occupation employing a significant proportion of female workers do women earn the same as their male colleagues.

Do women earn less than men because of their confinement to the lowest-paying jobs? Or are these jobs low-paid because women fill them? This chicken-and-egg question takes the analysis to the heart of the matter.

One justification sometimes given for paying

1970 and 1980 Average Incomes for Men and Women from the Largest Female Occupations of 1971

Occupation (Classification number)	Average Income for Men ($)		Average Income for Women ($)		Women's Income as a % of Men's	
	1970	1980	1970	1980	1970	1980
All occupations	6,574	21,623	3,199	13,773	48.7	63.7
Secretaries and stenographers (4111)	7,312	18,774	3,952	12,798	54.0	68.2
Sales clerks, commodities (5137, 5135)	4,262	17,538	1,803	9,697	42.3	55.3
Bookkeepers and accounting clerks (4131)	5,828	16,804	3,660	12,629	62.8	75.2
Elementary and kindergarten teachers (2731)	7,041	24,170	5,378	20,310	76.4	84.0
Waiters (6125)	2,992	10,851	1,442	7,681	48.2	70.8
Tellers and cashiers (4133)	3,813	14,049	2,325	10,294	61.0	73.3
Farm workers (7182)	1,784	10,158	1,322	8,424	74.1	82.9
Nurses, except supervisors (3131)	5,795	18,550	4,566	18,025	78.8	97.2
Typists and clerk-typists (4113)	5,110	16,338	3,066	11,788	60.0	72.2
General office clerks (4197)	5,364	16,594	3,326	12,315	62.2	74.2
Sewing machine operators (8563)	4,663	12,676	2,660	9,369	57.0	73.9
Personal service workers (6149)	2,583	12,230	1,554	9,378	60.2	76.7
Janitors (6191)	4,220	13,838	1,892	9,630	44.3	69.6
Nursing aides and orderlies (3135, 3134)	4,839	15,221	3,069	13,748	63.3	90.3
Secondary school teachers (2733)	9,152	26,580	6,762	23,130	73.9	87.0
Other clerical workers (4199)	5,552	18,276	3,032	13,348	54.9	73.0
Receptionists and information clerks (4171)	4,144	15,907	2,805	11,204	67.7	70.4
Chefs and cooks (6121)	4,000	13,026	2,299	9,561	57.5	73.4
Supervisors, sales, commodities (5130)	8,255	20,148	3,716	12,520	45.0	62.1
Packaging workers (9317)	3,524	15,390	2,520	10,907	71.5	70.8
Barbers and hairdressers (6143)	4,655	13,378	2,627	9,702	56.4	72.5
Telephone operators (4175)	4,480	16,762	3,108	11,787	69.4	70.3
Library and file clerks (4161)	3,850	13,845	2,847	11,771	73.9	85.0

Included are all the occupations which in 1971 contained at least one percent of the female labour force. The occupations are listed in the order of the number of women in them. Only those workers with some employment income are included in the calculation of average income.

women less is that female workers are not the *real* breadwinners — men are. Women are financially dependent on men. A woman's place is in the home; she does not really need a salary. If she works, it's for so-called "pin money", a little extra on the side for her personal whims.

In fact men frequently do not earn enough to support a family by themselves. In addition, many women no longer wish to be totally dependent on their husbands' wages. There are also 1.5 million mother-led families with children under six in Canada. Those women need an income to support themselves and raise their children.

Another justification for paying women less is what's seen as their uncertain or unreliable participation in the workforce. For instance, Geoffrey Hale, representing the Canadian Organization of Small Business, denies the existence of any discrimination against women. He argues that people of either sex get high-paying jobs simply on the basis of merit — education and experience. But, according to Mr. Hale, "Someone who is in and out, in and out, in and out, is less likely to have secure, continually-growing rates of pay than people — whether women or men — who are in long-term careers."

Working women do not necessarily *want* to enter and leave the work-force on a regular basis. Of course, the last weeks of pregnancy and early months of a child's infancy can take a woman out of the work-force at several points in her life. But the *biological* role by itself does not necessarily restrict her access to better-paid jobs or a long-term career. Rather, it is a woman's "duties" at home that restrict her eligibility for interesting and well-paid work. The real discrimination may be the assumption that her *social* role is essentially that of a dependant, a wife complementing her husband, a mother exclusively responsible for nurturing their children. That is her "long-term career".

A hidden justification for underpaying women is that their domestic work isn't paid, either. Cooking, cleaning, sewing and mending, raising children, caring for the sick and the infirm — these are vital tasks, often eulogized as such. But in fact domestic labour has been taken for granted and earns nothing at all. "No Occupation". Salary: zero. If that's what they're worth, why pay much more on the assembly line or at the typewriter?

Eliminating the ghetto would mean paying women the same as men who are doing jobs of comparable worth. For example, there is a gap of $1,784 between the maximum pay levels of female switchboard operators and male parking-lot attendants employed by the Ontario government. These could surely be described as jobs of comparable value.

Perhaps the economy does not need women to work without interruption. The "in and out" arrangement guarantees greater profits in many sectors. It is to the employers' advantage to have a reserve army of workers available when needed, with no choice but to accept lower pay, and vulnerable to dismissal when no longer needed. There is a vested interest in the sexual division of labour.

How often have women been heard to confess, "I'm just a housewife"? Low-paid jobs are usually not held in high esteem, and unpaid work is even less so. Women do both. If they want to "stay at home" and run a household or raise children, women should be able to do so. But either way, they cannot help feeling that society does not place much value on their contribution. If the traditional job ghettos were done away with, both women and men would be free to choose equally from among the variety of jobs — including homemaking and childrearing — that need doing.

The Double Day

If many women do move "in and out" of the paid work-force, it is because they have two jobs. A mother of two described her experience:

> All I have to say is that a working mother, when she has to work and leave her kids at home, it's pretty hard whether she's married or single. It's very hard. A mother that works and raises a family has to be pretty strong, very strong. I really feel sorry for the mother with the little kids — have to bundle them up in the morning and take them to the daycare centre and pick them up again at night. I wouldn't go through that again. It's too hard.

At the beginning and end of each weekday, many working women shop, provide meals for the family, transport the children to school or day-

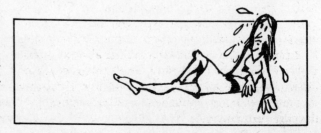

care, wash the clothes, do the dishes and clean the house. "The double day" is a term applied to these two daily shifts, one low-paid and the other unpaid. For in addition to eight hours on the job, the vital tasks of childrearing and housework are frequently a woman's to shoulder alone.

Clerical and service work is as important as assembling cars or managing a fast-food franchise. The childbearing is essential, the home-making is necessary. It's galling for women to hear how noble their calling is — yet have little freedom to choose what they do and also find their many responsibilities undervalued. It's especially difficult for a woman to live up to her own — and society's — expectations of what a mother "should be" while at the same time working as the breadwinner. Both roles are important. But given present arrangements at home and on the job, can they be humanly reconciled?

One problem for an ever-increasing number of parents is that very few subsidized daycare spaces are available. As a result, many women who both want and need to work must make the financial sacrifice of staying home with their children. Workers who are ineligible for the few subsidized daycare spaces find a good portion of their income gobbled up by expensive child care arrangements. It may be cheaper to arrange "informal" care in the home of someone who has her own children to look after anyway. This, the most common form of supervision, is often inadequate. Children being watched by a mother already overworked with housekeeping don't get the same attention, stimulation, creative play and companionship that they would get in a well-organized daycare programme.

> Adequate day care facilities are primarily the responsibility of the total community, including employers who benefit from the availability of women in the work force.
>
> It is the duty of the community which reaps the benefit of working mothers and pays for the plight of maladjusted children to take vigorous steps to meet the gaping need for adequate day care facilities. The community, on both the municipal and the provincial level, must assume the responsibility for setting and enforcing good standards for day care facilities, for ensuring that a sufficient number of such facilities is available to meet the need, and for bringing the cost of their use within the reach of the average family. The dimensions of the problem are too vast to consider any piecemeal approach adequate.
>
> At the same time, industry benefits even more directly from the services of working mothers. It is therefore incumbent upon industry to carry its share of the responsibility for providing sufficient day care services.
>
> *Lutheran Church in America — Canada Section,*
> **Fourth Biennial Convention,** *1969*

A mother explains the importance of daycare in overcoming the sexual division of labour:

> There can be no equality for women until we have equality in the home. As long as women have the primary responsibility for maintenance of the home and for child care, we will be less able than men to pursue job opportunities and our domestic commitment will be used to justify discriminatory employment practices. Free universal quality daycare is an essential element for equality of women in the labour force and for women's liberation in general.

Pin money, job ghettos, unequal wages and the double day represent obstacles that men generally do not face. Women, without denying their role in reproduction and the importance of nurturing children, do challenge the sexual division of labour and the double day. They are issuing a fundamental call for equal rights, equal dignity at home *and* on the job.

Women's Liberation

The past hundred years have been marked by important steps along the road known as *women's liberation.* The women's movement has won significant advances — the right to vote, the right to equal access to education, the struggle for equal pay for work of equal value. Yet many institutions still take advantage of women's secondary status and many men refuse to recognize them as equal partners at home and on the job.

The sixties and seventies saw a renewed feminist movement, which put new issues — everything from daycare to equal pay — onto the political agenda. Feminists have questioned basic assumptions about the place of women in relationship to men, the family and society. Of course the call to rethink such basic relations has elicited strong reactions on the part of both men and women.

Feminists have been labelled as angry "women's libbers" who aren't "real" women and don't appreciate motherhood. A 1983 magazine article about a feminist journalist (written by a generally-sympathetic male colleague) sketched this picture: "She is not just a feminist shouting down from a barren platform, but a whole woman, with frailties and silly obsessions and a love of children and dogs and cats." "Barren" (with its negative connotation of childlessness) juxtaposed with "whole" (communicating the idea of fulfillment) projects the caricature of feminists as a shrill, hard-hearted lot who surely hate kids, men and perhaps even dogs. What's behind the negative response? From among the many controversial issues, let's look at the role of the family and patriarchy, along with some common images of women.

Family

The family has been called a "haven" to which people can retreat from "a heartless world". But the heartless world with its economic hardships and cultural uncertainties has invaded the family to the point where the word "haven" does not describe the reality, if in fact it ever did.

The pressures on family life are illustrated by rising divorce and separation rates. Between 1952 and 1982 the divorce rates rose by six times. When marriages break up, it is the woman who usually gets custody of the children — often with little or no financial help from their father. The former wife becomes a single parent left to do the domestic work, provide financial support by working outside the home, and bring up the children.

Even if a family stays together, that does not mean that things are running smoothly. Some families enmesh their members in a web of fear and violence. The women's movement has contributed much to the recognition and public dis-

cussion of dramatic domestic problems. It is estimated that twenty-four thousand Canadians are battered wives. Indeed, wife battering is the single most important cause of injury to Canadian women. In addition, there is a connection to child abuse: One out of every four battered women was seriously abused as a child. The heavy caseloads carried by children's aid societies across the country testify to the numbers of children who are neglected, beaten or victims of incest.

Such incidents remained hidden behind the privacy of the home until the women's movement

forced them out into the open. Now there are shelters for women whose husbands or boyfriends attack them, where a battered woman can get counselling, help in finding a job, and the support of other women who have also suffered violence. Such shelters are urgently needed. Every time a new one opens, it's full within a week.

In the typical North American family, the father is "head" of the household but the mother is the real centre of domestic life. The father remains peripheral in many respects, especially to the raising of the children. The mother creates the home, provides emotional support for her husband, does all the domestic labour, brings up the children and, increasingly, earns a wage as well. The pattern is unfair to everyone. Women are demanding that it change.

In the words of one Canadian writer and mother,

Contemporary feminists have a much more complex view of mothering and the family than is generally thought. They no longer advocate (if, in fact, they ever did) doing away with the family or herding all children into state-run day care centres at six months. What they are doing is exposing some of the myths surrounding the family and women's place within it — myths which oppress not only women but men and children as well; and which prevent the family from being a vehicle for deep human love and commitment.

Thanks to a new awareness of the rights and duties of responsible parenthood, couples are sharing more equally than before the burdens and benefits of domestic work, from cleaning and cooking to parenting.

The pressures on family life are enormous. A more egalitarian pattern of family life contrasts with — and challenges — the father-led, mother-centred pattern. The questioning is having results, and those results spill beyond individual households to shape Canadian society.

> **As for us, let us recognize the ravages of sexism, and our own male appropriation of Church institutions and numerous aspects of the Christian life. Need I mention the example of the masculine language of our official — and even liturgical — texts?**
>
> **In our society and in our Church, man has come to think of himself as the sole possessor of rationality, authority, and active initiative, relegating women to the private sector and dependent tasks.**
>
> *Canadian Conference of Catholic Bishops,*
> **Intervention at the Synod of Bishops,** 1983

Patriarchy

What happens when, for reasons of tradition, culture and/or religion, men — simply because they are men — are assumed to hold all authority? The situation is called *patriarchy*, a very pervasive pattern of ideological assumptions and social structures.

An American churchwoman lists a series of examples where the pattern of patriarchy holds sway:

> Patriarchy is understood not only as the subordination of female to male but as a whole gamut of father-ruled social structures: master over slaves, aristocracy over workers, oligarchy over peasants, kings over subjects, racial overlords over colonized peoples, fathers over families, male religious leaders over the whole People of God.

The ideology and the structures reinforce one another. The belief in the secondary nature or status of women justifies the patriarchal structures; "father-ruled social structures" establish patterns of women's subservience to men.

In patriarchal societies, men control matters of finance, law, politics and religion. Men take on the role of protectors, leaders, representatives of and providers for women. The reasoning behind this is that, presumably, women are incapable of looking after themselves. The structural support comes from an unequal distribution of power.

Patriarchy may seem to have had a more obvious hold on pre-industrial Canada, but despite the advances Canadian society is still very patriarchal. Oppression based on sex determines the way both women and men see and live out the most basic relations, whether those relations are interpersonal, domestic, economic, social, cultural or religious. This oppression affects all women, men and children, but, like most forms of social injustice, its greatest negative impact falls on those who are poor.

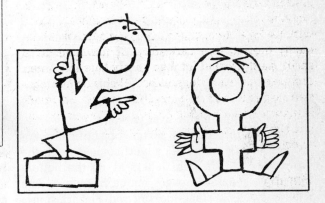

Women in particular racial or ethnic groups carry an extra burden. Immigrant women who do not speak English or French find it even harder to get work, obtain maternity leave and return to work than those who speak the language with ease. Immigrants, less certain of their rights under the law, can be more easily victimized by employers than women who have been in Canada all their lives.

Native women and women of colour, as "visible minorities", are not only subject to racial prejudice but also confront the same difficulties as white women in patriarchal society. Theirs is a double-edged discrimination and oppression.

Basic to feminist thinking is the belief that women and men are equal. By rejecting their consistently secondary, subordinate and subservient status, women question the patriarchal assumptions of Canadian society.

Images

A system based on patriarchy, and the difficulties women face within it, are neither new nor unique to Canada. In other societies and for thousands of years, women have lived in constant fear of assault, rape and violence. If women are subservient to men, then men can treat them as they wish.

In Canada, women are afraid to walk city streets at night. They live with the threat of wife-beating or (the more delicate phrase) "domestic violence", rape and the constant grind of sexual taunts and innuendo.

Domestic situations in which women depend on men for their economic survival — and at the same time are vulnerable to men — make it difficult to escape the violence. This is especially true when women have been culturally and socially conditioned to believe their only role and identity is that of wife and mother. When such a belief is deeply-engrained, a sense of duty makes it hard to run away, even if the home is a place of domestic horror.

Feminists campaigning against violence against women have frequently focused their efforts on the way women are portrayed in the media, in advertising and pornography. The stereotyping of women as sex objects — commodities to be bought, sold or possessed — reinforces male dominance over women.

An example of this sexual objectification of women is an automobile advertisement, with the word "Ferrari" in bold letters along the bottom and three separate images above the word. The first image is a sleek-looking red Ferrari sports car. It looks fast and expensive. Above this is a

bottle of Bordeaux wine lying on its side with the year 1928 visible on the label. It too is obviously expensive. The top image is a nude woman lying on her side, her body lit so that the curve of her hip is silhouetted along with a lock of blonde hair cascading over her shoulder. In small print are the two familiar words: "Decisions, decisions".

The advertisement causes the prospective (male) buyer to connect the three images. It suggests that all three *things* are desirable, high-quality and expensive commodities. The buyer must choose. It only takes money. Decisions, decisions.

> Pornography has an important function in society's oppression of women. It is the propaganda, the prop, supplying men with examples of society's model of masculinity. Pornography helps ensure women's sexual, social, political and economic oppression. It cannot be a coincidence that pornography exists in a society where women are raped, beaten by husbands, pushed into low-income work and generally not taken seriously.
>
> *United Church of Canada,*
> **Report of the Task Force on Pornography,** *1984*

Women are reduced to their bodies; their bodies — and even parts of their bodies — are reduced to the level of goods that the market offers to consumers. Similar images of women bombard us every day — in magazines, on billboards, on the bus, on television. They are used to sell cars, liquor, stereos or clothing. As women are demeaned as objects, so too are men constantly

discouraged from seeing them as equal persons. This process of objectification (see "reification/commodification" in chapter five) reinforces existing patterns of behaviour, so that violence against women and sexual harassment become everyday facts of life.

Towards Full Equality

The same society that wants woman at home gives her two jobs, pays her low wages and limits her choices; the same society that eulogizes the family and puts woman on a pedestal treats her as a disposable consumer good and an object of violence. The contradictions are glaring. On every count, whether the issue is domestic or economic, personal or social, women are discouraged from thinking of themselves as equal. That's why half the population has been described as "the second sex".

The law used to deny equality explicitly to women. They first won the right to vote in Manitoba in 1916. Only in 1929 were women recognized by the Canadian courts as persons. And it was not until 1940 that the women of Quebec could cast a ballot. In 1981, Canadian women succeeded in pressuring the federal government to include in the Charter of Rights of the country's new constitution a section guaranteeing women equal rights under the law.

This victory, after an intense political fight, was certainly a step forward for half the population. But the new constitutional guarantee represents only one more advance on the road towards full equality in all aspects of life. Women continue to struggle for more changes: They have asserted their own autonomy and dignity, especially through the suffrage movement and in trade union struggles.

At the present time there are many people seriously alarmed by the discontent among women. They say women are no longer contented with woman's work and woman's sphere.... Man has assigned woman her sphere. Woman's sphere is anything a man does not wish to do himself. This is a simple distribution of labour and easily understood and very satisfactory to half the population. Men have given a great deal of attention to women. They have told us what we are like. They have declared us to be illogical, hysterical, impulsive, loving, patient, forgiving, malicious, bitter, not any too honest, not very reliable. They have given us credit for all the good in the world and yet blamed us for all the evil.

These words were written around the time of World War I by pioneer women's rights activist Nellie McClung, who evidently realized that it would require more than adjustments in the law to achieve full equality for women. Only when patriarchy is abandoned will all people — men and women — achieve liberation from oppressive and exploitative structures and ideologies.

The domination of women by men on an individual level, in the family, is reproduced in the broader social and economic arena. The issues the women's movement has addressed, from rape and unequal pay to universal suffrage and daycare, have their roots in the way society is organized. Each advance towards greater dignity, equality and justice was won with great effort. It may be difficult to believe for those who feel threatened, but nevertheless, what the women's movement is struggling for contributes to the liberation of all Canadians.

Questions

• Geoffrey Hale, the same spokesman who claimed that the wage system is based solely on merit, also said that laws guaranteeing equal pay for work of equal value would be too expensive. Such laws have been passed only by the federal government and the government of Quebec and just apply to government employees. Is it enough to legislate equal pay for work of equal value? What other forms of social trans-

Resources

• Pat and Hugh Armstrong, *The Double Ghetto: Canadian Women and their Segregated Work*, Toronto: McClelland and Stewart, 1978. Careful statistical analysis of job ghettos, as well as several different explanations for the discrimination that women face in the work-force.

• Jennifer Penney, *Hard Earned Wages*, Toronto: Women's Press, 1983. Lively, moving and read-

formation need to be achieved in order to assure this right?

- Is women's traditional role in the family "natural"? To what extent is it socially-defined? What are some of the main factors that have contributed to women's secondary position in society? Is this rooted in personal relationships or social relationships?

- Ideology (see chapter ten): people's perceptions of their own social roles are linked with, and reinforce, the dominant social structures. Chauvinism (named after a soldier of Napoleon I) is defined in Webster's dictionary as unreasoning devotion to one's race, sex, etc. with contempt for other races, the opposite sex, etc. Did this chapter provide any new perspectives on these two notions of ideology and chauvinism?

- Should the fact that it is women who bear children and nurse them mean that women should be confined to the home for years? Should women have the exclusive, or even the primary, responsibility for child care and housework? Should the family be a place where such rigid roles prevail that women have but few options and are even subject to violence? Or, in a changing society, can a new kind of family allow women, men and their children to support one another mutually in all the tasks of life?

- What has been the position of the Christian churches on significant women's issues? In what ways has the role of the churches been liberating? in what ways repressive? Would the women's movement in Canada look to the churches for support in struggling for equal rights? On which issues? If not, why not? Are any of women's demands incompatible with the Christian message and way of life?

able stories of women's struggles in the workplace, based on interviews with women who have broken down the barriers to employment in "male" occupations.

- Maureen FitzGerald et al., eds., *Still Ain't Satisfied!* Toronto: Women's Press, 1982. An anthology of twenty-seven articles on the major personal, economic and social issues women have dealt with over the past ten years.

- "On the Bias," Development Education Centre, Toronto, slide-tape, 30 minutes. The experience of women working in the clothing industry.

- "Women Want...," International Cine-Media (International Women's Year Secretariat of the Privy Council), 1975, 16 mm, 27 minutes. Women's struggle for liberation, in different social sectors, is a struggle for equality and self-determination.

- "Heroes and Strangers," colour, 16 mm, 29 minutes. While most public attention on the family has centred on the mother's role and its demands, benefits and limitations for women, this film opens a discussion about the role of the father, suggesting that such discussion assures a more satisfying family life for both men and women. Contact Lorna Rasmussen, 467 Shaw Street, Toronto, Ont. M6G 3L4, ph. 416-531-3108.

- For further information, contact the Canadian Advisory Council on the Status of Women, Box 1541, Station B, Ottawa, Ontario, K1P 5R5, ph. 613-992-4975.

Chapter Fourteen

Canada in the Americas

Tiny Grenada, jewel of the eastern Caribbean, spice island of a hundred thousand people. In February 1979 a swift coup brought Maurice Bishop and the New Jewel Movement into power. For over four years the Bishop government worked to increase literacy, reduce unemployment and improve access to health care. It fought malnutrition with the regular free distribution of milk to poor children. Through regular parish meetings Grenadians were gaining an unprecedented voice in nearly every aspect of government policy.

Bishop's New Jewel Movement enjoyed good relations with Canada, Cuba and many Third World countries, but suffered the implacable hostility of the United States.

In October 1983 Grenada was suddenly shaken by the dramatic arrest and then murder of Prime Minister Bishop. President Reagan claimed that Grenada was on the verge of becoming a Cuban colony or an outpost of the Soviet Union, that it threatened the security of neighbouring islands, and that American citizens (especially 600 students at the St. George's University medical school) were in danger. On October 25th, U.S. forces invaded Grenada.

Canadian foreign policy generally favours non-intervention and the peaceful resolution of conflicts. In the case of an invasion, how did Canada relate to Grenada and respond to the United States? This chapter analyzes Canada's foreign policy, specifically towards the Caribbean and Central America. It looks at Canada's principles and traditions in foreign affairs, and at citizen participation in formulating foreign policy. Such an analysis, although directed outwards, is a look at ourselves — at the Canada that others see.

Canada Shut Out

Links between Canada and the Caribbean islands go back centuries and are formalized in shared membership in the Commonwealth. Important relationships include aid, trade, Canadian tourism, Caribbean immigration and diplomatic ties.

Canada was a good friend to Grenada in both diplomatic support and generous aid — nearly $1.6 million in bilateral aid in 1982-83 and nearly $500 thousand in support of projects undertaken by NGOs (Non-Governmental Organizations) such as OXFAM-Canada and CUSO. Canada's stated purpose in the Eastern Caribbean was to protect the region from the vagaries of Latin American politics and from direct U.S. interference.

During the critical ten days after Bishop's arrest, the press was reporting the build-up and movement of U.S. forces, especially on Barbados, as indications of U.S. intentions. Canada could have played a role to nullify the immediate excuses for intervention and thus lessen the likelihood of an invasion. External Affairs waited passively, however, and events overwhelmed its Caribbean policy.

The United States did not consult Canada beforehand "because of concerns on the security side that the invasion shouldn't be too widely known", according to Deputy State Secretary Kenneth Dam. The Reagan administration showed Canada neither respect nor trust. But even the opinion of the conservative British Prime Minister Margaret Thatcher, who opposed the military invasion of Grenada, did not carry any weight with the United States.

Canada's Caribbean allies did not inform Canada because they knew that Prime Minister Trudeau would disapprove. Jamaica and Barbados, "as facts show, were determined to support an invasion," Trudeau explained in the House of Commons. "They know that Canada is not in the habit of supporting invasions of other countries."

While underway the invasion endangered a number of Canadian aid workers. Before and afterwards, U.S. military authorities and local allies stymied Canadian evacuation attempts by refusing Canadian transport planes permission to leave Barbados or to land in Grenada. The invasion did receive the popular support of the Grenadian population anguished by Bishop's murder. But less drastic actions — such as diplomatic pressure, economic sanctions or a quick transition to civilian government — could have restrained the post-Bishop regime and guaranteed regional security.

The invasion of Grenada affected the political process not only in Grenada but also in the entire region. According to economist Kari Levitt, a specialist in Caribbean studies:

> The effectiveness of the Caribbean community, which would have been able to normalize the Grenada problem subsequent to the murder of Prime Minister Bishop, was destroyed by the actions of the governments of Barbados, Jamaica and the small islands of the Eastern Caribbean.

The invasion represented an irreversible setback for the Caribbean — and a diplomatic debacle for Canada. The government's limited expression of opposition to the invasion had no restraining influence on the subsequent projection of U.S. military power in the Caribbean.

Jamaica later apologized to Canada for failing to inform one of its closest allies of a momentous development in its "sphere of influence". But "the Commonwealth Caribbean", editorialized Toronto's *Globe and Mail*, "really isn't a Canadian sphere of influence after all. This middle power mythology has been rudely shattered by the military invasion of Grenada." Did Canada have a real "sphere of influence"? Is the role of "middle power" an effective stance or just a cover-up for inaction? Has Canada proven itself incapable of an active role in the Americas? Such are the painful questions raised by the tragic October of Grenada.

The cries for justice multiply and become more anguished each day. Their message must be heard in national and international conferences where relations among nations are discussed.... It is imperative that representatives of many peoples speak out with united voice in defence of the victims of repression.

Inter-Church Committee on Human Rights in Latin America, **Submission to the United Nations Commission on Human Rights,** 1982

Internationalism

Canadians have a positive image of their government playing an important, distinctive role in promoting global peace and development.

Lester B. Pearson, career diplomat and politician, was awarded the Nobel Peace Prize for his peacekeeping efforts in the Middle East before becoming Prime Minister. After leaving public office Pearson chaired a World Bank study of Third World development. The Pearson report, published under the title *Partners in Development,* urged the North to co-operate with the South in eradicating world poverty and challenged each developed country to bring its Third World aid up to a level of 1 per cent of its GNP.

Pearson's internationalist spirit was carried forward by Prime Minister Pierre Elliott Trudeau in his efforts to promote "a revolution in international morality". Trudeau first tried to bridge the concerns and energies of the First and Third Worlds through a North-South dialogue culminating in the Cancún Conference of 1981. During his last year in office (1983-84), Trudeau launched a peace initiative aimed at promoting demilitarization by resuscitating talks between the superpowers of East and West.

Its internationalist principles have involved Canada in alleviating tensions within both axes of global conflict: East-West superpower confrontation and North-South economic and political inequalities. Canada's image is that of a helpful mediator and of a contributor to world institutions, such as the United Nations, which promote international law. "Much of Canada's post-war self-confidence", argues political scientist Stephen Clarkson, "was based on the sense that it had a useful role to play as a middle power unsullied by imperialist ambitions." Canadian internationalism means an enlightened involvement in foreign affairs, opposed to both isolationism and interventionism.

Canada shows a growing awareness of its own international interests. Today the nuclear arms race is the most burning international issue as it poses an increasing, nearly unimaginable danger to each one of us and to our children. In an all-out confrontation between the United States and the Soviet Union, Canada's own airspace would provide the site of such a nuclear war. Even if Canadians survived the war itself, our northern climate would condemn us to death in the first post-nuclear winter. The Second Cold War of the mid-eighties catches Canada up in the deteriorating relations between West and East.

Canada has interests, too, as a highly dependent trading nation, 30 per cent of whose GNP is generated by exports. It stands to benefit economically from the future prosperity and stability of its Third World partners. An acute economic crisis, on the other hand, would threaten Canada's share of global trade and cost its banks an estimated $25 billion in bad loans to Latin America and the Caribbean alone. Humanitarian and security concerns, especially in this hemisphere, motivate Canada's interest in international affairs.

Despite its good image and intentions, Canada's record is a mixed one. Canada promotes North-South dialogue, but its aid remains well below the targets of the Organization for Economic Co-operation and Development (in 1984-85, less than half of Pearson's 1 per cent) and largely tied to the purchase of Canadian goods and services. When acting as a mediator, as on the International Control Commission in Viet Nam, Canada sometimes fails to act impartially and objectively.

A report from the North-South Institute in Ottawa sums up Canada's international resources and opportunities in this way:

First, it is clear that Canada can do very little *on its own* to solve major world problems. Second, however, in a tautly-interdependent world, with political, military and economic power being increasingly dispersed over many regions, world problems can no longer be managed by the superpowers. These problems must be managed collectively. Among the disparate group of "middle powers", from both North and South, with enough clout and credibility to lead in defining new collective management, and in radically improving existing multilateral systems, Canada emerges, insistently and naturally, because of both its traditions and its interests.

With its tradition of helpful fixer and its clear interests, with the needs so urgent and the stakes escalating, why would Canada not act?

Real Constraints

Of the various factors conditioning Canada's international role, the most important is the massive bundle of relationships with the United States. "No other two countries in the world", says External Affairs, "have so complex and extensive a relationship as Canada and the United States." The dependence has become so pervasive that in Canada political relations with the United States are often treated as a domestic rather than an international issue.

Economic and military relationships exemplify two kinds of dependence:

- Canada and the United States are each other's most important supplier and customer (two-thirds of Canadian exports, valued at $55.5 billion in 1981, go to the United States).
- U.S. direct and portfolio investment in Canada totals about $70 billion, translating into U.S. control of 30 per cent of Canada's mining sector, 47 per cent of oil and gas and 34 per cent of manufacturing.
- Militarily Canada is tied to the United States through NATO (North Atlantic Treaty Organization) and four bilateral agreements covering: continental air defence (NORAD); bilateral defence policy planning (Permanent Joint Board of Defence); military equipment development and production; and the testing of military systems (such as the Cruise Missile).

Just as economic and military, so too political and cultural ties overwhelmingly favour the United States. There are several festering bilateral disputes: fishing rights, border demarcation, foreign investment, acid rain and the Auto Pact deficit. In the hope of retaining Washington's goodwill for resolving these issues, Canada tends to refrain from any serious deviation from U.S. policy.

The invasion of Grenada dealt Canadian foreign policy a considerable defeat. But even before that event, the crises in Central America were putting Canada's internationalist reputation and traditions to the test.

> **Our mandate to expose and condemn violations of human rights in Latin America is not only based on statements of Church leaders and councils, but it is also in response to the cries of the victims themselves, who clamour to heaven for redress: the grieving mothers of the disappeared and murdered, the tortured political prisoners, the peasants driven from the land they have toiled on for generations, the homeless orphans traumatized at seeing their parents killed before their eyes. . . .**
>
> *Inter-Church Committee on Human Rights in Latin America,* **Submission to the United Nations Commission on Human Rights,** *1982*

Central America

European colonization brought poverty to Central America. Malnutrition, scandalous levels of infant mortality, disease and a short life have been the lot of the region's poor for centuries. During the twentieth century the standard of living deteriorated steadily as the peasant majorities lost access to agricultural land.

Today Central America hosts multiple crises. Subjugated, long-suffering peoples are struggling for social justice and to see their countries become modern nations. Citing each country briefly:

- *Guatemala* — "More than 100,000 civilians have been murdered by government forces in the last decade", 15,000 between early 1982 and December 1983, with entire communities wiped out by military units.

- *El Salvador* — Indiscriminate aerial bombing — some of it guided by sophisticated electronic scanning — is escalating the war's civilian death toll. The casualties, according to María Julia Hernández, a human rights lawyer with the Archbishop of San Salvador's Legal Aid office, "are children, women, old people. I am not talking guerrillas."
- *Honduras* — The original "banana republic" is the poorest and most undeveloped country in Central America. Chosen to be a second Canal Zone by the United States, its fledgeling democracy is drowning in a flood of military aid, and human-rights violations are on the increase.
- *Nicaragua* — Externally-based *contras* (or counter-revolutionaries), largely drawn from the ranks of dictator Anastasio Somoza's former National Guard, rely on U.S. "covert" aid to make military strikes. Nicaraguan communities, rather than strategic targets, are attacked. From January 1982 until March 1984 civilian victims totalled 747 people.
- *Costa Rica* — Self-styled as the Switzerland of Central America for its democracy and neutrality, Costa Rica has been the historical exception to the regional pattern of poverty and repression. There is a relatively better distribution of income, but the need for land reform persists and the country is under pressure to militarize. Cut-backs in social services, imposed by the International Monetary Fund as the condition for maintaining Costa Rica's credit-worthiness, are causing misery to spread.

"Central America in 1984", reported the Inter-American Dialogue (a private group of leading hemispheric academic and political personalities), "is a region at war. Polarization, violence, repression, and destruction are prevalent. The human suffering is staggering; 150,000 people have been killed and almost 1.5 million have been displaced in the last five years."

The roots of Central America's revolutions,

French President François Mitterand told a joint session of the U.S. Congress,

lie deep in the legacy of the past. Thus, the peoples of Central America have a long history marked by military oppression, social inequality and the confiscation of economic resources and political power by the few. Today, each of them must be allowed to find its own path toward greater justice, greater democracy and greater independence and must be allowed to do so without interference or manipulation.

But the United States interprets indigenous aspirations for social justice as externally-provoked threats to its own security.

During most of this century, the United States used to enjoy complete, unquestioned pre-eminence over all of Latin America. Canadians have occasionally debated the relative merits of being in the "front yard" of the United States, but Latin America has always languished in its "back yard", where national aspirations never success-

	Vital Statistics 1981				
	Population (000's)	Life Expectancy (years at birth)	Infant Mortality (aged 0-1, per 1000)	Per capita Income (U.S. $)	Adult Literacy (per cent)
Guatemala	7,100	59	66	1,198	40
El Salvador	4,750	63	75	680	50
Honduras	3,700	59	86	640	40
Nicaragua	2,700	57	88	897	90
Costa Rica	2,500	73	27	1,520	90
Grenada	111	69 (1979)	27.6 (1976)	625 (1980)	95
Canada	25,000	75	10	11,400	99

fully overcame Washington's preponderant political and military role.

"As the dominant power in the area for a century, the United States bears considerable responsibility for the conditions that burst into revolutions," says Cornell Professor Walter LaFeber. Twentieth-century Central American history is a pattern of frustrated reform and aborted social change.

The U.S. administration considers its image to be at stake. Its determination to "draw the line" in Central America has transformed the region into a militarized platform in order to make credible its threats against the Soviet bloc. Washington's tactics are superimposing East-West dynamics of confrontation on North-South dynamics for change and thrusting the region into the Cold War.

For example, when U.S.-supplied and -deployed mines damage a Soviet ship entering a Nicaraguan harbour, it takes very little imagination to see a future incident providing the catalyst for a direct and uncontrollable confrontation between the superpowers. "The more people [i.e., U.S. military] you have on the spot, the more chance you have of casualties and the more chance you have of confrontation with Sandinista troops and their Cuban advisors or the Salvadorean guerrillas," Senator Jeff Bingaman said. "The risk taking has increased," he said, "and so have the chances of an incident that could be used to justify direct American military involvement." Central America, dragged into the currents of global tension, is a potential "nuclear trigger".

President Miguel de la Madrid of Mexico warned that "The risk of a generalized war, the scope and duration of which no one can foresee, is growing." This must be avoided by:

> rejecting interventionist solutions of any kind. To that end let us apply the principles and rules of international law established by the countries of the American continent: self-determination, non-intervention, equality of states before the law, peaceful solution of conflicts and international cooperation for development.

Washington's penchant is to turn back the clock and reassert its past pre-eminence over all the Americas through a reliance on traditional military intervention. This leaves the Americas, especially Central America, poised on the verge of regional war: a tragic mistake of epic proportions.

> The growth of militarism and its renewed alliance with the United States in this hemisphere, provide both reason and necessity for a fresh restatement of Canadian official commitment to fundamental human rights in this hemisphere, and to the liberation of particular neighbours from particular yokes of repression.
>
> The voices which can speak for the oppressed in the Western Hemisphere are very few. Thus, when Canada fails to act ... the loss is felt particularly and deeply.
>
> *Inter-Church Committee on*
> *Human Rights in Latin America,*
> **Submission to the United Nations**
> **Commission on Human Rights,** *1982*

Canadian Connections

Given that geography, history and language have distanced us from Central Americans, Canadians may have long seemed aloof from the trials and tribulations of their Central American neighbours. Today social, political and economic crises increasingly tie us together and force Central America into our political lexicon.

In fact Canada has not been entirely absent from Central America. Canada's economic interests in the region are modest but growing. In the early 1900s William Van Horne brought his expertise to Guatemala to build a railway in partnership with an American general and the United Fruit Company. INCO at one time had the region's largest single foreign private investment, its $250-million nickel mine in Guatemala (it proved unprofitable and was prematurely closed). But direct investment is not as significant for Canadian business interests as loans and trade. Exact banking information is unavailable but 1978 statistics, indicative of Canadian involve-

ment, showed the Royal Bank to be the second-most important private creditor to Nicaragua.

Between 1970 and 1981 two-way trade with the region grew by over 470 per cent to $350 million. These ties have been strengthened by an increase in Canadian development assistance to the region. The Canadian International Development Agency (CIDA) is required to tie at least 80 per cent of bilateral aid to purchases of Canadian goods and services. Aid boosts trade. Aid commitments, which averaged approximately $10 million per year in the late seventies, doubled to about $20 million annually by the mid-eighties. Central America, which comprises only 8 per cent of Latin America's population, receives nearly 50 per cent of CIDA's total aid budget for the region (excluding the Caribbean).

Over the years Ottawa has occasionally taken a distinctive stand in hemispheric affairs. In the early sixties Prime Minister John Diefenbaker refused to cut relations with Castro's Cuba. More recently Prime Minister Pierre Trudeau proclaimed Canada's belief in hemispheric political pluralism:

In our view, states have the right to follow whatever ideological path their peoples decide. When a country chooses a socialist or even a Marxist path, it does not necessarily buy a "package" which automatically injects it into the Soviet orbit. The internal policies adopted by countries of Latin America and the Caribbean, whatever these policies may be, do not in themselves pose a security threat to this hemisphere.

This enlightened approach is in the Canadian tradition and only needs to be put into practice.

A group of Canadian academics, associated in Canada-Caribbean-Central America Policy Alternatives (CAPA), reports:

Canada maintains high credibility with Latin America. As the continent's second-wealthiest country, it is also in the unique position of being close to both the United States and Western Europe. These factors enable Canada to resolve conflicts, to bridge political and even ideological gaps between hostile countries or forces, to unravel complex and highly-charged issues, and thus to fulfill a significant positive role as a middle power in the Americas.

A continuing deterioration of events in Central America is obviously not in Canada's interest. Given a proven ability to act, Canada should contribute actively to a peaceful resolution of the regional crises. But can Canada challenge the United States over Central America without suffering retaliation?

The example of Mexico

In the past Canada has relied on acquiescence with U.S. foreign policy in the hope of gaining reciprocal benefits in bilateral conflicts. Stephen Clarkson analyzes Canada-U.S. relations and concludes that "Trading good Canadian deeds internationally for American concessions bilaterally proved remarkably unsuccessful in the late Seventies and early Eighties." Is there any alternative, whereby Canada could gain greater autonomy, defend its sovereignty, win respect and be treated more as an equal by Washington in its bilateral dealings?

Mexico, like Canada, is a contiguous neighbour of the United States, sharing a myriad of complex and difficult bilateral issues. Moreover, due to its foreign debt (some $80 billion in 1984), Mexico is extremely vulnerable to Washington's economic policies. Despite that, there is every indication that Mexico's highly principled and involved foreign policy on Central America has prompted Washington to take Mexico more seriously.

"The countries of Latin America seek, in conditions of equality and mutual respect, a new kind of relationship with the United States," Mexican President Miguel de la Madrid told a joint session of Congress. "They want to do away with any shadow of subordination while preserving sovereignties and national identity. For us, independence is not a part of our past but a daily conquest. It is the supreme value of our history."

Mexico is not alone. Other middle powers — Argentina, Brazil, Colombia and Venezuela — have also emerged to challenge the historic hegemony of the United States. If Canada is confident enough to join them, it would help lay to rest Latin America's logical reservations about the strength of Canada's backbone.

"Sometimes Latin America wishes for more from Canada regarding the United States," a Mexican official complained to *Globe and Mail* reporter Oakland Ross. "When the accounts are settled, Canada is always in favour of the United States."

Canada is very much the welcome if reluctant debutante on the inter-American scene.

According to CAPA, as a close American ally, Canada:

> has every reason to question Washington's ideologically-led commitment to a narrow course of action. Canada's special responsibility is to help develop "face-saving" options for an administraton caught in a cycle of escalating militarization. Canada could help the U.S. both grapple with the changes at its doorstep and accept its changing regional status.

The Canadian government appears to appreciate the gravity of the situation in Central

America. There are a number of obvious and positive steps that could be taken:

- In Central America itself Canada must overcome its handicap of insufficient diplomatic presence. The embassy in Costa Rica covers that country as well as Nicaragua, El Salvador and Panama.
- The Canadian government needs to develop its own information, analysis and perspective, rather than rely on U.S. sources. These range from the U.S. media through the State Department to the intelligence agencies that co-operate with the RCMP and the Canadian Security Agency.
- The Canadian foreign service, with a mentality of dependence on the United States, must overcome its self-limiting and short-sighted timidity. Traditional and novel diplomatic tools — not just those of quiet diplomacy — need to be applied in an adroit, aggressive, creative and energetic manner.
- Canada should support regional peace initiatives, such as the Contadora process (spearheaded by Mexico, Venezuela, Colombia and Panama), with more than mere words.

- Canada and the United States, as External Affairs noted in spring 1984, have agreed to disagree on Central America. But verbal disagreement by itself contributes little to resolving the regional crisis. The Canadian government must act on Canada's own global interests, which admittedly differ from those defined by the U.S. administration, while at the same time staying on a good footing with its most important neighbour.

- In the fast-moving world, as the Grenada invasion showed, Canada cannot rest content on the pious expressions of laudable principles. To remain trapped in a sort of psycho-political dependence on the United States betrays Canada's global *and* domestic interests. That is why Central America turns out to be a decisive litmus test of Canadian foreign policy in the eighties.

> **The choice confronting the people in Jesus' time confronts the Churches in Canada today and, in many ways, Canada itself as one nation among other nations. We are not the most powerful of nations. We are in the ambiguous middle — neither the gross violators, nor the wielders of power. Yet the inter-connectedness of our world brings the human rights issues of the world not only to our attention, but also to our doorstep.**
> *Inter-Church Committee on Human Rights in Latin America,* **Submission to the United Nations Commission on Human Rights, 1983**

Foreign Policy Becomes Democratic

Many Canadians got started on social analysis through concern about an international issue: starvation in Biafra, martial law in the Phillipines, the grape and lettuce boycott in California, the war in Viet Nam, repression in Chile and Argentina, the challenge of development in Zambia and Tanzania, the struggle against racism in Rhodesia and South Africa, the ongoing conflicts in the Middle East. The terrible poverty, malnutrition, injustice and violence that characterize the lives — not just of a few unfortunates — but of whole peoples and entire regions motivated many of them to begin doing social analysis. They raised critical questions, rejected self-serving explanations, co-operated in acts of solidarity, and sought to change unjust structures. Many solidarity groups and learner's centres were organized in the sixties and seventies to raise consciousness and protest atrocities overseas. The 1973 coup in Chile shocked Canadians, and thousands of Chilean refugees contributed to the awareness in Canada of what's happening in Latin America.

Grass roots interest in Central America began to mushroom in the late seventies. The dramatic "option for the poor" made by many Christians there, the tragic social costs of the externally-prolonged struggle, and worry about the ominously deteriorating security of the hemisphere all served to capture attention and concern. The Canadian churches have consistently spoken and acted on Latin American issues through several ecumenical coalitions: Ten Days for World Development (1973), the Taskforce on the Churches and Corporate Responsibility (1975), the Inter-Church Committee on Human Rights in Latin America (1976), the Inter-Church Committee on Refugees (1980). Through these coalitions, the churches have informed public opinion, put pressure on repressive governments, and contributed to the positive evolution of Canadian policy.

Thanks in no small part to the work of the church coalitions, the late seventies saw more Members of Parliament getting involved in criticizing our Latin American policy. In 1981 the first Parliamentary sub-committee was formed to examine Canada-Latin America relations. In its 1982 concluding report the Sub-Committee on Canada's Relations with Latin America and the Caribbean proposed that Central America be a region of concentration in Canada's foreign policy and that Canada take the initiative in promoting regional discussions.

Since 1982 Canadian scholars and researchers have worked together in CAPA (Canada-Caribbean-Central America Policy Alternatives) to develop effective, flexible and pragmatic options that the Canadian government might adapt in its relations with the region.

Various educational, solidarity, church, academic and labour groupings have carved out a role in the definition of foreign policy. The result has been to begin making the policy more effective and more democratic.

"The true north strong and free", the refrain from our national anthem, is a proud phrase that projects an image of strength and independence. That image by itself is more myth than reality. The fact, as we have seen, is that Canada is a modest, dependent power, yet with its own important resources, traditions and interests in international affairs. More and more citizens are asking that all these means be devoted energetically towards global justice and peace.

Questions

- What do you know about institutions that mediate international relations — for example, the International Monetary Fund, the World Bank, the United Nations, the World Court. In whose interests have they been set up and maintained? What role does Canada play in them?

- Review some of the ways in which people in your area — through NGOs, churches, trade unions and solidarity groups — have shown support for the people of Central America. In what ways have these same groups criticized Canadian policy towards the region? What role have human rights criteria played in the formulation of our foreign policy on Central America — what role should they play?

- What does the U.S. government mean by its "national security interests"? Do these interests justify the military presence of the United States in Central America? How does the U.S. government back up its claim that the conflicts in Central America are a ferment inspired by the Soviet Union and its proxy, Cuba? How would you sort out the East-West from the North-South issues in those conflicts?

- List all the links that bind Canada and the United States together. Compare these with a list of all the differences between the two countries. What effect do economic ties have on political

Resources

- Stephen Clarkson, *Canada and the Reagan Challenge: Crisis in the Canadian-American Relationship*, Toronto: James Lorimer in association with the Canadian Institute for Economic Policy, 1982. The book meticulously traces Canada-U.S. relations up to 1982, destroying the myth of the "special relationship" and identifying the growing divergence of interests between the two countries.

- Hugh O'Shaughnessy, *Grenada: Revolution, Invasion and Aftermath*, London: Sphere Books, 1984. British journalist O'Shaughnessy points an accusing finger at both superpowers. The Caribbean, he writes, was "sucked into a superpower confrontation which it had, until then, successfully avoided." He predicts an increasing embitterment of Eastern Caribbean politics and higher defence costs for all countries of the region.

- Latin American Working Group (LAWG) has been providing documentation, analysis and public education since 1966. For further information on particular countries or issues, or for the names of local solidarity groups, write to LAWG at P.O. Box 2207, Station P, Toronto, Ont. M5S 2T2, tel. 416-533-4221.

- *Central America Update*, a bi-monthly co-publication of LAWG and the Jesuit Centre,

Questions (cont'd)

relationships? To what extent could Canada pursue its own foreign policy more independently of the United States? Is there a role for Canada as a middle power between the two superpowers?

• The media focused great attention on Grenada at the time of the invasion. How was that event cast for public consumption? Has Grenada been in the news recently? What has happened in that country since the invasion? What kind of presence does Canada have in Grenada, and what role does the United States play?

Resources (cont'd)

reports on events in the region, analyzes the response of U.S. and Canadian policy, and lists the latest resources. A one-year subscription is $11. P.O. Box 2207, Station P, Toronto, Ont. M5S 2T2.

• The national ecumenical coalitions involved in Central American and Caribbean issues are:
   Inter-Church Committee on Human Rights in Latin America, 40 St. Clair Avenue East, Toronto, Ont. M4T 1M9, ph. 416-921-4152.
   Inter-Church Committee on Refugees, 40 St. Clair Avenue East, Toronto, Ont. M4T 1M9, ph. 416-921-4152.
   Taskforce on the Churches and Corporate Responsibility, 129 St. Clair Avenue West, Toronto, Ont. M4V 1N5, ph. 416-923-1758.
   Ten Days for World Development, 85 St. Clair Avenue East, Room 315, Toronto, Ont. M4T 1M8, ph. 416-922-0591.

• CAPA (Canada-Caribbean-Central America Policy Alternatives) brings together Canadian academics and researchers interested in Central America and the Caribbean. CAPA is linked with similar networks in the region, the United States, South America and Europe. CAPA, 947 Queen Street East, Toronto, Ont. M4M 1J9, ph. 416-469-1123.

Chapter Fifteen

We Have Just Begun

"Would you like a coffee?"

The example of a cup of coffee, which launched the questioning in *Getting Started* fourteen chapters ago, rounds it out in this chapter with the description of a unique trading company. It's the story of one solution. But many, many solutions are needed to all the problems unearthed by social analysis. This book, while not spelling out the solutions, suggests that an inevitable corollary to social analysis is the search for positive action. That search has to be guided by certain priorities, from addressing the needs of the poor and dominated classes to the necessity for participation. That search, as we will see, also carries social analysis into the realm of the political — and joins that realm closer to everyday life.

The Bridgehead Story

"There's a fortune in your teacup — but who gets it?" The poster on the wall of the small, in-home office of Bridgehead Trading suggests a business intent on something other than corporate growth and maximum profit. The "bottom line" here is clearly not shareholders' dividends.

The Toronto-based company was set up in 1981 with the idea of bridging the gap between struggling Third World food producers and concerned consumers in Canada. This meant, in effect, taking on the multinational corporations (MNCs) which, by controlling processing, marketing, technology and capital, control the prices paid for Third World commodities. The strategy of Bridgehead Trading was to bypass the MNCs that dominate the trade in food from the Third World.

Bridgehead's small warehouse occupies the basement of a church in a Toronto Greek neighbourhood. The walls are lined with cartons of vacuum-packed coffee and tea-bags, boxes of cashew nuts and cashewnut butter. Angie Pritchard, one of the four co-founders of Bridgehead, is justifiably proud of the firm's success. In 1983 sales of Sri Lankan tea, Nicaraguan and Tanzanian coffee and Mozambican cashews doubled over the previous year to a quarter-million dollars. In 1984 they were expected to double again and reach half a million dollars.

"Bridgehead is marketing products made in

the Third World," Angie Pritchard explains, "retaining enough of the profits to cover operating costs and then sending the remaining funds back to the Third World." In one project, for example, Bridgehead returned $4,000 to Nicaragua to help set up a coffee vacuum-packing plant.

The Bridgehead members aim to keep operating costs low in order to return as much as possible to the original source of the product. This reflects a trade structure that is markedly different than the norm. MNCs typically concentrate their processing and packaging (along with the jobs these activities create) in the industrialized countries. As Canadians know to their own cost, the value of a finished product is many times greater than the value of the raw materials it is made from. Therefore, to encourage local processing, Bridgehead's policy is to import its food as ready-to-sell as possible from the country where it was grown.

In other words, Bridgehead Trading is confronting some of the questions asked about the cup of coffee in chapter one. Bridgehead is trying to restructure some of the relationships between all those people who get the cup of coffee ready, from the seedling stage to serving the drink.

Bridgehead Trading is an example of social analysis leading to action. Its founding members had been working in development education, raising Canadians' awareness of the inequality and injustice of an international economic system dominated by western corporations, banks and governments. According to this analysis, Canadians were condemned to serve as accomplices in the economic exploitation and political oppression of agricultural workers in the Third World. Was there any way — besides a boycott of certain products — to act in solidarity with those farmers and food industry workers?

From Words to Action was the title of the timely 1979 Labour Day statement of the Canadian Conference of Catholic Bishops:

> It is not enough to see injustice, disorder, and violence at home and abroad and to worry about the future. These conditions will not improve on their own. We, the people, have the responsibility to change them.

With this statement as the catalyst, Bridgehead Trading took form.

"After years of analyzing global poverty, you have to do something, take a stab at it yourself," says Peter Davies of Bridgehead. "We didn't start out as another sort of charity — but as a way of

bringing producers and consumers together in new and fairer relationships."

Bridgehead Trading was born out of social analysis. It is based on a sharp critique of unjust marketing structures, national no less than global. It counters the excesses of the profit motive by recycling funds. Its alternative trading pattern challenges the dominant structures of ownership, marketing, distribution and retail sale. It expresses solidarity and eschews the unfair competition of giant MNCs versus tiny Third World producers. Compared with the dimensions of the problem it is trying to address, Bridgehead Trading is at once a most modest and a very successful operation.

Bridgehead also gets further analysis started. Its very success raises questions about the food industry in Canada. If alternative trading makes sense, why are there not thousands of bridge-building companies? If alternative trading makes sense for Third World producers, could Canadian farm products be marketed in a similar way?

The Game

Think of the struggle for social and economic survival in Canada as one great game. According to the Canadian sense of fair play, everyone has a good chance to win and no one should triumph at the expense of others. The final goal of the game is power — which in essence means some kind of control over the rules of the game. Relatively few people ever achieve that goal, unfortunately.

Commercials on TV serve up the Canadian game in its slickest form. Secure and youthful families, made happy by the products they consume, relax on warm summer afternoons. There's always clean air, good food and abundant energy.

But for people who do social analysis, the TV commercials raise questions: Where are the blizzards, the polluted rivers, the Indians, the bag ladies, the unemployed? What about the housing crisis, the upheaval caused by microtechnology, the old folks shunted off to the side?

According to conventional wisdom, there must be something wrong with people who ask such questions.

- They have proven unable to compete in Canada as it is. They're just poor losers.
- They resent the success of others. As moralizers and chronic complainers, they enjoy criticizing. They like to take all the fun out of the game.
- They exaggerate the plight of the poor and disadvantaged, who after all are relatively few in an otherwise prosperous and egalitarian country.
- They overlook the countless benefits of life in Canada and don't know how good they have it. They are simply ungrateful.
- They have an anarchistic or subversive streak in them. They seem to be addicted to change for its own sake.

But there is a different explanation for why people ask such critical questions. Social analysis, which begins with the ordinary problems of everyday life, soon makes it clear that commercial advertisements portray a false Canada. In the real Canada, the environment is imperilled, machines threaten to displace workers, many people live out on the edge and corporate rather than human values often seem to prevail.

The game is rigged, social analysis tells us, and the deck is stacked. The stated rules and principles are one thing, but how they work is quite another. Behind the rhetoric of "a just society" and "equal opportunity" and "free competition", most of the relatively few winners are predetermined by accidents of birth: class, sex and race. Some people have a head start. Many others — like women, the aged, natives, the poor and unemployed who can't find decent work or homes — never get into the official game at all.

Getting Started analyzes Canadian society from the viewpoint of those who have been cheated or unfairly penalized. The analysis speaks up for those who remain on the sidelines and have no role to play.

But is it enough to point out, over and over again, that the game is rigged? Does social analysis, and the concerns it nourishes, translate into anything besides talk and more analysis?

"What can we do?"

Spontaneously bursting into action may satisfy one or two people for a little while but it rarely proves effective. Action deserves careful planning. Just as analysis is best developed in the give-and-take of discussion, so action is best decided upon together too. The decisions to be made are many: pursuing a question further, getting into deeper research, joining a group, contacting other people, taking collective action.

The question of action seems to come "at the end", yet social analysis is oriented towards action right from the start. Social analysis, as defined in *Getting Started*, means *raising questions about society and seeking answers*. It helps *to develop a critical awareness of the world*, that is, of how and against whom the deck is stacked, how the rules are bent or broken, and for whose benefit. By uncovering concrete, particular instances of foul play that people can *do* something about, social analysis also helps *to lead towards social justice.*

"We can't afford to change"

Social analysis seems to cry out for answers, but easy answers, ideal models of society or perfect social organizations waiting to be copied do not exist. Thorny problems abound everywhere. Even Bridgehead Trading, a real success story, is no easy answer. A package of recipes for change or one overarching scheme of reforms won't be found in *Getting Started*.

If there are no answers, then what is the point, many will ask themselves, of getting involved in social analysis and change? (See the "Social Paralysis Quiz", at the end of chapter one.) Here are several reasons why Canadians feel reluctant to get involved:

- Some are comfortable and don't want to be disturbed — even though their comfort starkly contrasts to the pain of many others.
- Others feel sorry for the victims of injustice. They hope the poor, whether in Canada or the Third World, will get a better shake. But these sentiments are short-circuited by other values, for example, faith in "the marketplace" or in "freedom of opportunity". Believing there are no class barriers in Canada — just as there are supposed to be no racial or sexual barriers — people also believe the poor can "make it" if they only put in the effort: They will gradually move into the middle class and their problems will be solved.
- Some Canadians who do admit to the existence of social injustices are blocked by the fear that any potential solution will prove as expensive and messy as the original problem.
- Many Canadians long for peace and security but are convinced they can do nothing to change the injustices that inevitably lead to poverty, violence and war. Their longing remains abstract and sentimental.

Personal comfort and security, vague longings for peace, empty sympathy for the unfortunate, fear of future complications — these attitudes leave many Canadians paralyzed and powerless. The dominant ideology either denies that the problems are real or claims they can be solved by tinkering. This only reinforces the sense of paralysis. Proposed solutions are easily dismissed as idealistic, partial and unfeasible. Thus the status quo is — apparently — justified.

But *not* addressing the issues proves very costly. For the status-quo argument overlooks the tremendous human, economic and social costs of accepting the current patterns of social and economic relationships. Each chapter of this book demonstrates that the present situation is an all-too-messy and unfair one. The system not only fails to work, it cannot work for significant numbers of Canadians:

- women, old people, native people;
- the unemployed and the underemployed;
- those victimized by the crisis in medicare or threatened by the revolution in micro-technology;
- several million in search of decent affordable housing;
- all of us who are losing the right to a safe and healthy environment.

The decision to maintain things as they are contains its own acute contradictions and holds out little promise for the future. The burden of proof should be on those who would claim that change will be too costly and painful. Anyone who begins to do social analysis will quickly be forced to ask, "How can we afford not to change?"

Beyond Paralysis

The stories of South Riverdalers confronting lead pollution (chapter four), telephone operators unionizing at Bell to deal with technological change (chapter eight), native people furthering their land claims (chapter twelve), and Bridgehead Trading challenging world trade patterns (earlier in this chapter) — these are all good examples of solutions in progress. In each case, people confronted an injustice, figured out what was wrong, developed a strategy and began to build an alternative. Other examples may be found in the *Resources* at the end of nearly each chapter, where further readings and groups to contact are listed.

Envisaging alternatives and shaping solutions involves people's feelings and values. How do social analysts sort out the various voices, the conflicting interests, the competing needs, rights and demands? A simple principled commitment provides the guiding thread. In the words of David Hollenbach, a Catholic social philosopher:

> The needs of the poor take priority over the wants of the rich. The freedom of the dominated takes priority over the liberty of the powerful. The participation of marginalized groups takes priority

over the preservation of an order which excludes them.

These three priorities make challenging criteria for orienting social analysis and grounding the solutions that emerge. Many people in Canada would affirm them wholeheartedly, at least in theory. But can they be put into practice? Yes, if the problem is concrete and if it carries with it the possibility of concrete solutions.

First, the needs of the poor, the imprisonment of the dominated and the exclusion of the marginalized need to be clearly considered. To come to an appreciation of these needs, this imprisonment and exclusion *in the concrete* is a task of social analysis. Social analysis, by providing the necessary tools for understanding the real problem in particular cases (instead of producing merely vague feelings about social injustice in general), can help people to honour these priorities in practice.

Second, people need to envisage concrete, viable solutions — solid alternatives to the problems analyzed. People need to imagine change. Most chapters of *Getting Started* contain examples of people working together — often with the help of others from outside their group or class — and solving their own problems. Stories of change taking place, the failures no less than the successes, need to be exchanged among people doing social analysis.

The moral of all the stories: The way things are is not how they have to be.

Participation

In the mid-eighties two top corporate executives, Brian Mulroney and John Turner, were anointed leaders of the two main Canadian political parties in the same Ottawa hockey arena. These events, embellished with American-style hoopla and months of wearying media hype, represented a high-water mark in coverage of federal politics.

The process of selecting a national leader — whom Canadians get to vote for or against — seems no more participatory than the "vote" about what will be on the supermarket shelf (see chapter six). Unless they were journalists or a relative handful of delegates, few Canadians participated in any significant way. Maybe it's normal for people who feel powerless to also feel apathetic about party politics. Some would argue there's more participation in a Stanley Cup play-off.

What falls within the realm of the political? At first sight, politics refers to elections, town councils and legislatures. Between elections Canadians tend to leave not only party politics but also social issues in the hands of parliamentarians and aldermen. That is a pity. Federal, provincial and local representatives can be made responsive to pressure from their constituents and be enlisted to help resolve certain issues. Letter-writing, personal lobbying and even the ballot-box have proven useful. Public administrators can also be identified, informed and pressured to help solve social problems. These methods, however, are effective only to a degree.

Though politics includes the public management of many (and often the most important) aspects of daily life, very many Canadians remain excluded from social, economic and political decisions. They take part only in the most peripheral ways. Leadership conventions and elections bring a kind of selective change from the top-down, but do not often result in any significant shift of policies or power.

Social analysis is both a condition for, and a form of, participation. Without social literacy (see chapter five), people cannot take an intelligent — much less an active and creative — part in the issues unfolding around them. At the same time the very activity of social analysis, especially in a group, helps to "lift the fog" and overcome ideological confusion (see chapter ten). It can lead right into effective action.

Through social analysis, citizens can overcome their sense of intimidation — or cynicism — in the face of bureaucracy and conventional politics. The experience of social analysis can gradually involve people more and more in the management of their own lives. At the same time, to do social analysis in Canada is to realize how truly complex and ambiguous is the Canadian game. It is not a simple conflict of good guys versus bad. There is no central conspiracy that has complete power over the rules.

The only just — the only democratic — approach to these complexities is found in the arduous, risky process of participation. In this way, the notion of democracy expands beyond the ballot-box, the notion of politics stretches to include daily life.

Participation, not a new theme, runs through all of *Getting Started*:

- *Part One* — Confronting basic health, housing and environmental problems, people gather information, develop their own expertise and set up alternative organizations. A committee to fight pollution, a tenants' group, a neighbourhood taskforce to set up a health centre — the participants may solve the immediate problem and at the same time win some control over fundamental aspects of their lives.
- *Part Two* — Many basic issues have economic roots and, besides, the economy itself displays many shortcomings. Who is going to solve these immediate and structural problems? A just, participatory and sustainable society requires whole new ways of organizing production, work and consumption. Beginning to provide the needed creativity are all sorts of union initiatives, new small businesses, workers' and consumers' co-ops, government projects and self-help groups — or, in other words, people participating in what we might call economic democracy.

- *Part Three* — A different light is cast on basic and economic issues when looked at from the viewpoint of others. Each group — old people, native people and women — promises to contribute to society in important ways, but this cannot occur unless the members of these groups gain a new level of self-determination. Third World peoples struggling for their own liberation not only win our solidarity for their struggle but also provide us an inspiring example for our own.

Participation grows and increases in three interrelated steps: basic control, economic democracy and political self-determination. At no stage does participation provide ready-made solutions; but it does provide the *means* of approaching the solving. Participation is not a platform or a stopgap measure, much less is it just a means or a temporary tactic. Participation is a goal that makes many other goals possible. It is one very important fruit of social analysis.

At the same time, participation is a first step and often a very small one. The crime, as the philosopher Edmund Burke once said, is to do nothing because we fear we can do only a little. But small changes are important in themselves. Moreover, they can generate a so-called *critical mass*, a movement that eventually makes a heretofore impossible change inevitable. Each of these local, partial solutions helps to improve the workings of society. At the same time, few of those solutions will endure or fulfill their total promise without large-scale structural transformations of this country.

People come together to analyze a problem. They overcome social paralysis and discover a power of their own. They run into blocks, difficulties and obstacles. As they confront them, they generate more power. They move beyond the ballot-box. They press for significant change, demanding adequate public notice and more opportunity for input when major decisions are made. Social analysis guides this progression through basic economic and social issues. Participation nourishes the connections among people across the country who are doing social analysis, working on concrete issues locally and regionally, contributing in novel ways.

What can happen in Canada if people link up together, raise questions together and participate together in a collective analysis and a search for collective solutions? We have truly just begun.

Resources

Users of *Getting Started* who want to reflect further on social analysis or compare the approach taken in this book with other approaches will find the following resources helpful:

- Joe Holland and Peter Henriot, *Social Analysis: Linking Faith and Justice*, revised edition, Maryknoll, N.Y: Orbis Books, 1983. This book introduces social analysis as part of the pastoral cycle and analyzes U.S. society through three models of social change — traditional, liberal and radical. The concluding chapter on practical methodology discusses elements of social analysis (structures, history, values) as in chapter five of this book; how the different kinds of structures (economic, political and cultural) each generate their own set of questions; and how the information gathered can be analyzed and judged.

- GATT-Fly, *AH-HAH! A New Approach to Popular Education*, Toronto: Between The Lines, 1983. This novel approach begins by identifying the key social categories — the economy, political structures, economic structures — in a local context and generating questions from them. It follows up with something close to the rules of social literacy in chapter five here: the need to generalize, to look at history, to link up the various structures, to see how they fit together in a system.

- Christian Movement for Peace, *People Living for Justice*, five volumes, Dubuque: Wm. C. Brown, 1983-1984. Each volume introduces students to social analysis through the treatment of concrete social justice issues. The five themes are human labour, women's issues, militarism, economic questions of human development and human rights issues. This explicitly Christian approach relies on the Bible to provide ethical criteria for judging the particular issue being analyzed. Besides high school teachers, it will appeal to those interested in the task of theological reflection.

- John W. Foster and Virginia R. Smith, eds., *Signs of the Times: Resources for Social Faith*, new edition, Toronto: United Church of Canada, 1984. Excerpts from articles and talks on a wide variety of social issues, both Canadian and international.

- John R. Williams, ed., *The Canadian Churches and Social Justice*, Toronto: Anglican Book Centre, 1984. The Canadian churches' controversial statements on social, political and economic issues from 1970 to the present — from which many of the boxed quotations in this book were taken — are here republished in one handy volume.

- Canadian Conference of Catholic Bishops, *Witness to Justice: A Society to be Transformed:*

Resources (cont'd)

Working Instruments, 1979. The three parts of this very complete collection of resources treat the relationship of faith and justice, a dozen justice issues in Canada, and a dozen issues of justice in the Third World.

- Elizabeth Amer, *Yes We Can! How to Organize Citizen Action*, Ottawa: Synergistics Consulting, 1980. Chapter 4 contains helpful suggestions on where to go for information: libraries, government offices, periodical indexes, public interest groups (a list of these at the back of the book).

- Rick Arnold and Bev Burke, *A Popular Education Handbook: An educational experience taken from Central America and adapted to the Canadian context*, Toronto, n.d. Available in local CUSO offices and international resource centres, or order directly from CUSO Development Education, 151 Slater Street, Ottawa, Ont. K1P 5H5.

- CUSO, *How You Can Get Involved in Canada*, revised edition, Ottawa: CUSO Development Education, 151 Slater Street, Ottawa, Ont. K1P 5H5, 1983. This very practical resource lists groups in Canada on an issue-by-issue basis as well as regionally, and provides a comprehensive list of alternative media sources.

- For further information on alternative trading organizations, write to OXFAM Trading, 251 Laurier Avenue West, Room 301, Ottawa, Ont. K1P 5J6, ph. 613-237-5236.

- For further information on the social analysis project connected with *Getting Started*, to send criticisms or new ideas, contact the Jesuit Centre, 947 Queen Street East, Toronto, Ont. M4M 1J9, ph. 416-469-1123.

References

Each endnote is identified by the page number, the left-or right-hand column ("a" or "b"), and the line number. Sub-titles do not count as lines. Thus "10a43" identifies the reference to the quotation on page 10, the left-hand column, 43 lines from the top.

Preface

10a43: *33rd General Congregation*, Rome, 1983, paragraph 47.

Chapter One
Welcome to Social Analysis

16a7: Canadian Conference of Catholic Bishops, *A Society to be Transformed*, Ottawa, 1977, no. 12.
16a30: Canadian Conference of Catholic Bishops, *Ethical Choices and Political Challenges*, Ottawa, 1984, p. 2.

Chapter Two
In Sickness and in Health

20a22: D.U. Himmelstein and S. Woolhandler, "Medicine as Industry: The Health-Care Sector in the United States," *Monthly Review* 35 (April 1984), p. 14.
20b5: E.M. Hall, *Canada's National-Provincial Health Program for the 1980's*, Ottawa, 1980, p. 2.
20b12: M.A. Baltzan, "Deductible insurance could rationalize medicare," *Canadian Medical Association Journal* 126 (1982), p. 550.
20b46: National Council of Welfare, *Medicare: The Public Good and Private Practice*, Ottawa, 1982, pp. 53-59.
21a24: P.E. Enterline et al., "The distribution of medical services before and after 'free' medical care — the Quebec experience," *New England Journal of Medicine* 289 (1973), pp. 1174-1178.
21a26: A. McDonald et al., "Effects of Quebec Medicare on Physician Consultation for Selected Symptoms," *New England Journal of Medicine* 291 (1974), p. 651.
21a34: P. Manga, "Income and Access to Medical Care in Canada," in D. Coburn et al., eds., *Health and Canadian Society: Sociological Perspectives*, Toronto, 1981, p. 340.
21b15: J.E. Bennett and J. Krasny, "Health Care in Canada," in Coburn, *op. cit.*, pp. 40-66.

21b21: P. Starr, "The Laissez-Faire Elixir," *The New Republic,* April 18, 1983, p. 19.

21a28: Ontario Ministry of Health, *Final Report of the Task Force to Review Primary Health Care,* Toronto, 1982, p. 1.5. G.L. Stoddart, *Paying for Health Care: The Canadian Perspective Today,* Hamilton Program for Quantitative Studies in Economics and Population, Research Report 2, January 1982, pp. 9-10.

21a32: Montreal *Gazette,* Sept. 12, 1983.

21a50: Ministry of National Health and Welfare, *Preserving Universal Medicare,* Ottawa, 1983, p. 21.

22a24: P. Rich, "Don't look now, doctor, but . . . Profession highest paid in Canada," *Medical Post,* Feb. 8, 1983, p. 18.

22a28: Toronto *Globe and Mail,* Jan. 12, 1983.

22a29: *CBC-Radio News,* Oct. 23, 1982.

22a32: E. Holmes, "O.M.A. Income Survey: No Surprises in 1980," *Ontario Medical Review* (1982), p. 378.

22a45: National Council of Welfare, *op. cit.,* Appendix B.

22b14: H. Krahn, "An argument for opting out," *Canadian Medical Association Journal* 126 (1982), p. 1340.

23a13; *Toronto Star,* Jan. 22, 1983 and Montreal *Gazette,* Sept. 12, 1983.

23a28: Ministry of National Health and Welfare, *op. cit.,* p. 12.

24b8: T. McKeown, *The Role of Medicine: Dream, Mirage or Nemesis,* Princeton, 1979.

24b27: City of Toronto, *Brief to the Health Services Review '79,* Toronto, 1980, p. 2.

24b46: Bureau of Epidemiology, Health and Welfare Canada, *Cancer Patterns in Canada, 1931-74,* Ottawa, n.d, pp. 177-81 et passim; Statistics Canada and Health and Welfare Canada, *Cancer in Canada,* Ottawa, 1982, p. xviii.

25a18: E.P. Eckholm, *The Picture of Health: Environmental Sources of Disease,* New York, 1977, p. 90.

25b47: V. Kelman, "Community Health Centres," *Canadian Dimension* 13 (May 1979), pp. 43-46. L. Lee, "A Community Oriented Approach to Primary Health Care," *Canadian Family Physician* 29 (1983), pp. 2319-2325.

Chapter Three
The Housing Drama

29b1: Toronto *Globe and Mail,* Nov. 13, 1982.

29b11: M. Goldberg, *The Housing Problem: A Real Crisis?* Vancouver, 1983, p. 89.

30a16: R. Block, "Shelter for the poor," *Maclean's,* March 12, 1984.

30a22: J. McClain and C. Doyle with the Canadian Council on Social Development, *Women and Housing:*

Changing Needs and the Failure of Policy, Ottawa, 1984, pp. 73-74.

30a32: *Today,* Jan. 30, 1982.

30b16: H. Aubin, *City for Sale: International Financiers Take a Major North American City by Storm,* Montreal/Toronto, 1977, pp. 22-26.

30b26: D. Capponi, *Phoenix Rising,* November 1982.

30b33: Toronto *Globe and Mail,* Dec. 7, 1981.

31a9: Capponi, *op. cit.*

31b21: J. Fleming, "Developers: the cost of survival," *Maclean's,* April 2, 1984.

31b27: Financial Post Corporation Service, 1982.

31b38: *Report of the Federal Task Force on Housing and Urban Development,* 1969, quoted in G. Barker et al., *Highrise and Superprofits,* Kitchener, 1973, p. 98, italics in original.

32b47: Toronto *Globe and Mail,* Feb. 9, 1984.

32b50: Toronto *Globe and Mail,* March 15, 1983.

33a4: CMHC, *Annual Report,* 1983 and CMHC *Capital Budget,* 1984 Calendar Year.

33a25: J. Lorimer, *The Developers,* Toronto, 1978, p. 64.

33a35: United Church of Canada, *ISSUE* 26 (1982), p. 3.

34a11: Personal interview, Toronto, Ont., Jan. 18, 1984.

34a16: Toronto *Globe and Mail,* April 13, 1982.

34a28: D. Martin with S. Goetz-Gadon, *The Great Apartment Sale: The Tenants' Perspective,* Toronto Metro Tenants' Legal Services, 1984.

34a35: Toronto *Globe and Mail,* April 23, 1982.

34b31: Toronto *Globe and Mail,* Nov. 17, 1983.

35a28: *Today,* Jan. 30, 1982.

37a25: Canadian Conference of Catholic Bishops, *Decent Housing For All,* Ottawa, 1976, paragraph 7.

38a6: *Ibid.,* paragraph 11.

38a16: B. Ward, *Human Settlements, Crisis and Opportunity,* Ottawa, 1974, p. 2.

Chapter Four
Our Planet Earth

41a2: J. Nriagu, "Properties and the Biogeochemical Cycle of Lead," in J. Nriagu, ed., *The Biogeochemistry of Lead in the Environment,* New York, 1978.

41a4: National Academy of Sciences, *Lead in the Human Environment,* Washington, 1980.

41b10: National Research Council, *Effects of Lead in the Canadian Environment,* Ottawa, 1978.

41b14: Toronto *Globe and Mail,* April 9, 1983.

41b30: J. Nriagu, "Lead in the Atmosphere," in Nriagu, *op. cit.*

41b31: Environment Canada, *Lead and Gasoline*, Ottawa, 1983, p. 2.

41b35: H.V. Warren, R. Delevault and W. Fletcher, "Metal pollution — a growing problem in industrial and urban areas," *Canadian Mining and Metallurgy Bulletin* (July 1971), pp. 1-12.

42a2: H.E. Hawkes and J.S. Webb, *Geochemistry in Mineral Exploration*, New York, 1962, p. 367.

42a12: J.F. Jaworski, *Effects of Lead in the Human Environment — 1978; Quantitative Aspects*, Ottawa: National Research Council of Canada, 1978, Publication no. 16736, p. 628; Brunswick Mining and Smelting Corp. Ltd., *Proposed Electrolytic Zinc Reduction Plant, Belledune, New Brunswick, Environmental Impact Assessment*, 1981, p. 133.

42a15: T.M. Roberts, W. Gizyn and T. Hutchinson, "Lead contamination of air, soil, vegetation and people, in the vicinity of secondary lead smelters," in D.D. Hemphill, ed., *Trace Substances in Environmental Health — VIII*, Columbia, Missouri, 1974, pp. 155-166.

42b8: V.P. Garnys, R. Freeman and L. Smythe, *Lead Burden of Sydney School Children, Parts 1 and 2*, Kensington, Australia, 1979; H.L. Needleman et al., "Deficits in Psychological and Classroom Performance of Children with Elevated Dentine Levels," *New England Journal of Medicine* 300 (1979), pp. 689-695.

42b34: For two accounts of the South Riverdale lead controversy see C.C. Lax, "The Toronto lead-smelter controversy," in W. Leiss, ed., *Ecology Versus Politics in Canada*, Toronto, 1979, pp. 57-71, and R. Howard, *Poisons in Public: Case Studies of Environmental Pollution in Canada*, Toronto, 1980, chapter 5.

43a18: South Riverdale Community Health Centre, *Health Lines*, Toronto, 1984, p. 6.

43a43: Working Group on Lead, *Studies on the Relationship of Environmental Lead Levels and Human Lead Intake*, Toronto: Ontario Ministry of the Environment, 1974.

43a48: Robertson Committee, *Effect on Human Health of Lead from the Environment*, Toronto: Ontario Ministry of Health, 1974.

43b6: Toronto Residents' Associations, *Submission to the Environmental Hearing Board*, Toronto, 1975.

43b14: Environmental Hearing Board, *Lead Contamination in the Metropolitan Toronto Area*, Toronto, 1976.

43b50: City of Toronto Department of Public Health, *South Riverdale Blood Lead Testing — 1983*, Toronto, March 1984, p. 1.

43b53: Toronto *Globe and Mail*, April 20, 1984.

44a2: *Canada Gazette*, Part 1, Feb. 18, 1984, p. 1421.

44a6: Dr C. Patterson in National Academy of Sciences, *Lead in the Human Environment*, Washington, 1980, p. 272.

44b22: Toronto *Globe and Mail*, Nov. 27, 1973.

44b52: Lax, *op. cit.*, pp. 61-62.

45b2: *Ward Seven News*, Toronto, April 8, 1983.

45b37: Toronto *Globe and Mail*, April 6, 1984.

47b22: Toronto *Globe and Mail*, Oct. 14, 1982; emphasis added.

Chapter Five
Social Analysis Again

52a12: E. Gaber-Katz, "The Politics of Literacy: Educating for Continuity," in L. Rainsberry, ed., *Out of the Shadows*, Toronto, 1983, p. 56.

52a21: A. Thomas, *Canadian Adult Basic Literacy Resource Kit*, Toronto, 1979, p. 22, cited in H. Alden, *Illiteracy and Poverty in Canada: Toward a Critical Perspective*, University of Toronto Master's Thesis, 1982, p. 2.

52a23: Gaber-Katz, *op.cit.*, p. 59.

56a14: J. Holland and P. Henriot, S.J., *Social Analysis: Linking Faith and Justice*, Maryknoll, New York, 1983, p. 28.

Chapter Six
Lost in the Supermarket

60a29: M. and R. Friedman, *Free to Choose*, New York, 1981, p. 57.

60a47: *Canadian Grocer*, June 1982.

60b5: Statistics Canada, cited in D.P. Ross, *The Canadian Fact Book on Poverty*, Toronto, 1983, p. 7.

60b9: National Council of Welfare, *1983 Poverty Statistics*, Ottawa, August 1983, p. 3.

60b-graph: D.P. Ross, *The Canadian Fact Book on Income Distribution*, Toronto, 1980, p.12.

61b17: Ontario Public Interest Research Group (OPIRG), *The Supermarket Tour: A Handbook for Education and Action*, Waterloo, 1978, p. 43.

62a28: *Canadian Grocer*, May 1982.

62ab-graph: Toronto *Globe and Mail*, Dec. 12, 1983.

63a25: Toronto *Globe and Mail*, Nov. 2, 1983.

63b30: OPIRG, *op. cit.*, p. 13.

64b33: Diane Francis, "Swallowed Alive," *Canadian Business*, July 1981, p. 56.

65a8: Corporation and Labour Unions Returns Act, *Report for 1981*, Table 9.

65a-graph: Francis, *op.cit.*, p. 58

65b6: *Ibid.*

65b44: P. Newman, *The Canadian Establishment*, Vol. I, Toronto, 1975, p. 55.

66a25: Newman, *op. cit.*, p. 65.

66ab-graph: Statistics Canada, *Productivity — Commercial Industries — Indexes*, 14-201; *National Income and Expenditure Accounts*, 13-001; *Public and Private Investment in Canada*, 67-205; the same data may be found in *Bank of Canada Review* (annual publication).

67a55: GATT-Fly, *Power To Choose: Canada's Energy Options,* Toronto, 1981, p. 28.

67b-graph: R.L. Sivard, *World Military and Social Expenditures, 1982,* Leesburg, Virginia, 1982, p. 19.

67b7: R.J. Barnet and R.E. Muller, *Global Reach: The Power of the Multinational Corporations,* New York, 1974, pp. 14-15.

67b22: Statistics Canada, *Economic Review,* 1983, Tables 68 and 71.

70a16: Canadian Conference of Catholic Bishops, *Sharing Daily Bread,* Ottawa, 1974, paragraph 1.

Chapter Seven
The Plague of Unemployment

72b17: Social Planning Council of Metropolitan Toronto, "Hidden Unemployment," *Social Infopac 3* (February 1984).

73b24: *Toronto Star,* April 9, 1983.

73b36: Toronto *Globe and Mail,* Sept. 12, 1983.

74b27: Adam Smith, *The Wealth of Nations* [1776], New York: Random House, 1937, p. 355.

75ab-graph: Statistics Canada in *CUPE Facts,* February 1983

75b23: Personal interview, Sudbury, Ont., April 24, 1983.

76b-graph: U.S. Bureau of Labour Statistics in *CUPE Facts,* February 1983.

77a7: Toronto *Globe and Mail,* April 14, 1983.

77b25: Personal interview, Bathurst, N.B., Jan. 18, 1984.

78a2: Toronto *Globe and Mail,* March 2, 1983.

78a55: Toronto *Globe and Mail,* Sept. 9, 1983.

79a39: *Financial Times,* March 19, 1984.

79b41: Canadian Conference of Catholic Bishops, *Ethical Reflections on the Economic Crisis,* Ottawa, 1983.

Chapter Eight
Microtechnology and the Future

81a21: Toronto *Globe and Mail,* Feb. 10, 1983.

81b29: Toronto *Globe and Mail,* May 4, 1983.

82a43: IBM ad, *The London Times,* Jan. 14, 1982.

82b33: Toronto *Globe and Mail,* May 13, 1983.

83a24: E.P. Thompson, *The Making of the English Working Class,* Harmondsworth, 1969, chapter 14.

83a34: Quoted in *Canadian Interchange,* no. 38, 1981.

84b30: Northern Telecom, "TOPS For People and Profit," cited in J. Kuyek, *The Phone Book,* Toronto, 1979, p. 69.

85a16: Quoted in Kuyek, *op. cit.,* p. 69.

86a25: H. Menzies, *Computers on the Job: Surviving Canada's Microcomputer Revolution,* Toronto, 1982, p. 148.

86a29: B. DeMatteo, *The Hazards of VDTs,* Toronto: Ontario Public Service Employees Union, 1981.

86a40: Menzies, *op. cit.,* p. 126.

86a44: See J. Rada, *The Impact of Microelectronics: A Tentative Appraisal of Information Technology,* International Labour Organization, Geneva, 1980; Labour Canada, *In the Chips: Report of the Labour Canada Task Force on Microelectronics and Employment,* Ottawa, 1982; C. Norman, "Microelectronics at Work: Productivity and Jobs in the World Economy," *Worldwatch Paper* no. 39, Washington, 1980.

86b25: M. Siemiatycki, "The Microchip Battleground," *CBC-Radio Ideas,* March/April, 1983.

87a13: Quoted in Siemiatycki, *op. cit.*

87a21: *Ibid.*

87b2: Cited in A. Gorz, *Farewell to the Working Class,* Boston, 1982, p. 130.

Chapter Nine
Energy To Burn

91a6: "Bye, bye, nuclear power," *Canadian Dimension,* July/August 1982, p. 32.

92a8: *Nairobi to Vancouver, 1975-1983: Report of the Central Committee to the Sixth Assembly of the World Council of Churches,* Geneva, 1983.

92b17: *Saint John Evening Times-Globe,* March 29, 1983.

92b44: *Toronto Star,* July 3, 1983.

92b49: *Financial Post 500,* Summer 1984.

93a21: Gatt-Fly, *Energy Monitor 3,* October 1982.

93b7: Toronto *Globe and Mail,* Feb. 25, 1982.

93b31: GATT-Fly, *Power To Choose: Canada's Energy Options,* Toronto, 1981, p. 77.

94a-graph: GATT-Fly, *op. cit.,* p. 116.

94b6: A. MacDonald, "The Political Economy of Energy," *CBC-Radio Ideas,* March 1981, p. 29.

94b15: *Ontario NDP Backgrounder on Darlington,* Oct. 13, 1983.

95a26: Quoted in T.R. Berger, *Northern Frontier, Northern Homeland: The Report of the Mackenzie Valley Pipeline Inquiry,* Vol. I, Ottawa, 1977, p. 112.

96b8: *Proceedings of the 111th Annual Meeting of the Canadian Medical Association*, Ottawa, June 1978, resolution 30.

98a7: MacDonald, *op. cit.*, p. 21.

99a25: *Toronto Star*, July 3, 1983.

Chapter Ten
Media and Ideology

102a18: *Royal Commission on Newspapers*, 1981, p. 90.

102a25: S. McFadyen et al., *Canadian Broadcasting: Market Structure and Economic Performance*, 1980, pp. 20-21.

102b9: *Royal Commission on Newspapers*, p. 76.

103a29: *Time*, Aug. 15, 1977, quoted in E. MacLean, *Between The Lines*, Montreal, 1981, p. 129.

103a34: *Royal Commission on Newspapers*, p. 91.

103b9: Quoted in *Financial Post*, July 16, 1983.

104a35: T. Gitlin, *The Whole World is Watching*, Berkeley and Los Angeles, 1980, p. 42.

105b52: B. McDougall, "The rape of East Timor," *CIJ Review* 1982, pp. 47-51.

106a10: R. Cirino, *Don't Blame the People*, New York: Random House, 1971.

108a33: S. McKay, "A cautious antitrust bill," *Maclean's*, April 16, 1984.

Chapter Eleven
Aging — Out of Sight

114a24: Data for industrial nations as a whole from P. Townsend, "The Structured Dependency of the Elderly: A Creation of Social Policy," *Aging and Society*, March 1981; for Canadian data, J. Synge, "Work and Family Support Patterns of the Aged in the Early Twentieth Century," in V. Marshall, ed., *Aging in Canada: Social Perspectives, Toronto, 1980.*

115a36: Quoted in *Report of the Special Committee of the Senate on Aging*, Ottawa, 1966, p.71.

115b22: K. Collins, *Women and Pensions*, Ottawa, 1978, cited in S. Neysmith, *A Portrait of the Aging Canadian Woman: Or How a Resource Can Be Defined as a Problem*, mimeo, 1980.

116a21: *The Retirement Income System in Canada*, Vol. I, p. 14, cited in J. Tindale et al., *Distributional Justice and Income Security for the Canadian Aged*, mimeo, 1982.

116b2: Neysmith, *op. cit.*

116b19: Health and Welfare Canada, cited in Tindale, *op. cit.*

117a16: Neysmith, *op. cit.*

117a52: J. Edwardh, *Old Age in Two Urban Neighbourhoods: An Ecological Study of Old People in Syracuse, N.Y.*, Master's Thesis, 1974.

118a1: Simone de Beauvoir, *Old Age*, Harmondsworth, 1977, p. 244.

118a33: C. Schwenger and J. Gross, "Institutional Care and Institutionalization of the Elderly in Canada," in Marshall, *op. cit.*, p. 254.

118a41: V. Ross, "The coming old-age crisis," *Maclean's*, Jan. 17, 1983.

118ab-graph: Statistics Canada Projection, cited in B.J. Powell and J.K. Martin, "Economic Implications of Canada's Aging Society," in Marshall, *op. cit.*, p. 205.

118b34: Personal interview, Toronto, Ont., May 25, 1983.

119a15: S. Ward, "Private nursing homes find gold in caring for the old," *Financial Post*, April 14, 1984.

Chapter Twelve
A Home and Native Land

123a34: W. Currie, Aug. 20, 1969, quoted in P. Petrone, *First People, First Voices*, Toronto, 1983, pp. 172-73; see p. 22.

124a40: Cited in P.A. Cumming and N.H. Mickenberg, eds., *Native Rights in Canada*, second edition, Toronto, 1979, pp. 113-14.

124b26: D.J. Dickie, *All About Indians*, Toronto, 1925, p. 34.

125a13: E. Jacobson, *Bended Elbow*, Kenora, 1975, p. 21.

125a-graph: A.J. Siggner, *An Overview of Demographic, Social and Economic Conditions Among Canada's Registered Indian Population*, Research Branch, P.R.E., Department of Indian Affairs and Northern Development (DIAND), 1979, in *Indian Conditions: A Survey*, DIAND, 1980, p. 15.

125b-graph: Medical Services Branch Statistics, Statistics Canada, February 1976, in *Indian Conditions*, p. 15.

126a-graph: *Annual Report, 1978: Medical Services Branch*, Health and Welfare Canada; Statistics Canada; *Trajectory of Indian Health Care*, U.S. Department of Health, Education and Welfare; in *Indian Conditions*, p. 19.

126b-graph: *Annual Report, 1978: Medical Services Branch*, Health and Welfare Canada; 1977, DIAND (Indian Population); 1976, Statistics Canada (National Population); in *Indian Conditions*, p. 19.

127a16: Statement made at the International Non-Governmental Organization Conference on Indigenous People and the Land, Geneva, September 1981, published in *Ontario Indian* 5:3 (March 1982), p. 32.
127b5: Quoted in Royal Commission on the Northern Environment, *Issues, Toronto, 1978,* p. 75.
128a13: Port Severn Band, quoted in *ibid.,* p. 56.
128b35: Quoted in *ibid.,* p. 57.
129a22: *Scarboro Missions* 64:3 (March 1983), p. 29.
129b50: P. Puxley, "The Colonial Experience," in M. Watkins, ed., *Dene Nation: The Colony Within,* Toronto, 1977, p. 117.
130a14: Jacobson, *op. cit.,* p. 21.

Chapter Thirteen
"A Woman's Place . . ."

134a8: Quoted in L. Rasmussen et al., *A Harvest Yet To Reap: A History of Prairie Women,* Toronto, 1976, p. 84.
134a29: R. Sedgewick, "The Proper Sphere and Influence of Women in Christian Society," November 1856, in R. Cook and W. Hutchison, *The Proper Sphere: Women's Place in Canadian Society,* Toronto, 1976, p. 3 (emphasis in original).
134a39: *Ibid.,* p. 21.
134b27: Employment and Immigration Canada, *Labour Market Development in the 1980s,* July 1981, p. 15.
135a13: W. Clement, *The Canadian Corporate Elite,* Toronto, 1975, pp. 266-67.
135a25: *1981 Census,* Volume 1, Table 3.
135ab-graph: P. and H. Armstrong, *The Double Ghetto: Canadian Women and their Segregated Work,* Toronto, 1978, p. 39. With additional information from *1981 Census,* Volume 1, Table 3.
135b6: Toronto *Globe and Mail,* April 28, 1984.
136a26: Quoted on *CBC-Radio Sunday Morning,* May 29, 1983.
136b37: Quoted in P. and H. Armstrong, *A Working Majority: What Women Must Do For Pay,* Canadian Advisory Council on the Status of Women, 1983, p. 203.
137b36: P. Schulz, "Minding the Children," in FitzGerald et al., eds., *Still Ain't Satisfied,* Toronto, 1982, p. 124.
138a23: *Toronto Life,* September 1983.
138a41: Statistics Canada, 84-205, 1982.
138b5: Toronto *Globe and Mail,* Nov. 11, 1983.
138b19: S. Cole, "Home Sweet Home," in FitzGerald, *op. cit.,* p. 61.
139a6: K. McDonnell, "Room to Breathe," *New Internationalist,* December 1982.
139a47: M. Riley, O.P., *Center Focus,* Issue 58, January 1984.

141a37: *Toronto Star,* Feb. 26, 1984.
141b19: N. McClung, "Women Are Discontented," n.d., in Cook and Hutchison, *op. cit.,* pp. 288-89.

Chapter Fourteen
Canada in the Americas

143b6: F. Ambursley and J. Dunkerley, *Grenada: Whose Freedom?,* 1984, pp. 83-84.
144a19: Toronto *Globe and Mail,* Oct. 27, 1983.
144a31: Canada, *House of Commons Debates,* Oct. 25, 1983.
144a44: Ambursley and Dunkerley, *op.cit.,* p. 87.
144a54: K. Levitt, *Canada and the Grenada Crisis,* Toronto: Canada-Caribbean-Central America Policy Alternatives (CAPA), November 1983, p. 5.
144b13: Toronto *Globe and Mail,* Oct. 26, 1983.
145a12: Toronto *Globe and Mail,* Jan. 19, 1981 quoted in R. Carty and V. Smith, *Perpetuating Poverty,* Toronto, 1981, p.3.
145a31: S. Clarkson, *Canada and the Reagan Challenge,* Toronto, 1982, p. 278.
145a50: A.R. Megarry, "Canada should boost foreign aid," Toronto *Globe and Mail,* June 21, 1984.
145b1: Seven major Canadian banks, Annual Reports, 1983.
145b14: C. Taylor, *Snow Job: Canada, the United States and Vietnam (1954 to 1973),* Toronto, 1974.
145b31: North-South Institute, *Review '83 — Outlook '84,* Ottawa, 1984, p. 3; emphasis in original.
146a6: Department of External Affairs, "Relations Between Canada and the U.S.A.," *Canadian Foreign Policy Text* (83/2), April 1983.
146a16: External Affairs, *op. cit.*
146a21: External Affairs, *op. cit.*
146b45: Fact sheet from the Coalition for a New Foreign and Military Policy, fall 1983 (Washington, D.C.); Council on Hemispheric Affairs (COHA), *Human Rights in Latin America 1983,* Washington, 1984, p. 37; ICCHRLA, "Why Don't They Hear Us?": Report of a Canadian Inter-Church Fact-Finding Mission to Guatemala and Mexico, Toronto, 1983.
147a8: *Washington Post,* quoted in *Central America Update* insert, May 1984.
147a14: ICCHRLA, *Canadian Policy and Central America: Renewing the Dialogue,* Toronto, June 1984.
147a22: Speech of D. Ortega, Co-ordinator of the Government of National Reconstruction, to the Council of State, Managua, May 4, 1984.
147a41: Inter-American Dialogue, *The Americas in 1984: A Year for Decisions,* Washington, 1984, p.2-1 (Mimeo version).
147ab-graph: World Bank, *World Development report 1983,* Oxford University Press; PACCA, *Changing*

Course: Blueprint for Peace in Central America and the Caribbean, Institute for Policy Studies, Washington, 1984; Ambursley and Dunkerley, op. cit.

147b11: New York Times, March 23, 1984.

148a6: W. LaFeber, Inevitable Revolutions: The United States in Central America, New York, 1983, p.18.

148a33: New York Times, April 23, 1984.

148a46: Toronto Globe and Mail, May 16, 1984.

149a2: Central America Report, July 17, 1978, p. 223.

149a25: Canadians in the Third World: CIDA's Year in Review 1982-83, Ottawa, 1984, pp. 75-82.

149b9: Speech of P.E. Trudeau to the Commonwealth Caribbean Heads of State Meeting, St. Lucia, February 1983.

149b24: CAPA, From Acquiescence to Action: A Brief by CAPA on Canada's Policy Toward Central America, Toronto, 1984, p. 4.

150a15: Clarkson, op. cit., p. 283.

150a38: New York Times, May 17, 1984.

150a50: Toronto Globe and Mail, May 3, 1984.

150b12: CAPA, op. cit., p. 5.

152a3: House of Commons issue no. 78, Minutes of the Proceedings and Evidence of the Standing Committee on External Affairs and National Defence Respecting: Canada's Relations with Latin American and the Caribbean. Including the Twelfth Report (Routine Business), the Thirteenth Report (South America), and the Fourteenth Report (Final Report — Latin America and the Caribbean), 1982.

Chapter Fifteen
We Have Just Begun

156a4: Oshawa This Week, June 8, 1983.

156a48: Canadian Conference of Catholic Bishops, From Words to Action, Ottawa, 1979, paragraph 1.

156b2: Personal interview, Toronto, Ont., May 2, 1984.

159a2: D. Hollenbach, S.J., Claims in Conflict: Retrieving and Renewing the Catholic Human Rights Tradition, New York: Paulist Press, 1979, p. 204.

Index